AN INTRODUCTION

PROGRAMMING IN SIM

HUMBERSIDE
LIBRARIES

UNITED FLOURISH WE

LS/77

COMPUTER SCIENCE TEXTS

COMPUTER SCIENCE TEXTS

An Introduction to Programming in SIMULA

R. J. POOLEY

BSc, MSc
Department of Computer Science
University of Edinburgh
Edinburgh EH8 7TJ, UK

BLACKWELL SCIENTIFIC PUBLICATIONS

OXFORD LONDON EDINBURGH

BOSTON PALOALTO MELBOURNE

© 1987 by
Blackwell Scientific Publications
Editorial Offices:
Osney Mead, Oxford, OX2 0EL
8 John Street, London, WC1N 2ES
23 Ainslie Place, Edinburgh, EH3 6AJ
52 Beacon Street, Boston
  Massachusetts 02108, USA
667 Lytton Avenue, Palo Alto
  California 94301, USA
107 Barry Street, Carlton
  Victoria 3053, Australia

First published 1987

Set by Setrite Ltd Hong Kong, and
Printed and bound in Great Britain

Distributed in North America by
Blackwell Scientific Publications Inc.
PO Box 50009, Palo Alto
California 94303, USA

British Library
Cataloguing in Publication Data

Pooley, R.J.
  An introduction to programming in
  SIMULA. — (Computer science texts)
  1. SIMULA (Computer program
  language)   I. Title II. Series
  005.13′3   QA76.73.S55

  ISBN 0-632-01611-6
  ISBN 0-632-01422-9 Pbk

Library of Congress
Cataloging-in-Publication Data

Pooley, R.J.
  An introduction to programming in
  SIMULA.

  (Computer science texts)
  Bibliography: p.
  Includes index.
  1. SIMULA (Computer program
  language) I. Title. II. Series.
  QA76.73.S55P66 1986   005.13′3
  86-20711
  ISBN 0-632-01611-6
  ISBN 0-632-01422-9 (pbk.)

Contents

Introduction

This book covers most of what SIMULA contains. Any omissions are of features which originated in Algol 60 and are now generally regarded as out of date. For those who wish to check for themselves, there are still plenty of Algol 60 textbooks available. What is more important is which way to go to develop the really powerful features unique to SIMULA.

Only a handful of textbooks have been written describing SIMULA. Several are not available in English. The only one that I can unreservedly recommend is *SIMULA Begin* (see reference section) and even that is rather behind on the new developments in the language. What it does have is a marvellous feel for what is special about SIMULA.

For up-to-date information on the world of SIMULA users, the Association of SIMULA Users (ASU) publishes a quarterly newsletter, organizes conferences and workshops, etc. They are also a pleasant, sociable bunch who are delighted to help newcomers. Their address is:

> The ASU Secretary,
> c/o SIMULA A.S.,
> Dag Hammarskjoldsvei 35,
> N-0513 Oslo 5,
> Norway.

Membership is currently free.

In some ways SIMULA's name gives a misleading impression. It is a general purpose language which suits the development of simulation packages uniquely well. It is not a simulation language. (Indeed, a group of us were driven at a recent SIMULA Standards Group meeting to propose that SIMULA should be seen as the acronym for SIMple Universal LAnguage.)

On the other hand, SIMULA has been used very extensively in simulation work, particularly in discrete event and combined simulation. When I proposed writing this book, some people expressed disappointment that it was not going to be about simulation in SIMULA. There are two answers to them. Firstly, maybe one day I will write such a book, but this is needed more urgently. Secondly, there already exist some excellent books on the subject. I would like to recommend two in particular.

A System for Discrete Event Modelling on SIMULA, by Graham Birtwistle, describes both a rudimentary amount of SIMULA and how the DEMOS simulation package can be used to extend SIMULA and make discrete-event simulation easy. The package is a joy to use and constitutes what class SIMULATION would be like if it were to be written today. To use it you have to buy the package, but it is a good investment. If you are interested, contact E.R.C.C. (see implementors list).

The Process View of SIMULATION, by Bill Franta, is a seminal work on this area. It outlines a general theory of simulation using a process-based approach and shows how it could be implemented in SIMULA. Well worth reading, perhaps after some experience with DEMOS, but using only SIMULA.

SIMULA has been fully standardized since it was first formulated, around 1968. From the start the name was trademarked and can only be applied to implementations meeting the standard. It is hoped to gain acceptance for the 1986 SIMULA Standard as an ISO standard.

This helps to guarantee that nearly all programs which run on one machine will run on any other which has a SIMULA system. It does not, however, mean the SIMULA is rigidly fixed. Extensions are made regularly to add to its power.

The guarding of the standard is the responsibility of the SIMULA Standards Group (SSG) which contains representatives of all the recognized implementations. Changes and additions have to be approved by this body.

Working with the SSG is the SIMULA Development Group (SDG), which is responsible for investigating new features and problems with existing features. It contains the SSG members plus other interested parties and is less formal than the SSG.

If you have suggestions for changes, or would like to raise problems you have found which you think are due to bad design of SIMULA, you should write to the chairman of the SSG. If you want to become involved in this work yourself, you should write to the chairman of the SDG. Both can be contacted at the address given for the ASU.

I hope you find this book as interesting to read as I did to write. I certainly learned a lot that I did not expect to. On the other hand, I hope reading it will not be as hard a task as writing it. The rest is up to you.

See you at the next ASU conference, I hope.

Chapter 1

Fundamental concepts.
Statements, declarations and comments

What is a computer program?

A computer program (program is always spelt in the American way) is a series of instructions which contains all the information necessary for a computer to perform some task. It is similar to a knitting pattern, a recipe or a musical score. Like all of these it uses a special shorthand, known in this case as a programming language.

This book describes how to write and understand programs written in the language SIMULA. The definition used is the 1986 SIMULA Standard, which extends and clarifies the language previously known as SIMULA 67. The 67 stood for 1967, the year in which this earlier version was first defined.

These should not be confused with the older language known as SIMULA 1, which is an ancestor of SIMULA 67 and thus of today's SIMULA.

A few old references to SIMULA (notably a 1966 article in CACM) will mean SIMULA 1. More often SIMULA 67 is intended. Many implementations of SIMULA will not yet have all the features given in the 1986 standard, although they will probably have more than those defined in 1967. Wherever sensible, this book tries to warn its readers of features which may not be universally available. In addition, it is usually a good idea to check the documentation for the particular SIMULA system to be used, in case it has any peculiarities of its own. SIMULA is highly standardized, but differences may still be found.

You may already be familiar with other programming languages such as FORTRAN, BASIC or PASCAL. Even so you will find this introduction essential, since SIMULA views the world rather differently in some ways. In particular, SIMULA expects you to organize or structure your program carefully. It also allows you to describe actions as if they were happening simultaneously or in parallel.

If the next paragraph seems confusing, read it now and see how much you can understand, then come back after each chapter until it makes complete sense. Do the same for any other parts of this book

1

which are not clear at first reading. Remember that in learning a new computer language you are trying to take in many concepts which only make sense together, so that often several re-readings of what will later seem obvious points are necessary.

A SIMULA program is made up of sequences of instructions known as blocks, which act independently to varying degrees, but which are combined to produce the desired overall effect. The simplest programs contain only one block, known as the program block. All other blocks follow the same basic rules, so let us have a look at the single-block program, example 1.1.

```
begin
  integer Int1;
  comment The first SIMULA program written for this book;
  Int1:=3;
  OutInt(Int1,4);
  OutImage
end
```

Example 1.1 A simple example

This is not the simplest possible program. We could have written

> begin end

and had a complete program block. This tells us the first rule about all blocks. **A block always begins with the word *begin* and ends with the word *end*.** *begin* and *end* are called 'keywords', since they are reserved for special purposes and may not be used for anything else.

A note on letters and 'cases'

Although the programs shown in this book use both capital letters, which are known to computer programmers as 'upper case' characters, and small, 'lower case', letters, you are free to use whichever case you prefer. A SIMULA program is interpreted as if all its letters, which are not enclosed in double quotes, were first converted to upper case. You can even write BegIN or eNd.

The right ingredients

So we have to put *begin* and *end*. What about the text in between?

This is made up of instructions to the SIMULA system, which are of two types: *declarations* and *statements*. There are also pieces of the text which are ignored by the SIMULA system and which simply help any human who reads the program to follow what is happening. These are called comments.

Declarations

In example 1.1, the first instruction after the word *begin* is a declaration:

    integer Int1;

Declarations in a block show how much of the computer's memory is going to be needed by that block. They also show into how many sections it is to be divided, how big each is to be and to what sort of use each will be put. Each of these sections is given a name, by which the program will refer to it.

The program block in example 1.1 has only one declaration. It starts with the 'type' keyword *integer*, followed by a name or 'identifier', Int1.

The type (integer in this example) says what the section of memory will be used for. In example 1.1 it will be used to hold a whole number, which is called an integer in SIMULA. Once a section of memory has been given its type in this way, it may not be used to hold something of a different type.

Since this location will hold an integer, its required size will also be known to the SIMULA system. All items of the same type require the same amount of space in the memory to hold them.

The identifier Int1 is now the name of the space reserved in this way. We may sometimes refer to the value held in this space as Int1 also. This is a useful shorthand, especially when we are not aware what the current contents are.

If we want to use more locations, we can declare them in the same way, being careful to give the correct type to each. Thus we might write

    begin
       integer Int1;
       real Real1;
          etc.

which gives us a location of type real and called Real1, which we can use in this block. The possible types and their uses are explained more fully in Chapter 3.

If we want to have more than one location which can hold a whole number, then we can declare a second integer, with a different identifier. We might do this by writing

```
begin
    integer Int1;
    integer Count;
        etc.
```

or, alternatively, by writing

```
begin
    integer Int1, Count;
        etc.
```

which many people find neater. This style is called a declaration list, with a series of identifiers of locations with the same type separated by commas.

Comments

The next line is a comment. It begins with the keyword *comment*, is followed by some text and ends in a semi-colon.

```
comment The first SIMULA program written for this book;
```

It has no effect on what the program does, but it contains some information on what the program is or does. In example 1.1 it tells us which version of the program we are looking at. This is often very useful.

As well as forming lines on their own, comments can also be used in certain places within instructions or combined on the same line as them. This will be shown in the next chapter.

When you are writing programs in independent sections, as we will be, you may not look back at a 'working' component for some time. It is also possible that someone else may need to change what you have written. The design of the overall system should tell him what the component is supposed to do, but the details of how it works may not be obvious. To help everyone understand your programs, you should include comments in them.

Statements

The other instructions in our example are all statements. They tell the SIMULA system what it is to do.

We shall be looking at the different sorts of statements which exist in SIMULA in detail later. For the moment, let us look briefly at those in the example to get a flavour of the possibilities.

The first one is an 'assignment' statement. It tells the system to place something in one of the locations declared for use by this block. In this case the value three is to be stored in the integer location declared as Int1. Since this value is of a type which matches that declared for the location, the statement is legal SIMULA.

The next statement uses something called OutInt, which is a 'procedure' and is available in all SIMULA systems. OutInt will write out the first number in the parentheses — ordinary brackets — after it. It writes it as a whole number at the end of the line, or 'image', which is currently being created. The second number is used to tell the system how much space to use on the line, when writing out the first number.

The final statement uses OutImage. Like OutInt, OutImage is a procedure and is available in all SIMULA systems. Such standard procedures are known as 'system procedures'. They are not keywords, since you may declare a different meaning for them within a block if you wish.

OutImage causes the line which is currently being created — the current image — to be written to the printer or terminal and a new line to be started. You have probably noticed that it does not have any parentheses or numbers after it. These numbers, known as 'parameters', are only present when the procedure needs information from the program to carry out its task.

What do we do with our program?

So now we have what we think is a legal SIMULA program. Unfortunately it is on paper and, whilst we know what it should cause to happen, the SIMULA system cannot read from the page. How then do we get the SIMULA system to obey our program?

The first step is to write our program, known in full as the 'source program', in some medium which the computer housing the SIMULA system can manipulate. Older machines may require you to punch the text on paper tape or cards, but today most machines will handle text files. These are stored in the computer's memory on some magnetic medium such as a disk or tape. You can usually create them by typing them into the system using a text editor. You will need to check the documentation for the computer that you intend to use, especially the SIMULA user's guide or programmer's reference manual.

Once you have created this 'machine readable' version of the source program, the part of the SIMULA system known as the 'compiler' must be used to read the source and create a sequence of 'machine instructions', which tell the computer what the SIMULA program wants to do. This is known as 'compiling' the program.

Machine instructions are different on different types of computer. If you want to move a SIMULA program from one computer to another type of computer, you must re-process the source, with the compiler of the SIMULA system on the second machine. This is sometimes referred to as recompiling the program on the second machine.

Once you have compiled the program, you may have to 'link' the file of machine instructions which has been generated by the compiler. Not all computers require this step. The file produced by the compiler is known as the object file and the translation of your source program which it holds is known as the 'object program'.

Linking — sometimes called linkage editing — merges the object program version of your program with the standard programs already available in the SIMULA system — the 'runtime system' or 'runtime library'. These allow reading and writing, standard maths functions and so forth to be used; OutInt is made available in this way. Where linking is not necessary, these standard procedures are found by the command which runs the program.

Details of how to compile and, if necessary, link your program should be available to you in the user's guide or programmer's reference manual for your SIMULA system. Where on-line 'help' information is available on your computer, this may provide a useful summary. Where you have access to professional advisers or more experienced SIMULA users, you may be able to save a lot of time by asking them for help, but you should still read the documentation carefully, since not everyone uses all the features of a large programming language like SIMULA.

The final product of compilation and linking is a translation of your original SIMULA source into instructions which your computer can obey. You can now 'run' the file containing these and see your program work. Again you should consult the documentation for your computer for details of how to do this.

NB The ability to compile and run SIMULA programs depends on having access to a computer with a SIMULA system. If your computer currently does not have this system, you may be able to buy one, but they are not available for all computers. The suppliers of those systems known to the author are listed at the back of this book. If your computer is not listed, write to SIMULA A.S., who may be able to help. Their address is given in the list. Readers in the United Kingdom might wish to contact the author.

Summary

Each chapter will end with a brief summary of what the author thinks you should have learned from it.

- In this chapter we have looked informally at what a program and a block are. We used a very simple program, made up of only one block to illustrate this.
- We discovered that a block is a series of instructions, preceded by the keyword *begin* and followed by the keyword *end*.
- Instructions are either declarations, which reserve and name locations, in which information of one particular type may be kept, or statements, which tell the SIMULA system to perform some action.
- Lastly we looked at how to compile and run our program on a computer.

Exercises

When the author was learning to write programs, he was told the most important rule, 'There is no such thing as an armchair programmer'. The simplest exercise can often teach even an experienced programmer something new. Avoid the temptation to miss out examples as they will often lead on to the material covered in the next chapter.

This chapter has introduced a lot of ideas. You may feel completely bewildered. Do not despair. By using the ideas in successive chapters and examples you will soon become familiar with them. To start with, try three fundamental, but by no means unimportant, exercises.

1.1   Using this chapter and the documentation for your SIMULA system, compile and run our example. Note carefully the printed output from the compiler and what files are produced by it.

1.2   Nearly all compilers allow you to produce a printed listing of your program when it is being compiled. Most will allow you to specify things about the appearance of this listing, for instance whether the lines will be numbered for you and whether a cross-referenced index of identifiers is to be appended. Try producing listings using any options available on your SIMULA system.

1.3   Try exercise 1.1 again, changing the source program by (a) leaving out each line in turn, (b) leaving out one of the semi-colons, (c) adding in the extra declarations shown in this chapter, and (d) swapping lines around, especially moving *begin*, *end* and the declaration of Int1.

Note carefully the differences in messages from the compiler and when running the program in each case. See if the listing is different when messages are printed by the compiler.

Chapter 2

The nature of correct programs. Basic rules of syntax and semantics

Rules and penalties

Chapter 1 gave an example of a correct program. When you altered it as you were asked to in exercise 1.3 and recompiled it, some of the results will have been incorrect programs. (If you have not yet completed the exercises in Chapter 1, you should do so now. It will be much easier for you to follow this chapter.)

The compiler will have printed error messages for some of these variations. It may also have printed warnings. Sometimes, though probably not in any of your attempts at exercise 1.3, the compiler will report success in producing the machine instruction version, but the part of the SIMULA system which runs the program, which we call the runtime system, will print an error message or warning during the execution of the program.

Clearly, there are rules to be followed in writing programs. In Chapter 1 some were mentioned in passing, but only two were spelt out. One was that every block starts with the keyword *begin* and finishes with the keyword *end*; the other was that the rest of a program is made up of declarations and statements.

To be correct, a program must follow all the rules of SIMULA. Sometimes the compiler can detect mistakes; sometimes they only show up when we run the program; sometimes, but very rarely, the compiler and runtime system both fail to detect an error, with unpredictable results.

Even when a program compiles and runs without producing error messages, the program is only correct if the actions performed are those intended. In this case we have written a correct SIMULA program, but not the correct program to perform the task required. This book will teach you to write correct SIMULA programs. It can only guide you towards writing programs which perform correctly. The rest is up to plain common sense, planning and persistence — the three Ps of programming.

When it comes to writing correct SIMULA programs, there are two sets of rules. Although it is not always sensible to separate them, the error messages from the compiler may refer to mistakes in this way and so we will look at them briefly now.

Syntax rules

The commonest errors reported by a compiler are those which do not obey the grammar or 'syntax' of the language. Often they are the result of typing errors. If you still have not managed exercise 1.1, this is probably because of a syntax error caused by mistyping.

The rule that a program block must start with *begin* and finish with *end* is a syntax rule.

Syntax of declarations

The declarations

        integer Int1;

and

        integer Int1, Count;

both follow the syntax rules for declarations. A declaration has to be a keyword giving the type, followed by an identifier list. An identifier list is either a single identifier or a series of identifiers, separated by commas, with the option of as many spaces as desired either side of the commas.

The syntax rules for SIMULA, like those for most programming languages, are very strict. You cannot omit the space which indicates the end of the keyword *integer*, without breaking the syntax rules for a declaration.

Sometimes breaking the rules for one sequence, will produce a syntactically correct piece of SIMULA, with a different meaning. For instance, if we had mistyped the comma in the second declaration above, hitting the semi-colon key instead, we would have got the following

        integer Int1; Count;

which clearly violates the syntax rules for a declaration.

As we shall see later, this sequence could still be correct SIMULA, meaning the declaration of an integer called Int1, followed by a call on a procedure called Count. The grammar of the sequence is correct, but its meaning is now different and wrong. In this case the compiler would still probably report the error, but as one of the second category of compiler-detected errors, which are dealt with below.

Before considering this second category, let us look at some more syntax rules. These still deal with our earlier examples and will probably answer some questions which have occurred to you already.

Syntax of identifiers

We have used the word identifier as the technical term for the name given to something in our programs. So far we have not considered what an identifier must look like.

The identifiers which we have used so far are:

> Int1
> Count
> OutInt
> OutImage
> Real1

Notice that procedure names are identifiers and follow the same rules. Keywords have the same syntax as identifiers, but they are not available for the programmer to define or redefine.

The meaning of an identifier is defined by a declaration. System identifiers, like OutInt and OutImage, are already defined outside the program, but can be redefined inside it. This, however, is straying into our second category of rules. The syntax rules are as follows.

- An identifier is a sequence of letters, numbers and underline characters (the last are known sometimes as break characters). An identifier must start with a letter.
- Some systems set a limit on the number of characters in an identifier. Others allow long identifiers, but only look at the first so many characters. You should consult the documentation for any system before using it, especially when moving a program from one system to another.
- Letters are often called 'alphabetic characters', numbers 'numeric characters' or 'digits'. Mixtures of these two types are called 'alphanumeric characters'.

The following are valid identifiers:

```
TOTAL
A1
NEW4SUB6
MAX__SIZE
G43
I
```

Syntax of blocks

We have already looked at the syntax of blocks informally, now let us be a little more formal. The rules for a block are as follows.

- A block starts with the keyword *begin*, which, like all keywords, must have at least one space following it or be the last word on a line.
- This keyword is followed by a list of declarations or a list of statements or a list of declarations followed by a list of statements. Statements and declarations are separated by semi-colons or keywords. All declarations must come before any statements in a block.
- A block ends with the keyword *end*.
  Examples 2.1−2.3 are valid blocks.

```
begin
   integer I
end
```

Example 2.1

```
begin
   Result := 4
end
```

Example 2.2

```
begin
   integer I;
   real Arc;
   I := 5;
   Arc := 3.2;
   OutInt(I,3);
   OutImage
end
```

Example 2.3

Although all these blocks are syntactically correct, example 2.1 will not result in any actions, since it contains no statements. Example 2.2 will cause an error to be reported, since there is no declaration to set aside space and define a type for Result before it is used in the statement.

Exercises

You are probably getting rather impatient with all these rules. Let us try out a few of them. In each of the following program blocks, find and correct the syntax errors.

2.1

```
begin
   integer I1.I2;
   I1:= 3;
   I2:= I1
   OutInt(I2,4);
   OutImage
end
```

2.2

```
begin
   Res:= 4;
   integer Res;
   OutInt(Res,6);
   OutImage
end
```

2.3

```
begin
   OutInt(609;6);
   OutImage
end
```

2.4

```
begin
  Outtext("Line one");
  OutImage;
  Outtext "LINE TWO";
  OutImage
end
```

You should also go back to the error messages you got in Chapter 1 and see if you can understand them better now.

What about statements?

The only major component of our program blocks for which we have not given proper syntax rules is the statement. In fact statements can have many different forms and we need only concern ourselves with a few at a time. We have used two forms of statement so far — procedure calls and assignments — and we can give some rules about these. In addition, we can note that a block can be used in place of a simple statement. In this case it is called a 'sub-block' or a block which is 'local' to the program block. The reason for such local blocks will become apparent later, but their use is a major feature of SIMULA.

A procedure call is an identifier (the name of the procedure) followed in some cases by a parameter list which is enclosed in brackets. The parameter list is a list of identifiers, constants and expressions, separated by commas. (See example 2.4.)

We have already defined identifiers. We shall define constants properly in the next chapter. Expressions are sequences of SIMULA which give values. They are dealt with briefly when we consider assignments below and more fully in mathematical appendix A. Those of us who are not interested in mathematics should only need an informal understanding of expressions and can omit this appendix without missing anything.

Assignment statements have an identifier followed by optional spaces, followed by the assignment 'operator', followed by optional spaces, followed by an expression. The assignment operator is the sequence colon followed by an equal sign, :=. Before giving an informal description of expressions, it is probably best to consider the assignment statements given in example 2.5.

OutImage   No parameters. Moves output to next line.

Outtext("HI")   One parameter, a text, which is printed on the current line. In this example a text constant is used as the parameter.

OutInt(643,3)   Two parameters, both integers, separated by a comma. Prints out the first integer on the current line, padding on the left with spaces if this produces fewer figures than the second integer. Either or both the integer constants given as parameters in the example could have been replaced with identifiers or expressions.

Example 2.4 Procedure calls

Res := 3

Count := Last

Count := Last + 1

Message := "PLEASE TYPE YOUR NAME"

Next   :=   Average*Number + 2

Example 2.5 Assignment statements

The use of spaces before and after the assignment operator has no effect on the correctness of the statement. This applies to all 'operators' in SIMULA.

Expressions

Several kinds of expressions are shown to the right of the assignment operator in these examples. The simplest of these is a constant, such as 3 or "PLEASE TYPE YOUR NAME". These are explained more fully in the next chapter. An expression can also be a single identifier, such as Last in the second example.

The remaining examples show identifiers and constants separated by operators. Thus

Last + 1

is the identifier Last followed by the addition operator followed by the constant 1.

Average*Number + 2

is the identifier Average followed by the multiplication operator followed by the identifier Number followed by the addition operator followed by the constant 2. We shall not attempt a complete definition of expressions, but explain them as we need to use them. These examples should give a feel of what is meant.

A note on operators

The commonest arithmetic operators are given below. For a complete outline of mathematical operators, see appendix A.

> +   Addition
> −   Subtraction
> *   Multiplication
> /   Division with non-whole numbers (reals)
> // Division with whole numbers (integers)
> := Assignment

Saying what you mean

As we looked at the rules for writing parts of SIMULA programs, we found that it was possible to write SIMULA whose syntax was correct but which was still illegal. There are extra rules to be obeyed. These spell out the meaning of a sequence of SIMULA. When the way we write the parts of such a sequence is correct, it is still possible that we have put these parts together in a way which has an illegal meaning. These rules of meaning are sometimes called the semantic rules or, more simply, semantics of the language.

English has syntax and semantics in the same way, although they are far more complex than those for SIMULA. Let us look at an example in English of a sentence whose syntax (or grammar) is correct, but whose semantics (or meaning) is nonsense.

'The dish ran away with the spoon.'

This sentence obeys the normal rules of English grammar. The reason that it would be rejected as nonsense is that the nouns, 'dish' and 'spoon', are defined in such a way that they do not fit the verb, 'ran away'. By changing the nouns or the verb we can produce a sentence with the same syntax, but with a sensible meaning, such as

'The dish belonged with the spoon.'

In SIMULA we could produce the same effect in the following program block.

```
begin
    text T1;
    T1:= 3
end
```

Here the operator ':=' acts like the verb and 'T1' and '3' act like nouns. 'T1' and '3' represent types which cannot be assigned to one another. The statement 'T1:= 3' is nonsense because the meaning of 'T1' is wrong.

Let us take one more example from English, before we spell out the most important rules for the SIMULA building blocks we have used so far.

'Come to my arms my beamish boy.'

Lewis Carroll delighted in writing syntactically correct nonsense, like jabberwocky. The sentence above illustrates a favourite device. The only word that makes this nonsense is 'beamish'. From its position in the sentence we know that this must be an adjective describing 'boy', but there is no such adjective. It has no known meaning. Our minds may be able to infer some meaning (this is a large part of the fun of nonsense poetry) but that does not make unambiguous sense out of nonsense.

The following SIMULA program block contains a similar use of a meaningless concept, i.e. one which has no properly defined meaning.

```
begin
    T1:= 3
end
```

This time we have not defined T1 as having a type which fails to match '3'. T1 has not had any type defined for it at all. It has not been declared before being used and therefore no space has been reserved for it and no type has been allocated to it.

So, let us consider a few rules about how we must write SIMULA
to avoid semantic errors.

Semantics of declarations

- The same identifier cannot be declared twice in a block.
- The identifier is used to name a space in the computer's memory
  which is large enough to hold a value of the type specified. Whenever the identifier is used subsequently, it refers to this space and
  this type of value.

Semantics of procedure calls

- A procedure call must have the correct number of parameters.
- Each parameter must be of the correct type. This is explained in
  more detail in the next chapter.
- The actions of the procedure are performed, using the parameters
  to provide information for the procedure if necessary.

Semantics of assignments

- The type of the expression to the right of the assignment operator
  must be 'compatible' with the type of the identifier on the left.
- The value of the expression on the right will be stored in the
  location reserved for the identifier on the left.

Semantics of expressions

- The types of the quantities in an expression must be compatible.
  The type associated with the value of an expression is determined
  by the types of the quantities in it, except when the division
  operators are used. In this case the type is the same as the operator,
  i.e. integer for '//' and real for '/'.
- The working out of an expression by the SIMULA system, known
  as its 'evaluation', is done in the following order:
  (a) Working from left to right all multiplications and divisions are
      performed;
  (b) Working from left to right all additions and subtractions are
      performed.
  This is explained more fully in appendix A.

Semantics of blocks

- Any identifier used in a statement in a block must already have been declared.
- The statements in the block are performed in the order indicated.

Syntax and semantics of a comment

A comment is a special sequence in SIMULA which is treated as a space by the compiler. It contains a message which explains what is going on around it in human terms. Its syntax is quite simple.

A comment is:

- the keyword *comment*, followed by any sequence of characters ending at the first semi-colon, or
- the character !, followed by any sequence of characters ending at the first semi-colon, or
- any sequence of characters following the keyword *end*, ending at the first occurrence of the keyword *end*, *else*, *when* or *otherwise* or a semi-colon or the end of the program.

Example 2.6 shows a program which uses all of these forms. It is very fully commented. In practice you will probably not need this sort of detail, but better too many comments than too few. In our worked examples I shall include comments, partly to help you understand things and partly to get you into the habit of using them. They will help you see what is going on, but only in the important places.

A word of warning is needed here. Be very careful to end your comments properly. If you forget a semi-colon or keyword, as appropriate, you will lose some of the following program, since it will be treated as part of the comment. In particular, remember that the end of a line does not end a comment, as the first instance in example 2.6 shows.

To be consistent we need the semantic rules for comments. Comments have no meaning in the program.

Summary

This has been a longer chapter and has introduced a lot of important ideas. You should not worry if you do not see the point of some of it yet. Whenever we come to look at a new feature in SIMULA you will see how the concepts of syntax and semantics help define the ways in which the feature can be used. Within a few chapters you will find that

```
begin
   comment Double space removal program,
            first version, Rob Pooley, March 1984;

      text T; ! Holds the text to be processed;

      InImage;                    ! Reads the text into SysIn.Image;
      inspect SysIn do            ! Refer to SysIn not SysOut;
      begin
         T :- Blanks(Image.Length); ! See the next chapter;
         T:=Image;                    ! Copies the characters into T;
      end;
      if T.GetChar=' ' then        ! First character is a space?;
      begin
         if T.GetChar=' ' then     ! Second character is also?;
            T:=T.Sub(2,T.Length-1); ! Remove first character;
      end;

      comment Now write out the text;
      OutText(T);
      OutImage
   end Double space remover
```

Example 2.6 The use of comments

you are using words like syntax without noticing. In the meantime, you may need to refer to this chapter while reading some of the following chapters, until you feel confident.

- We have looked in this chapter at the rules that tell you how you must write your program for the compiler to be able to make sense of it. These are called the 'syntax' of SIMULA.
- We have defined the syntax of comments, identifiers, declarations, some types of statements and blocks. We have looked at, but not given any definite rules for, expressions.
- We have looked at how meaningless programs can be written, even when the individual parts of the program are correct. The rules that define the meaning of the program are called the 'semantics' of SIMULA.
- We have seen the important semantic rules for those parts of SIMULA whose syntax we had described earlier.
- We have looked at the rules for comments, which have no meaning, only syntax.

Exercises

Correct the errors in the following program blocks.

2.5

```
begin
   integer First;
   First:= 3;
   Second:= First
end
```

2.6

```
begin
   integer Next;
   Next:= 4;
   OutText(Next);
   OutImage
end
```

2.7

```
begin
   text Line;
   Line:= "MESSAGE ONE";
   OutImage(Line)
end
```

2.8

```
begin
   integer I;
   I:= "3";
   OutInt(I+2,4);
   OutInt(I−4,I,3);
   OutImage
end
```

2.9

```
begin
   integer One, Zero;
   One:= 1;
   Zero:= 0;
   One:= One // Zero
end
```

What is different about 2.9?

Chapter 3

Simple types

The importance of types

So far we have seen three types: integer, real and text. The only one we have looked at in any detail is integer. In fact SIMULA contains several other types as keywords or combinations of keywords. In addition it is possible for you to create combinations of these simple types and give them names, by using the *class* mechanism. In this chapter we will look at the simple types which are already defined in SIMULA.

Types in assignments

A type is given in a declaration so that the SIMULA system knows how much space to allow for the declared quantity. The system checks whenever a new value is stored into this location that the value is of the same type. If the types are different then the system may do one of two things.

1   It may 'convert' the quantity being stored to that of the location. This is only possible between the types integer and real and their short and long variants.

2   If conversion between the types is not specified in SIMULA, the system will report a semantic error.

SIMULA will only convert one type to another where this has a clear meaning. In practice this is only the case for arithmetic values, i.e. types which represent numbers. Even there it may need clarification. Unlike some languages, it is not enough that the two types take up the same amount of space in the computer. Try examples 3.1 and 3.2 to see how your SIMULA system handles such situations.

Clearly we must be very careful how we use types. Even where we are allowed to mix types, we must be careful that we understand what will happen when a value of one type is converted into a value of another type. For instance, what would happen in example 3.1 if the value assigned to RealVal was 3.5 or 3.9? Is it rounded up or down?

```
begin
   integer IntVal;
   real RealVal;
   RealVal := 3.2;
   IntVal := RealVal;
   OutInt(IntVal,4);
   OutImage
end
```

Example 3.1 A legal assignment of one type to another

```
begin
   character CharVal;
   integer IntVal;
   CharVal := '3.2';
   IntVal  := CharVal;
   OutInt(IntVal,4);
   OutImage
end
```

Example 3.2 An illegal assignment of one type to another

Allowing the system to convert things in this way is sometimes known as 'implicit conversion'. SIMULA also provides procedures which can be used to carry out type conversion in a controlled way. In general it is safer to use these 'explicit conversion' procedures, so that it is obvious when reading the program what is happening. We shall look at the rules used in implicit conversion at the end of this chapter.

Types in expressions

The rules about mixing types in assignments also apply in expressions. For instance, we are not allowed to add together an integer and a text. Try compiling and running examples 3.3 and 3.4.

To complete this brief look at types in expressions, here are some rules of thumb about what happens when you mix arithmetic types in expressions and implicit conversion is performed.

● Where real and integer values are mixed in an expression, they are all converted to real values.

● Where the real division operator, /, is used in an expression, all values in the expression are converted to real values.

```
begin
   integer IntVal;
   real RealVal;
   IntVal := 2;
   RealVal := 69.54;
   RealVal := IntVal + RealVal - 4;
   OutFix(RealVal,2,6);
   OutImage
end
```

Example 3.3 A legal mixing of types in an expression

```
begin
   character CharVal;
   real RealVal;
   CharVal := '2';
   RealVal := 69.54;
   RealVal := CharVal + RealVal - "4";
   OutFix(RealVal,2,6);
   OutImage
end
```

Example 3.4 An illegal mixing of types in an expression

- Where the integer division operator, //, is used in an expression, the values must be integer or an error is reported.

This subject is covered in more detail in the mathematical appendix B.

Types of parameters

Exactly the same rules apply where values are passed as parameters as apply when they are assigned. In effect the parameter given is assigned to a location with the type specified for that parameter. This will be discussed further in Chapter 5.

Standard types

We shall now look at each of the simple types provided in SIMULA. For those who wish to use SIMULA for mathematical programming, appendix B contains more information on the use of arithmetic types.

integer

As we have seen, values are of type integer if they are whole numbers. They may be positive, negative or zero.

On any particular SIMULA system there will be a largest positive and a smallest negative number which can be held in an integer location. The documentation for a particular system will tell you what these limits are. There are system constants which contain them and these may be used in your programs to check that your values do not exceed them. They are called MaxInt and MinInt respectively, and are described in Chapter 20. Such limits do not normally cause problems.

In our programs we have used integer constants to represent values being assigned to our integer locations. An integer constant is a whole number written as a sequence of decimal digits, i.e. any digit in the range 0−9. This may be preceded by a minus or, less commonly, a plus sign. A minus sign indicates a negative value; a plus sign has no effect. See example 3.5.

```
2
45678231
−432
+ 1245
```

Example 3.5 Integer constants

Spaces after the plus or minus are ignored. Spaces between digits are not allowed.

It is also possible to give integer constants in other number bases. This is described in mathematical appendix C.

real

A real value is a number which is not necessarily whole. It is held in a form which allows it to contain a fractional part. In common speech it is what is known as a 'decimal' number or decimal fraction, i.e. it is written with a decimal point separating the whole and fractional parts of the number.

A real value is restricted both by a largest/lowest range and by the number of significant decimal places which can be held. Again this will be explained in detail in the documentation for your SIMULA system.

There are two system real constants, MaxReal and MinReal, which may be used to check them in your programs. These are described in Chapter 20. Again they will not cause problems for most users.

Most of us are used to writing decimal numbers (decimal fractions) in what is technically known as 'fixed point' notation. The decimal constants used in examples so far are in this form. It can be described as two strings of decimal digits (in the range 0–9) separated by a full stop or period. Like integers, they may be preceded by a minus or plus sign. See example 3.6.

```
5.7
236.0
3246.8096
−45.87
+ 46.876
```

Example 3.6 Legal fixed-point real constants

The use of spaces is not allowed between digits or between a digit and the decimal point.

Mathematicians often use another notation to write decimal values, especially where these are very large or very small. This way of writing them is known as 'floating point' and is also allowed for writing real constants in SIMULA. It is described in mathematical appendix B, since most programmers will never use it.

character

A character holds a value which represents a single character. SIMULA allows you to use any of the characters in the 'character set' of the computer that you are using plus the characters defined by the International Standards Organization (ISO) character-set standard. (This is sometimes known as the ASCII character set.) More details on character sets are given in Chapter 12.

It is important to stress that a character has a different type from a text (see below).

We normally think of a character as something written on a page. In the computing world this sort of character is often referred to as a 'printing character'. It is probably easy enough for us to accept that a space is also a printing character. It is rather harder to grasp that a character can produce other effects, such as making the printer start a new line or a new page. These are non-printing 'control characters'. Some of these character values produce very complex effects in certain printers or terminals and no effects or different effects in others.

In general terms, the values held in character locations are those which are sent as instructions to printers, terminals and other hardware devices. Most of these instructions control the printing and formatting of written information. The simplest merely instruct the device to print a visible character.

Character constants are normally written as single characters, enclosed in single quotes. Note carefully that a single character enclosed in double quotes is a text constant and may not be used as a character.

Control characters cannot be written in this way. They use their internal integer value (see Chapter 12), written as an integer constant and enclosed in exclamation marks, inside single quotes. This notation can also be used to write printing characters, but is very clumsy. See example 3.7.

```
'A'
'b'
'4'
'%'
' '
'''
'!3!'        Control character, enclosed in exclamation marks.
```

Example 3.7 Legal character constants

Note that case, i.e. the difference between capital and small letters, is significant in character constants. Thus 'A' and 'a' are not equivalent. Note also how a single quote is represented as a character constant.

Boolean

A Boolean quantity can only have two values. These are True and False.

The use of Boolean quantities may not be intuitively obvious and we merely mention them here. They will be considered in more detail when we look at conditional statements and loops.

A Boolean can be assigned the value of any conditional expression and can be used wherever a conditional expression might be used, e.g. in an *if* statement or a *while* loop.

Boolean constants can only be represented by the keywords True and False.

text

A text variable is used to refer to and manipulate sequences of characters. A sequence of characters is often known as a 'string'. In the examples using text variables so far, we have often assigned strings as the values to be placed in locations declared as type text. From this it might seem that a text and a string are the same thing. In fact a text is more complex than a string and we shall spend most of Chapters 5 and 8 looking at what a text really holds.

Text constants are strings, i.e. sequences of characters, surrounded by double quotes. Each character in a string can be any of those in the ASCII (ISO) standard set.

A character in a string can also be represented by its internal integer value enclosed in exclamation marks. See Chapter 12 for details of internal representation.

When a string is too long to fit onto a single line of your SIMULA program, it can be continued on the following line by typing a double quote at the end of the first line and again at the start of the second line. These quote characters are ignored and the value of the constant is the string on the first line followed by the string on the second line.

"The cat sat on the mat"

"34.56"

"%"

"This string is typed on two lines, but will be treated as if it"

"was on a single line, without the second and third double quotes."

"This string has a control character !10! embedded"

""""""

Example 3.8 Legal text constants

Note that the last string show in example 3.8 will contain only one double quote. When you want to have a text constant which contains one double quote you must type two, so that the compiler knows that it is not the end of the string. Another example showing this is:

"This string contains only one"", but we must type two."

Note also that the single character text constants "%" and """" are not the same as the character constants '%' and '"'. They have different types.

Initial values

An identifier of a certain type, which is not declared as a constant (see later in this chapter), is often referred to as a 'variable' of that type, since, unlike a constant of the same type, its value can be changed by assigning to it. When we declare such a variable, the SIMULA system places an initial value in the location identified. This value is the same on all SIMULA systems on all computers for all variables of a given type.

Thus it is quite legal, and meaningful, in SIMULA to write

```
begin
   integer IntVal;
   OutInt(IntVal,4);
   OutImage
end
```

since the initial value placed in the location identified by IntVal will be printed. This will be the value initially given to all integer locations.

The values placed in each type of location are given below.

integer	0
short integer	0
real	0.0
long real	0.0
character	The ISO NULL character, which is 'invisible'.
Boolean	False.
text	NoText, the empty text, referring to an empty string. Equivalent to "".

Implicit conversion of reals and integers

When a real value is assigned to an integer location, or vice versa, we have said that the value will be converted to one with the type of the location. When integers are converted to reals, no problems are involved in understanding what will happen. The values 3 and 3.0 are usually thought of as identical and such a conversion presents no ambiguities.

On the other hand, when reals are converted to integers, the result depends on how we deal with the fractional part of the real value. How do we get rid of the figures to the right of the decimal point?

If we go back to our earlier examples we might use them to produce example 3.9. Running this would show the outcome of implicit conversion of reals to integers.

```
begin
    integer I1, I2, I3;
    I1:= 3.2;
    I2:= 3.9;
    I3:= 3.5;
    OutInt(I1,4);
    OutInt(I2,4);
    OutInt(I3,4);
    OutImage
end
```

Example 3.9 Implicit conversion and rounding

Clearly more than one outcome is possible.
    If all reals are rounded up the output will be

        4   4   4

if down

        3   3   3

and if to the nearest integer value

        3   4   4

or

        3   4   3

the last two depending on whether 3.5 is regarded as nearer to 3 or 4.

Since no armchair programmers are allowed, you should now try compiling and running the program and see for yourself what happens.

What happened? It was clear enough, I hope. When implicit conversion is relied upon, SIMULA converts reals to integers by rounding to the nearest integer value. 3.5 is rounded up.

There is more on this subject in mathematical appendix B.

Constant declarations

Constant declarations were introduced into SIMULA very recently and are still regarded as controversial by many people. They should be used with some restraint if you want to move your programs to other systems. Older SIMULA systems will not have constant declarations.

A constant declaration allows an identifier to be assigned a value in its declaration. This identifier may not then be assigned another value. This can be very useful when using the same value frequently in a program, especially when the value is easily mistyped or has no obvious meaning.

Example 3.10 shows the use of a real constant declaration to represent Pi in a program which calculates the area and circumference of a circle whose radius is typed in.

Any declaration of an identifier of the types in this chapter followed by an equal sign followed by a constant of matching type is a legal constant declaration.

It is also legal to use an expression containing constants and identifiers from earlier constant declarations as the right-hand side of such declarations. This can aid readability by showing the way in which some named constants are used to derive others.

Summary

- We have looked in some detail at the importance of the type associated with a value. In particular, we have noted that values can only be stored in locations of the same type. Attempts to store them in locations of a different type will result in implicit conversion to the type of the location or an error being reported.
- We have seen that mixing of types in an expression is restricted in a similar way. So is the use of types of parameters.
- We have looked at the standard types in SIMULA, namely in-

```
begin
   real Pi = 3.14159;        ! A constant declaration;
   real Radius;         ! A variable declaration;

   Radius: = InReal;         ! Read in the radius;
   OutText("Radius =");
   OutFix(Radius,6,12);
   OutText("Area =");
   OutFix(Pi*(Radius**2),6,12);      ! Area = Pi times radius squared;
   OutImage;
   OutText("Circumference =");
   OutFix(2*Pi*Radius,6,12);         ! 2 times Pi times Radius;
   OutImage
end..of..program
```

Example 3.10 Constant declaration

teger, real, Boolean, character and text, defining them and looking at how constants of each type are written.

- We have looked at the rules controlling implicit conversions between reals and integers.
- We have seen the initial values given to locations of each standard type.
- We have seen how constant identifiers may be declared.

Exercises

Correct the following programs.

3.1

```
begin
   integer IntVal;
   Int Val: = '3'
end
```

3.2

```
begin
   character LETTER;
   LETTER: = "J"
end
```

3.3

```
begin
  OutInt("34",2);
  OutImage
end
```

3.4

```
begin
  OutText('There's many a slip');
  OutImage
end
```

3.5

```
begin
  OutText("She whispered,"I love you."");
end
```

What will be the value printed by each of the following? Compile and run them to check.

3.6

```
begin
  integer IntVal;
  IntVal:= 5.2 + 3.5;
  OutInt(IntVal,4);
  OutImage
end
```

3.7

```
begin
  real RealVal;
  RealVal:= 3 / 2;
  OutFix(RealVal,2,6);
  OutImage
end
```

3.8

```
begin
  real RealVal;
  RealVal:= 3 // 2;
  OutFix(RealVal,2,6);
  OutImage
end
```

If you do not enjoy mathematical examples, please try these any-way. This is the last time I shall ask you to try any exercises of this kind, unless you are reading the mathematical appendices. From now on only the simplest of arithmetic will be used and only to help us do more interesting things.

Chapter 4

Conditional statements

What do computers do?

It may seem a little late in this book to ask such a question, but we have really taken for granted what computers are and what they can do. If we are to use them as fully as possible, we need to understand exactly what they are capable of.

Most people probably used to think of computers as giant, super-fast calculating machines. More recently the idea of very small micro-computers has changed that image somewhat. More importantly, the use of computers in word processing and graphics (particularly computer games) has introduced many more people to the use of computers in information processing and decision making.

As programmers, we can consider computers as performing three sets of functions, which can be combined in our programs to achieve a wide range of tasks.

1   Movement of information — reading a magnetic tape and printing on a lineprinter; reading the input from a keyboard and storing in random access memory; reading the input from a 'joystick' and moving a picture on a screen.

2   Arithmetic calculations — we have seen some examples of this already.

3   Comparison of information and choice of actions depending on the result — this chapter will look at the basic mechanisms for this.

Conditions and choices

The ability that makes computers more than calculators or fancy type-writers is the ability to perform different actions according to some condition or conditions, which it can determine to be either true or false. Computers can be told, 'Check this condition. If it is true then do the following, otherwise do this other thing'. In some cases the other thing is nothing. Put crudely, computers can make choices.

What they cannot do, or, at least, as far as the author is aware, not yet, is decide which condition to test, or whether the actions which follow are really sensible. They must be told these things, and programming languages have mechanisms for doing so.

In SIMULA, the most important construction for making choices is the 'conditional statement' or, as it is often known, the *if* statement.

What is an *if* statement?

Example 4.1 contains a simple example of an *if* statement.

```
begin
   integer Int1;
   Int1:=InInt;
   if Int1=2 then OutText("YES");
   OutImage
end
```

Example 4.1 Simple use of an *if* statement

This program will read in a whole number and compare its value against 2. If it is equal to 2 then the program will print YES, otherwise a blank line will be printed. Compile and run it to make sure.

From this example we can see the syntax of an *if* statement. An *if* statement starts with the keyword *if*, followed by a condition, followed by the keyword *then*, followed by a statement. The semantics are probably obvious to you as well.

The program checks the condition. If it is true, the statement is executed (or carried out, if you prefer), but if it is false, the statement is skipped. The next statement, if there is one, is then executed.

An *if* statement may be used wherever a simple statement may be used.

The *if−then−else* statement

Consider example 4.2 which uses *if* statements.

```
begin
   integer Int1;
   Int1 := InInt;
   if Int1=2 then OutText("YES");
   if Int1 ne 2 then OutText("NO");
   OutImage
end
```

Example 4.2 Uncombined *if* statements

Here we have added a second *if* statement to our first example, but all
that it does is check the opposite condition to the first. *ne* is the symbol
for 'not equal' in SIMULA. This program will print out YES if the
number read in is 2, otherwise it will print out NO. Again, try it and
see.

This might seem a useful device, but it is wasteful since the program makes the same check — is the number equal to 2? — twice and
decides its actions on the basis of whether the outcome is true or false.
In practice this combination is so useful that SIMULA provides a less
wasteful means of achieving the same result. Rewriting our example
using this concept we get example 4.3.

```
begin
    integer Int1;
    Int1:=InInt;
    if Int1=2 then OutText("YES")
            else OutText("NO");
    OutImage
end
```

Example 4.3 The *if−then−else* statement

A 'real' program

So far we have used only trivial examples to demonstrate features of
SIMULA. None of them has had a purpose apart from that. Although
writing and correcting such programs is interesting for a while, it soon
becomes boring. We are now going to begin to construct a series of
programs which have a very real and very practical purpose. If you
complete this book you will have built the basis of a suite of word-
processing programs, which will allow simple editing and formatting of
text files. You may then extend these to provide some very powerful
tools. We shall also look at some simple database tools, which will
allow you to store and retrieve information efficiently.

The important thing about writing large programs which perform
complex functions is to break the design into sections which perform
sub-tasks and which are simple enough to write easily. Our next
examples introduce simple programs, although ones which are more
complex than those we have seen so far. On its own each is not very
useful, but later on we will use it as a building block in our much more
powerful programs.

A 'top down' design

Sometimes, in explaining the programs we wish to write, we start from simple components and work towards the whole system. This approach is known as 'bottom up' design, for fairly obvious reasons. Where we are only designing a small part of our 'grand design' this approach is sufficient. There are not too many components to hold in our heads as we build up the program.

When the system we are designing gets bigger, this approach is not good enough. It would be very difficult to write down now all the parts of our formatting and editing system in this kind of detail, especially as we have not said exactly what we want the system to do. It is much more sensible to start at the highest level, with our overall system, and break this down step by step until we reach components which are simple enough to write in SIMULA in detail. This approach is called 'top down' design.

Figure 4.1 is a quick sketch of the design of our total system, concentrating on the line-formatting programs we are about to write. This shows a major advantage of top-down design: since the low level components are designed to operate as independently as possible, we

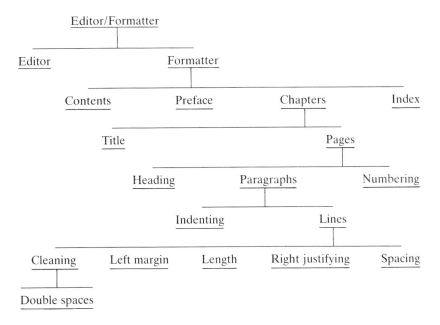

Fig. 4.1 Overall top-down design of Formatter/Editor.

can write and test them separately and then build up our overall system by combining tested units. The only important parts of each component are its function — what it does — and how it receives and passes on information from, and to, other components — its 'interface'.

This type of design allows us to begin work now, without losing sight of the overall plan. It is also possible to design components now and improve on them later if we discover better ways of implementing them. Most importantly, this form of design makes it easier to change parts of the system without upsetting other parts, since the degree of interdependence of components can be seen easily.

We shall fill in other branches as we learn more of SIMULA's capabilities. In fact we shall not finish the system. No piece of software is ever so good that extra or better features might not improve it. You should be able to add such refinements for yourself before we finish.

One last point about top-down designs: in reality it is impossible to start with a complete plan, along the lines shown, and write the final program from it. The process of implementing the program in SIMULA will show errors in it and suggest better solutions to some problems. Thus, we can change the design in the light of experience, but we should never change the program without making the same changes in the design. It is surprising how quickly you can forget what the program really does if you have not got a clear description of it. It is even worse if someone else has to look after a program written by you. Since we are writing 'real' programs, we must do the job properly.

Some simple starting points

We are going to write some programs now which can be extended to perform some of the functions associated with components in our plan. In fact they may prove useful in other places in the system as well. There are two that are simple to write using *if* statements and *if−then− else* statements. One will check if a text starts with a double blank and remove one blank if it does. The other will check if a line is longer than 60 characters and split it if it is.

Double-blank removal

This problem is easy to describe in English. We have a text variable, which may contain any number of printing characters (we assume no non-printing characters are present). If the first two of these are spaces (ISO blank characters), we want to remove one of them, to leave a shorter text.

A good way of writing programs is to write them in SIMULA as far as we can at the moment and to describe any parts which are missing in English. The program in example 4.4 shows this, with the genuine SIMULA parts in normal letters and the informal English descriptions in italics. We shall use italics in programs in this way from now on.

```
begin
    text T;
    read in a line of text and place it in T;
    if first character in T =' ' then
    begin
        if next character in T =' ' then
            remove the first character from T
    end;
    OutText(T);
    OutImage
end
```

Example 4.4 Informal description of double-space remover

There is one thing about the use of *if* statements which this program shows, even in this unfinished form. The *then* in an *if* statement must be followed by a statement. The syntax of SIMULA states that this following statement must not be a second *if* statement and so the second test is made by an *if* statement enclosed in a *begin−end* pair. In other words the statement following the *then* is a compound statement containing a single *if* statement. Any sequence of one or more statements, not containing declarations, and enclosed in the keywords *begin* and *end* is a compound statement and may be used, amongst other things, to hide a second *if* statement, following a *then*. Compound statements are explained more fully at the end of this chapter.

The condition in the second *if* statement is only checked if the condition in the first *if* statement is true. Thus we only check if the second character is a space after we have found that the first one is.

This can be extended so that the statement following the second *then* is a compound statement containing a single *if* statement, allowing us to check for triple spaces or any combination of three characters we choose. By further extension of this we can check four or any other number of conditions, where each is only checked if all those which precede it are true. This is often referred to as 'nesting' *if* statements inside one another.

Let us start to fill in the non-SIMULA parts of the program. As we are going to look at texts in some detail in the next chapter we shall have to cheat by learning some information about them early. We shall also have to use some facts about reading and writing in SIMULA which we will not cover in detail until Chapter 7.

Firstly, we need to read in a line from the program's input. We will assume that all input is coming from a terminal, but if you are using a different system the same program will work, taking its input from the batch input stream. The default input is referred to as SysIn. This will be looked at in detail in Chapter 7.

To read in from the normal input all we need to do is use a system procedure called InImage, which matches our output procedure OutImage. This reads in the next line (sometimes called the next 'record') and places its characters in a special text location called Image. This is predefined, like system procedures, and does not need to be declared. We can then copy Image into T.

As Image is inside SysIn, we enclose references to it in an *inspect* statement, which specifies SysIn as the place to find it. If we did not

```
begin
    text T;
    InImage;       ! Read into SysIn.Image;
    inspect SysIn do    ! To use SysIn.Image, not SysOut.Image;
    begin
        T :- Blanks(Image.Length);   ! Create a text of the required length;
        T := Image;       ! Copy in the contents of SysIn.Image;
    end;
    if first character in T =' ' then
    begin
        if next character in T =' ' then
            remove the first character from T
    end;
    OutText(T);
    OutImage
end
```

Example 4.5 More complete version of double-space remover

do this the Image contained in SysOut, the default output, would be taken. Now our program, as shown in example 4.5, is looking a bit healthier.

Using :=, we are not allowed to assign more characters to a text than it already contains. The use of the line

T:− Blanks(Image.Length)

fills T with the same number of space characters as the total number of characters in Image, allowing the assignment of the actual contents of Image. Blanks is explained in detail in the next chapter, but for the moment we will use it without further comment.

Now we need to check the first character in T. To do this we will use a procedure which gives the next character in a text as a *character* value. Each time it does so it moves along the text, without changing the characters in the text. It is called GetChar and is a part of the text itself. When we first looked at texts I said that they contained more than just the characters assigned to them. One thing every text contains is a set of procedures of its own.

GetChar is different from the procedures we have seen so far in two ways. Firstly, unlike system procedures, it is part of a text rather than of the whole program. Secondly, when it is called it 'returns a value' of type text. This means that it can be used to assign a text value. In fact the procedure InInt also returned a value, of type integer, in an earlier example in this chapter, but we did not investigate it fully. The whole subject of procedures will be considered in detail in Chapter 6. For the moment the use of GetChar in this example should be clear enough.

To call a procedure which is inside an object like a text, we use the name of the object, T, followed by a dot, followed by the procedure's name, GetChar. Image.Length is another example of accessing an attribute inside a text. Now our program, as shown in example 4.6, is nearing completion.

Finally, we need to find a way to remove the first character from T. To do this we will use two more procedures which are found inside each *text* object, Length and Sub. The first returns an integer value, which is the number of characters currently held in the text. The second is a procedure which returns a text which is a section of the characters in the original text.

Length has no parameters, but Sub takes two, both integers. The

```
begin
  text T;
  InImage;
  inspect SysIn do
  begin
    T :- Blanks(Image.Length);
    T := Image
  end;
  if T.GetChar=' ' then          ! Is the first character a space?;
  begin
    if T.GetChar=' ' then        ! Is the next character a space?;
      Remove the first character from T
  end;
  OutText(T);
  OutImage
end
```

Example 4.6 Almost complete double-space remover

```
begin
  comment Double space removal program,
          first version, Rob Pooley, March 1984;

  text T; ! Holds the text to be processed;

  InImage;                      ! Reads the text into SysIn.Image;
  inspect SysIn do              ! Refer to SysIn not SysOut;
  begin
    T :- Blanks(Image.Length); ! See the next chapter;
    T:=Image;                   ! Copies the characters into T;
  end;
  if T.GetChar=' ' then         ! First character is a space?;
  begin
    if T.GetChar=' ' then    ! Second character is also?;
      T:=T.Sub(2,T.Length-1); ! Remove first character;
  end;

  comment Now write out the text;
  OutText(T);
  OutImage
end Double space remover
```

Example 4.7 Complete double-space remover

first is the number of the first character in the text to be included in the text returned. The second is the number of characters from the original text to be included. Thus

    T.Sub(1,4)

returns a text containing the first four characters of T.

    Combining Length and Sub we can finish our program, or at least produce one that will work for most cases (example 4.7).

    Do not worry too much if this is not completely clear at first. With a little study you should get an idea of what is happening. An even better idea is to try compiling and running this program. Try various combinations of spaces at the start of the input you use.

Exercises

4.1   Try compiling and running the program below.

```
begin
  text T;
  T:- Blanks(1);
  T:= "  "; ! Single space;
  if T.GetChar='  ' then
  begin
    if T.GetChar='  ' then
      T:= T.Sub(2,T.Length)
  end;
  OutText(T);
  OutImage
end
```

Change this program so that whatever value is assigned to T it will not cause a runtime error.

4.2 What happens if the value assigned to T is NoText or ""? If your program does not cater for this case, change it.

4.3 Write a version of our original program which replaces three blanks at the start of a text with a single space.

4.4 Write a version of our original program which replaces two or three spaces with one.

4.5 Could we write a program which looks along the whole of a text and replaces all occurrences of double blanks? This may or may not be possible with our present knowledge of SIMULA. What facilities would make it possible and/or easier?

4.6 The following program was intended to write a greeting, but it only prints a blank line. Fix it.

```
begin
    comment This program is supposed to say hello
    OutText ("Hello")
    comment But all it does is print blank lines;
    OutImage
end of greeting
```

Line breaker

Our second example breaks lines at a length of 60 characters. It is rather crude, but we can improve it. This is another development technique which is widely used — stepwise refinement. Stepwise refinement works by getting part of the job working and moving, one step at a time, towards a complete solution.

Again we start with an informal half SIMULA description, in example 4.8.

```
begin
  text T;
  InImage;
   inspect SysIn do
  begin
    T :- Blanks(Image.Length);
    T:=Image
  end;
  if T.Length>60 then ! Line too long;
    Break T into two lines and print them
  else OutText(T); ! Otherwise write it out unchanged;
  OutImage
end
```

Example 4.8 Outline of a line breaker

This time we have filled in more of the program to start with. As you become more familiar with SIMULA, you will be able to write large parts of a program straight away. Do not be tempted to fill in more than the most routine parts, however, as you may need to revise your design as you go.

You have probably noticed that the program uses an *if–then–else* statement. This is because the statement following the *else* is not used if the statement following the *if* is executed. T will not be printed if it is split.

You have probably also noticed the comparison and the new symbol it uses, $>$. This replaces the $=$ and *ne* symbols that we have used before. It means 'is greater than', as you may have guessed from its use. A full list of the comparison operators, or 'relational operators' as they are known, is given in Table 4.1.

We are left to fill in the actions when the length of the line is greater than 60 characters. One immediate problem is that more than one action is required, yet only a single statement is allowed in this place in the *if–then–else* statement. Fortunately, we have already seen the answer.

Table 4.1 Relational operators

Symbol	Alternative	Meaning
$=$	*eq*	is equal to
$< >$	*ne*	is not equal to
$>$	*gt*	is greater than
$<$	*lt*	is less than
$> =$	*ge*	is greater than or equal! to
$< =$	*le*	is less than or equal to

Compound statements and blocks as statements

If you think back, I mentioned that a block in SIMULA can be used as a statement. More generally, we can use a sequence of statements enclosed in *begin* and *end* wherever we can use a simple statement.

In fact SIMULA uses the term 'compound statement' for such a sequence if it contains only statements and the term block where it contains its own declarations. Let us rewrite our program using each in turn to see this, first with a compound statement in example 4.9.

Note that we have used two new variables, which are only needed within the compound statement. We can rewrite this using a block and declaring these where they are used (see example 4.10). This prevents accidental assignment to them elsewhere, since variables declared inside a sub-block are not visible outside of it. They are, however, visible inside sub-blocks which it encloses.

In general it is safest to declare variables as close to the point where they are used as is possible.

```
begin
    text T, First, Second; ! Two new text variables used;
    InImage;
    inspect SysIn do
    begin
        T :- Blanks(Image.Length);
        T:=Image
    end;
    if T.Length>60 then ! Line too long;
    begin ! Break into two add print separately;
        First :- Blanks(60); Second :- Blanks(T.Length-60);
        First:=T.Sub(1,60); ! First 60 characters;
        Second:=T.Sub(61,T.Length-60); !Second part;
        OutText(First);
        OutImage; ! To separate the lines;
        OutText(Second)
    end else OutText(T); ! Print unchanged;
    OutImage
end
```

Example 4.9 Line breaker with a compound statement

```
begin
    text T; ! No new text variables here;
    InImage;
    inspect SysIn do
    begin
        T :- Blanks(Image.Length);
        T := Image
    end;
    if T.Length>60 then ! Line too long;
    begin
        text First,Second; ! Declare the variables here;
        First :- Blanks(60); Second :- Blanks(T.Length-60);
        First := T.Sub(1,60); ! First 60 characters;
        Second := T.Sub(61,T.Length); ! Rest of text;
        OutText(First); OutImage;
        OutText(Second)
    end else OutText(T); ! Print unchanged;
    OutImage
end
```

Example 4.10 Line breaker with a block as a statement

Summary

- We have seen the use of *if* and *if−then−else* statements to enable choices within our programs.
- We have seen how top-down design works and begun to outline the software that we shall build as our practical work in this book.
- Using *if* and *if−then−else* statements we have written programs which will form the basis for some parts of our system — double-blank removal and line breaking.
- We have seen the concept of stepwise refinement.
- We have seen how to replace simple statements with compound statements and blocks.

Exercises

4.7 Extend our line breaking program to cope with lines longer than 120 characters.

4.8 Could we extend the program to cope with lines even longer than this? How does this fit in with the problem in 4.5?

Chapter 5

While loops and basic properties of texts

Don't stop until I tell you

In the last chapter we twice considered the question of how to extend programs which assumed a maximum number of repeated tests, so that any number could be dealt with, as the data required. I hope you managed to deal with triple spaces and triple-length lines without too much trouble. Obviously it would be more of the same to cope with four spaces or lines longer than 180 characters and so on. But how can we cope with any number of repetitions?

This situation is obviously going to crop up in most real programs. To deal with it SIMULA has a statement known as a *while* loop. Example 5.1 shows it in use.

```
begin comment Read and Total a stream of Positive numbers,
            ending when a negative number is found;
    integer Total,Next;
    Next := InInt; ! Read in an integer;
    while Next>=0 do ! Only perform the next statement if
                        condition is true;
    begin
        Total := Total + Next; ! Update total;
        Next := InInt; ! Read in the Next integer;
    end; ! Go back to the start of the while loop;
    OutInt(Total,8); ! When the condition fails, print the total;
    OutImage
end
```

Example 5.1 A *while* loop

This is a simple program and it is explained by its comments. Let us look at the syntax of the *while* loop statement, which may be used wherever any simple statement may be used.

A *while* loop is the keyword *while*, followed by a condition, followed by the keyword *do*, followed by a statement.

In our example the statement following the *do* is a compound statement, but any kind of statement may be used.

This is very similar to the *if* statement, with *while* instead of *if* and *do* instead of *then*. The real difference is in the meaning — the semantics.

The condition is tested and, like an *if* statement, if it is not true, the rest of the *while* loop is skipped and the program continues after the *while* statement.

If, on the other hand, the condition is true, the remainder of the *while* statement, i.e. the statement following *do*, is executed, again like an *if* statement. When this statement has been completed, however, the program moves back to the *while* and tests the condition again. Thus the statement following the *do* is executed repeatedly for as long as the condition remains true.

To see this more clearly, let us consider some possible streams of input. The simplest is where the first number is negative. In this case the condition *Next>=0* is false the first time it is tested and the statement following the *do* is never executed. If we had used an *if* statement the effect would have been the same.

Another possible stream is one positive number followed by a negative number. Here the condition is true the first time and the number is added to *Total*. When the next number has been read the program moves back to *while*. This time the condition is false and so the statement after *do* is skipped and the total will be the value of the first number.

Exercise

5.1 Work through the case where two positive numbers are input, followed by a negative one. It is known as 'dry checking' when you try the program 'by hand' in this way.

Compile and run the program to make sure you were right.

Line breaker revisited

We can now extend our line breaker to deal with any length of line. Let us write it out informally, to get our design right.

The important things to consider when writing programs using *while* loops are:

1 What condition is to be tested?
2 Have all values used in the test been set the first time the test is carried out?

3 Are all the possible cases covered?

4 Are at least some of the values used in the condition potentially updated within the loop before each subsequent test?

Bearing this in mind, let us start with the program in example 5.2.

```
begin
  Set up initial values;
  while condition do
  begin
    Actions;
    Update values tested in condition
  end;
  Final actions
end
```

Example 5.2 General outline of a program using a *while* loop

The initial values are set by reading the line into Image as before and assigning its Length to an integer, LenLeft. The condition to be tested is that the unprinted part of Image is longer than 60 characters. Once this length is 60 characters or less, we want to print the remainder of Image as a separate line and this makes up the final actions. This gives us example 5.3.

```
begin
  integer LenLeft;
  inspect SysIn do
  begin
    InImage;
    LenLeft:=Image.Length;
    while LenLeft>60 do
    begin
      Actions;
      Update tested variables
    end;
    OutText(Image.Sub(1,LenLeft));
    OutImage
  end..of..inspect..SysIn
end
```

Example 5.3 Line breaker 1

This leaves the actions and updating within the loop to be filled in. The actions are to print the current first 60 characters of Image as a separate line. The updating must reduce LenLeft, otherwise the loop will go on indefinitely. The simplest solution is to remove the first 60 characters from Image and subtract 60 from LenLeft. Thus our complete program is example 5.4.

```
begin
    integer LenLeft;
    inspect SysIn do
    begin
        InImage;
        LenLeft:=Image.Length;
        while LenLeft>60 do
        begin
            OutText(Image.Sub(1,60));
            OutImage;
            LenLeft := LenLeft - 60;
            Image:=Image.Sub(61,LenLeft)
        end;
        OutText(Image);
        OutImage
    end..of..inspect..SysIn
end
```

Example 5.4 Line breaker 2

This time I have used a more concise way of printing the first 60 characters and, since Image takes the place of Second in the examples in Chapter 4, no extra text variables are used.

Exercise

5.2 Are there any line lengths which are not catered for? If you can think of any, modify the program to cater for them.

What is a text?

In the last chapter we saw some properties of *text*, which make it a much more complex type than *integer*, for example. Let us consider further what exactly a text is and what properties it has. In fact it is so complex that we shall only look at half of its properties here and leave the rest until Chapter 8.

So far we have seen that a text has a string of characters. This may be of any length from zero to some very large number. The maximum length is system dependent and you should consult the user's guide or programmer's reference manual for the SIMULA system you are using. It is unlikely to be too small for you.

We have also seen that a text contains procedures, which are inside it or 'local to it', to use the technical term. In fact a text variable is not quite what it seems.

Strictly speaking the location reserved for the text variable holds a reference to a sequence of characters. These characters are known as a text frame. A text reference contains a pointer to its text frame plus related variables and procedures. The use of these will, hopefully, soon become clear.

A text reference

The variables inside a text reference are not visible outside it. They are used by the procedures which form the visible attributes of a text, along with the text frame.

The major parts of a text, with examples of their use, are described below.

Text frame

The value part of a text is the string of characters to which its reference variable points. This is known as the text frame, referenced by that variable. It is a location in the computer's memory holding a sequence of characters and has a fixed length.

Two text frames may overlap and share some part or all of the same sequence of characters and, by implication, of the same location.

Length

The length of the string of characters in the text frame is held in a hidden integer in the text-reference variable. Its value can be obtained by calling the local integer procedure Length. We have used this in some earlier examples to find the length of a line of input (see example 5.5).

Note that the name given to the integer is irrelevant to the call of Image.Length. I have called it Length to demonstrate that the procedure

```
begin
   integer Length;
   InImage;
   inspect SysIn do Length := Image.Length;
   OutInt(Length,8);
   OutImage
end
```

Example 5.5 Use of Length

Image.Length is different from any use of Length on its own, in the program itself.

Pos

The position of the character which will be read next in the text frame is held in another hidden integer variable within the text reference. It can be read by calling the integer procedure Pos. When a text object is first created, Pos will give the value 1. After calling GetChar for the first time it will give 2 and so on. See example 5.6.

```
begin
   InImage;
   inspect SysIn do
   begin
      OutInt(Image.Pos,4);
      OutImage;
      Image.GetChar;
      OutInt(Image.Pos,4);
      OutImage
   end
end
```

Example 5.6 Use of Pos

You should get

1
2

as output when you run this.

More

More tells you when you have reached the end of a text. It returns either True or False, i.e. it is a Boolean procedure.

More gives the value True as long as the value given by Pos is between 1 and the value given by Length. Thus, once the last character has been read, More returns the value False (see example 5.7).

```
begin
   InImage;
   inspect SysIn do
      while Image.More do
      begin
         OutInt(Image.Pos,4);Image.GetChar;
         OutImage
      end;
end
```

Example 5.7 Use of More

When you run example 5.7 you should get output of the following form.

```
1
2
3
4
etc. until Image.Length
```

Constant

Boolean procedure Constant is a recent addition to the definition of text. It returns the value False unless the text frame for its text reference is non-writeable, in which case it returns True. Only text frames generated by reference assignment of a constant string (see below) or subtexts generated from these will cause Constant to return True. Any attempt to alter the contents of a text frame whose reference returns True for Constant will cause a runtime error to be reported.

As a very new feature, Constant will not be recognized by many older systems.

See example 5.8.

```
begin
  text T;
  T :- "Constant frame";
  if T.Constant then OutText("Correct") else OutText("Wrong");
  T :- Copy("Writeable");
  if T.Constant then OutText("Wrong") else OutText("Correct");
end
```

Example 5.8 Use of Constant

Sub and Start

We have already used Sub. Sub returns a reference to a text frame made up of a sequence of characters which are part of the original text. It has two integer parameters. The first specifies the number of the character in the original text frame which will be the start of the subtext. The second specifies the number of characters which will be in the subtext.

Example 5.9 will print out the following:

    Miser
    cord
    Mire

Make sure you understand why. Try running it for yourself.

Note that Sub does not copy the characters from the original text. It merely creates a text reference to part of the same location.

```
begin
  text T;
  T:-"Misericordia";
  OutText(T.Sub(1,5));
  OutImage;
  OutText(T.Sub(7,4));
  OutImage;
  OutText(T.Sub(1,2));
  OutText(T.Sub(5,1));
  OutText(T.Sub(4,1));
  OutImage
end
```

Example 5.9 Use of Sub

Recently, integer procedure Start has been added to the definition of text. It is used in conjunction with Sub, to keep track of where the current text frame starts within the original text frame of which it forms part. Only text frames generated by calls on Sub can cause Start to return anything but 1.

When a new text reference is generated by Sub, the value of Start in the new reference will be the value of Start for the text passed to Sub plus the offset within this of the text frame of the subtext, i.e. the first parameter of Sub minus 1. Start reflects the cumulative effects of any Sub calls which have produced the text frame of the current text reference.

Older systems will have Sub but not Start. See example 5.10.

```
begin
    text T1, T2, T3;
    T1 :- "123456789";
    T2 :- T1.Sub(3,7);
    T3 :- T2.Sub(3,5);
    OutInt(T1.Start,4);    ! 1;
    OutInt(T2.Start,4);    ! 1+3-1=3;
    OutInt(T3.Start,4);    ! 3+3-1=5;
    OutImage
end
```

Example 5.10 Use of Start

Text assignments

The oddest thing about texts is that there are two different kinds of assignment statement, using two different assignment operators. We have already used both, but now we can explain their differences.

There are text-reference assignments and text-value assignments. Examples are:

T:− Blanks(60);! Reference assignment;
T:= "Hello";! Value assignment;

The difference is very simple, but very important.

A text-reference assignment will replace the pointer in the text-reference location, which originally points to one text frame, with a different reference, which may or may not point to a different text frame. All the parts of the original text reference, including its current

Pos, Length etc., are replaced by the corresponding parts of the new text reference. Thus calls on T.Length and T.Pos may give different values before and after a reference assignment to T.

A text-value assignment will only replace the characters held in the text frame. None of the other parts are replaced and so calls on T.Length or T.Pos will return the same values before and after a value assignment to T.

Since a value assignment leaves the Length unchanged, we must be careful that the number of new characters being assigned is not greater than Length. In fact three cases are possible:

1   The number of characters being assigned is the same as Length. In this case the new characters simply overwrite the old contents of the text.

2   The number of characters being assigned is less than Length. In this case the leftmost characters in the text are overwritten by the new characters and the remainder by spaces. The value of Left.Length is unchanged in example 5.11b.

3   The number of characters being assigned is greater than Length. This will be a runtime error. The program will compile successfully, but at runtime will report an error.

Note that text-value assignment to a constant text frame is always illegal.

NoText

When you create a text variable it is set to point to NoText. NoText is an imaginary text frame with no characters. Thus it has a Length of zero and any value assignment to it will fail, except when the value is the empty text value, "". This is the reason we had to use Blanks in our early examples, to make what you should now recognize as a text-reference assignment to any text variable, before any value assignments were made to it.

Creating text objects

In general, we must make a reference assignment to a text variable before we use it for almost anything else. This points it at a text frame and sets the values for Pos, Length etc., but where does this object come from in the first place?

(*a*) Equal-length texts.

```
begin
  text Left,Right;
  Left :- Copy("FRED"); ! Length of Left becomes 4;
  Right :- Copy("DAVE"); ! Length of Right becomes 4;
  Left:=Right;
  OutText(Left);OutImage;
  OutInt(Left.Length);OutImage
end
```

(*b*) Left-hand text longer than right.

```
begin
  text Left,Right;
  Left :- Copy("FRED"); ! Length of Left becomes 4;
  Right :- Copy("JIM"); ! Length of Right becomes 3;
  Left:=Right;
  OutText(Left);OutImage;
  OutInt(Left.Length);OutImage
end
```

(*c*) Left-hand text shorter than right.

```
begin
  text Left,Right;
  Left :- Copy("FRED"); ! Length of Left becomes 4;
  Right :- Copy("CHARLIE"); ! Length of Right becomes
  Left:=Right; ! Causes a runtime error;
  OutText(Left);OutImage;
  OutInt(Left.Length);OutImage
end
```

Example 5.11 Possible cases of text-value assignment

In fact we have used several methods of text-object generation already, without explaining them in detail. Here is a more detailed look.

Blanks

The standard procedure Blanks creates a new text object containing only spaces. It has one integer parameter, which specifies the number of space characters it is to contain and, thus, sets its Length.

Start and Pos will initially be 1. More will be True. Constant will be False. See example 5.12.

```
begin
    text Empty;
    Empty :- Blanks(60);
    comment Point Empty at a text frame containing 60 spaces;
    OutInt(Empty.Length,4);
    OutImage
end
```

Example 5.12 Use of Blanks for text generation

Reference assignment of text constants

We have seen how text constants, or strings, are represented. When a text-reference assignment, whose right-hand side is such a constant, is made, a text frame is created containing the characters in the string.

One important property of the text frame created in this way is that it is regarded as constant or 'read only'. Any attempt to overwrite its characters will cause a runtime error.

The value of Length will be the number of characters in the string. Start and Pos will be 1. More will be True. Constant will be True. See example 5.13.

The text frame generated for each text constant in a program is regarded as occupying a unique location. This is important when we come to 'reference comparison' of texts. The only exception is an occurrence of the empty string, "", which is always assumed to generate a reference to the imaginary location of NoText.

```
begin
    text Full;
    Full:-"Any old string you like";
    OutInt(Full.Length,4);
    OutImage
end
```

Example 5.13 Text-constant reference assignment

Copy

In older SIMULA systems, reference assignment of text constants
was not allowed. If you are using such a system you will have to use
the standard procedure Copy to do the same thing. Copy will still work
on newer systems, so if you may need to move your programs around a
lot it might be safer to use it from the start.

Copy differs from constant text-reference assignment in that the
text frame created is alterable or 'writeable'. It is possible to overwrite
its characters. Thus Copy may be used for many purposes where text-
reference assignment of constants would not be suitable, even on
newer systems.

Copy can also be used to generate a reference to a copy of the text
frame of another text reference, not just a string. The second use of
Copy in example 5.14 shows this.

Rewriting example 5.13 using Copy, we get the first part of
example 5.14. This should have exactly the same effects, except that
attempts to overwrite Full would now be successful.

In the reference generated by Copy, Length is the length of the
string or of the text frame being copied. Start and Pos are 1. More is
True. Constant is False.

```
begin
   text Full, NewFrame;
   Full :- Copy("Any old string you like");
   OutInt(Full.Length,4);
   OutImage;
   NewFrame :- Copy(Full);
   OutInt(NewFrame.Length,4);
   OutImage
end
```

Example 5.14 Text generation using Copy

Line breaker again

Using the facts about reference assignment of text variables that we
have just seen, it is possible to write our line-breaking program more
neatly. It should now be obvious why we used the integer LenLeft to
hold the length of Image which remained. It is now possible to use
Image.Length instead (see example 5.15).

This version has another advantage, which probably is not apparent. In the version using value assignment, the Length of Image remains unchanged throughout, with more space characters following the visible characters after each assignment of Image.Sub. These characters are not present after the reference assignments in the new version. Since some output devices make a printing movement even for a space, their presence may slow down output. They also take up space in the computer's memory which is freed in the new version.

```
begin
   InImage;
   inspect SysIn do
   begin
      while Image.Length>60 do
      begin
         OutText(Image.Sub(1,60));
         OutImage;
         Image :- Image.Sub(61,Image.Length-60);
         comment Note the use of reference assignment which
                 updates Image.Length, unlike value assignment;
      end;
      OutText(Image);
      OutImage
   end
end
```

Example 5.15 Line breaker using reference assignment of texts

```
begin
   text T1;
   character Char;
   InImage;
   inspect SysIn do
   begin
      T1 :- Image;
      while T1.More do
      begin
         Char := T1.GetChar;
         if multiple space then replace with single space
      end;
      Remove trailing spaces;
      OutText(T1);
      OutImage
   end
end
```

Example 5.16 Informal description of multiple-space remover

Exercises

We have had quite a lot to absorb recently, so here are some examples to help your digestion. Then we will have another look at space removal and a final look, for the moment, at text objects.

5.3   Write a program to draw a Christmas tree, like the one below.

5.4   Write a program to count the number of characters before the first space in a text.

5.5   Write a program to count the number of words in a text, assuming that only spaces separate words.

5.6   Write a program to calculate the cost of sending a telegram, assuming that the whole message is contained in a single text. Assume that each word costs 10 pence.

5.7   Rewrite the last program assuming that words longer than 5 characters cost double and that the minimum charge is 50 pence.

5.8   Use Sub to write the message Merry Christmas using parts of the string "May Charlie stay for curry?".

5.9   Is it possible to rewrite the word-counting program to allow full stops (periods) and commas to be word separators? What extra SIMULA facility would be useful for this?

Double-blank remover, mark two

The problem with our double-blank-removing program is that it will only work when the double blank is at the start of the text. What we really need is a program to read along the whole of a text and remove any double blanks. Even better, it should remove treble and other multiple blanks as well.

Using our informal SIMULA description method, we can start with the program in example 5.16. The problems to be solved are how to detect multiple blanks and how to replace them with a single-space character. The first of these is fairly easy.

If the current character is a space, check to see if the next one is also. If it is not, carry on around the loop. If it is, check whether the next character is also a space and so on. When a non-space is found, move the remainder of the text to the left until only one space remains. Clearly the scanning along multiple spaces is another *while* loop. Let us write out the program so far, in example 5.17.

This is getting rather complicated, so let us have a look at what is going on in the case where a blank is encountered. It is always sensible to 'dry check' new parts of your program when they become more than trivial extensions.

First we check that this is not the end of the line, by using T.More. If we try to use GetChar when we are already at the end, it will cause a runtime error to be reported. If there is more to read, we note the current position in Position1. This is the position of the first character after the space and so we remove any spaces from here to the next non-space character.

We now read the next character into Char2 and begin our blank-removal loop. As long as Char2 is a space we read on, checking that we have not reached the end of the text. If we have reached the end, we do not need to trouble with this sequence of blanks, since they are at the end of the text. We shall see how to deal with such 'trailing blanks' in a moment.

If we do reach the end of the text while skipping through a sequence of blanks, we want to leave the loop and avoid further processing of this text. To achieve this we set a dummy value in Char2, which is not a space character, thus ending the *while* loop. Since we are not interested in removing any blanks, we reset our position to Position1.

Having completed the *while* loop, we check to see if Position2 is still the same as Position1. If it is then we have either not found any spaces following the first one or the current sequence of spaces is at the end of the text. In both these cases no spaces need be removed. If

```
begin
  text T1;
  character Char1, Char2;
  InImage;
  inspect SysIn do
  begin
    T1 :- Image;
    while T1.More do
    begin
      Char1 := T1.GetChar;
      if Char1=' ' then
      begin
        integer Position1, Position2;
        if T1.More then
        begin
          Position1 := T1.Pos; ! Remember current position;
          Char2 := T1.GetChar; ! Check Next character;
          while Char2=' ' do
            if T1.More then Char2 := T1.GetChar else
            begin
              Char2 := '£';
              Reset Pos to Position1
            end;
          Position2 := T1.Pos; ! Remember final position;
          if Position1 ne Position2 then move the rest left;
          Reset Pos to first character after blank
        end
      end
    end;
    Remove trailing spaces;
    OutText(T1);
    OutImage
  end
end
```

Example 5.17 Second stage of multiple-space remover

Position2 is different, we have skipped over some spaces in the *while* loop and want to remove them.

Having removed any extra spaces, we reset our position to that immediately following the single space, i.e. to Position1, and continue reading through the text looking for the next space, in the outer *while* loop.

Try following some texts through the program on paper. In particular, try to think of all the different cases which might occur. The choice of test data for your programs is very important. If you forget a case then your program will almost certainly fail the first time it is used in earnest.

We still have two parts of the program to fill in. Before we can do so we must look at some more properties of text objects.

GetChar and PutChar

We have seen how GetChar works, but let us quickly define exactly what it does. GetChar returns the character at the current position in a text and increments the position counter by one. Thus successive calls on GetChar will scan through a text character by character.

PutChar overwrites the character at the current position in a text with the value passed to it as a parameter. It has a single character parameter. It increments the position counter by one each time it is called.

In example 5.18 the program joins the character contents of two texts together. This is sometimes referred to as concatenating them.

```
begin
  text T1, T2, T3;
  InImage;
  inspect SysIn do
  begin
    T1 :- Copy(Image.Strip); ! Strip is explained next;
    InImage;
    T2 :- Copy(Image.Strip);
    T3 :- Blanks(T1.Length + T2.Length); ! Create enough space;
    while T1.More do T3.PutChar(T1.GetChar);
    comment T3.Pos is now T1.Length + 1;
    while T2.More do T3.PutChar(T2.GetChar);
    OutText(T3);
    OutImage
  end
end
```

Example 5.18 Text concatenation using GetChar and PutChar

SetPos

One of our problems in our space-removal program is solved immediately by the procedure SetPos. This takes one integer parameter.

SetPos resets the current position in a text to the value passed to it as a parameter. Using this we can rewrite our text-concatenation program more simply.

```
begin
  text T1, T2, T3;
  InImage;
  inspect SysIn do
  begin
    T1 :- Copy(Image.Strip);
    InImage;
    T2 :- Copy(Image.Strip);
    T3 :- Blanks(T1.Length + T2.Length);
    T3 := T1;
    T3.SetPos(T1.Length + 1);
    while T2.More do T3.PutChar(T2.GetChar);
    OutText(T3);
    OutImage
  end
end
```

Example 5.19 Text concatenation with SetPos

Strip

Another small problem is solved by the procedure Strip. This returns a text reference to the original text with any trailing spaces, i.e. any spaces at the right-hand end of the text, removed. Try the program in example 5.20 to see this at work.

```
begin
  text T;
  T :- Blanks(60);
  T := "FOUR";
  OutInt(T.Length);
  T :- T.Strip;
  OutInt(T.Length);
  OutImage
end
```

Example 5.20 Use of Strip

Main

The last part of a text object that we need to consider at this point is the procedure Main.

When a text variable is pointed at a subtext, by using Sub or Strip, the result is that the text variable points at a new text frame. This shares some of the characters in the original, main text, but has its own local Pos, Length and other attributes. Pos will be 1 and Length will be the length of the subtext.

It is still possible to refer to the main text from the subtext, however, by using the attribute Main. This procedure returns a reference to the text frame of which the subtext forms a part. For a text reference whose text frame is not a subtext of a larger one, Main points to that frame itself.

The reference generated by Main has Pos and Start equal to 1 and Length equal to the Length of the main text frame.

```
begin
    text T1, T2, T3;
    T1 :- "Now is the time for every good man";
    T2 :- T1.Sub(5,20);
    T3 :- T2.Sub(4,17);
    OutText(T2);
    OutImage;
    OutText(T2.Main);
    OutText(T3);
    OutImage;
    OutText(T3.Main);
    OutImage
end
```

Example 5.21 Use of Main

Example 5.21 should produce the following output:

    is the time for ever
    Now is the time for every good man
    the time for ever
    Now is the time for every good man

Multiple spaces finally removed

First consider example 5.22, where SetPos and Strip are added to our program. We have now catered for everything except the actual deletion process.

Example 5.23 adds the final stage — the removal of those blanks. Watch closely, as we are going to use a very powerful property of text-reference assignment.

```
begin
   text T1;
   InImage;
   inspect SysIn do
   begin
      T1 :- Image;
      while T1.More do
      begin
         character Char1, Char2;
         Char1 := T1.GetChar;
         if Char1=' ' then
         begin
            if T1.More then
            begin
               integer Position1, Position2;
               Position1 := T1.Pos;
               Char2 := T1.GetChar;
               while Char2=' ' do
                  if T1.More then Char2 := T1.GetChar else
                  begin
                     Char2 := '£'; ! Force loop to end;
                     T1.SetPos(Position1); ! Ignore spaces;
                  end;
               Position2 := T1.Pos;
               if Position1 ne Position2 then remove spaces;
               T1.SetPos(Position1)
            end
         end
      end;
      T1 :- T1.Strip;
      OutText(T1);
      OutImage
   end
end
```

Example 5.22 Adding SetPos and Strip to multiple-space deletion

```
begin
  text T1;
  InImage;
  inspect SysIn do
  begin
    T1 :- Image;
    while T1.More do
    begin
      character Char1, Char2;
      Char1 := T1.GetChar;
      if Char1=' ' then
      begin
        if T1.More then
        begin
          text T2;
          integer Position1, Position2;
          Position1 := T1.Pos;
          T2 :- T1; ! T2 holds current Pos, Length etc.;
          Char2 := T1.GetChar;
          while Char2=' ' do
            if T1.More then Char2 := T1.GetChar else
            begin
              Char2 := '£';
              T1.SetPos(Position1)
            end;
          Position2 := T1.Pos;
          if Position1 ne Position2 then
          begin
            T2.PutChar(Char2);
            while T1.More do T2.PutChar(T1.GetChar);
            while T2.More do T2.PutChar(' ');
            T1 :- T2
          end;
          T1.SetPos(Position1)
        end
      end
    end;
    T1 :- T1.Strip;
    OutText(T1);
    OutImage
  end
end
```

Example 5.23 The complete multiple-space remover

Chapter 5

The point to note is that when the text variable T2 is pointed at the text frame already pointed to by T, the effect is that a new reference is created with all its current values the same as T. As in a subtext, some of the characters are shared by both frames; in this case it is all the characters which are shared. When T.GetChar is used, it is only the Pos of T that is affected. That of T2 is unaffected.

When we are shuffling the characters to the left to remove unwanted spaces, we are able to pretend that T and T2 are entirely different texts. If we did not do this, we would have to copy into another text frame and then back again. This way of manipulating the characters in a text is very powerful, but must be fully understood and used with great care. It is only when the part of the text that we are copying from is ahead of the part that we are copying to that this method will work.

Summary

We are now writing programs which really do things.
- In this chapter we have seen the *while* loop and how it can allow an action or sequence of actions to be repeated as often as necessary.
- We have used informal SIMULA descriptions to allow us to develop our programs in stages.
- We have learned some of the attributes of a text object — Length, Pos, Sub, Start, Constant, Main, Strip, GetChar, PutChar and SetPos.
- We have learned the difference between a text variable and the text frame it points to.
- We have learned the difference between text-value assignment and text-reference assignment.
- We have seen how text objects are generated by Blanks, Copy or reference assignment of a text constant, noting that those generated by reference assignment of a constant may not be over-written.
- We have seen how two text variables pointing at the same sequence of characters can have different current positions.

Exercises

5.10 A computer fault has changed some small letter a's into ampersands, '&'. Write a program to scan a text and correct this.

5.11 A similar fault has changed every occurrence of the word 'and' to the word 'boe'. Write a program to correct texts which have suffered this fate.

Chapter 6

Procedures

Building blocks

We have written some programs which do real work, but at the moment they have to be run separately, with the input provided for each run. It is not obvious how we can use such separate programs to build a large, flexible piece of software.

One method would be to combine all the small programs that we write into one large program, using each program in the right order. We could use our multiple-space-removing program, followed by our line-breaking program, and so on. This is fine for programs that only need to be used in one place, but if the same function is required in several places we will need to duplicate the instructions each time. This is inefficient, making our programs much longer than they need to be. It can also make it tedious to follow the overall working of a large program, since a mass of detailed instructions tends to obscure the important features of the design.

As an example of a program which could be used in many places in our package, we might take the text-concatenation program. In fact this is such a useful thing to be able to do that we might wish that a language feature existed for it. Such a facility is now provided as part of SIMULA although, unfortunately, it is not yet available in most systems. We shall see it in Chapter 8. Fortunately, we are able to define our own procedures, which we can then use wherever we like inside the block where we declare them. In fact we can even build a library of our favourite procedures and use it in all our programs.

Declaring procedures

It is clearly not enough to declare a procedure in the way we declare an integer. The declaration

    procedure Concatenate

cannot magically tell the SIMULA system what we want Concatenate

74

to do. We must also supply the actions to match the name. Here is a valid procedure declaration:

```
procedure PrintName;
  OutText("Alice");
```

The syntax of the simplest procedure declaration is the keyword *procedure*, followed by the identifier to be used for the procedure, followed by a semi-colon, followed by a statement.

The statement following the semi-colon is known as the procedure body and specifies what is to be done each time the procedure is invoked or 'called' in the subsequent program. Calling the procedure is done by using its identifier as a statement in the program, exactly as we call system procedures.

Example 6.1 shows the use of our procedure, PrintName. Note the use of blank lines to make it easier to see where the procedure begins and ends. These are not compulsory, but make the program more readable to humans.

```
begin

  procedure PrintName;
    OutText("Alice");

  PrintName;
  OutImage
end
```

Example 6.1 Simple procedure use

We would normally want to have more than one statement in our procedure body. We can achieve this by using a compound statement or a block. Example 6.2 is our Concatenate program from Chapter 5 used as a procedure.

Parameters to procedures

This Concatenate procedure only joins texts which are read in by it. Having done so, it merely prints out the result. This would be much more useful if we could use it to combine any two texts in our programs and to assign the result to any text we choose. This can be done by specifying parameters in the declaration.

```
begin
  procedure Concatenate;
  begin
    text T1,T2,T3;
    InImage;
    inspect SysIn do
    begin
      T1:-Copy(Image.Strip);
      InImage;
      T2:-Copy(Image.Strip);
      T3:-Blanks(T1.Length + T2.Length);
      T3:=T1; T3.SetPos(T1.Length+1);
      while T2.More do T3.PutChar(T2.GetChar);
    end--of--inspect--SysIn;
    OutText(T3);
    OutImage
  end;
  Concatenate
end
```

Example 6.2 Concatenate as a procedure

We have already seen how parameters can be used to pass values to system procedures. Example 6.3 shows how to declare two texts as parameters to the Concatenate procedure.

```
begin
  procedure Concatenate(T1,T2); text T1,T2;
  begin
    text T3;
    T3:-Blanks(T1.Length+T2.Length);
    T3:=T1;
    T3.SetPos(T1.Length+1);
    while T2.More do T3.PutChar(T2.GetChar);
    OutText(T3);
    OutImage
  end;
  text Text1,Text2;
  Text1:-"Fred";
  Text2:-"Smith";
  Concatenate(Text1,Text2)
end
```

Example 6.3 Concatenate with parameters

This passes in our texts, T1 and T2, which are now used as parameters to the procedure. The identifier given for the procedure in its declaration is followed by a list of all the parameters to be used, enclosed in parentheses and separated by commas. The declaration

    text T1, T2;

following the semi-colon and before the *begin* is known as the type specifier and gives the type of each of the parameters.

Where more than one type of parameter is to be used, more than one type declaration must be given. Example 6.4 uses one text and one integer parameter.

```
begin
  procedure TextAndInt(T,I); text T; integer I;
  begin
    OutText(T);
    OutInt(I);
    OutImage
  end;
  TextAndInt("NUMBER",10)
end
```

Example 6.4 A procedure with more than one type of parameter

When execution of a procedure is complete, all quantities declared inside it are lost. This includes the final values of its parameters. The remaining question is how to get back the text containing the concatenated texts once Concatenate is complete. There are two ways of doing this in SIMULA and the first of these uses a different sort of parameter.

Parameter modes

The way of specifying parameters that we have used so far will always work for passing values into a procedure. If we want to get information out, we may have to add a mode specifier for some parameters.

This sounds confusing, but is easy to follow in practice. Example 6.5 is a final version of Concatenate.

Notice that, as well as specifying that T3 is of type *text*, we have specified that it is *name*. *name* is not a type but a mode. When a

```
begin
  procedure Concatenate(T1,T2,T3);
  name T3; text T1,T2,T3;
  begin
    T3:-Blanks(T1.Length + T2.Length);
    T3:=T1;
    T3.SetPos(T1.Length + 1);
    while T2.More do T3.PutChar(T2.GetChar);
  end;
  text Text1,Text2,Text3;
  Text1:-"Fred";
  Text2:-"Smith";
  Concatenate(Text1,Text2,Text3);
  OutText(Text3);
  OutImage
end
```

Example 6.5 Using a name parameter to return a result

parameter is defined as of name mode, any assignments to it alter the value of the variable actually passed in the call, rather than a local copy, as would have happened with the other parameters, which are passed by value.

In fact there are three modes: value, reference and name. Where a mode specifier is not given for a parameter, a mode of value or reference is assumed, depending on its type. Some modes are illegal for certain types. Table 6.1 is a complete table of the assumed (usually referred to as default), legal and illegal modes for parameters to procedures.

A simple type is integer, real, character or Boolean and any long or short variants of them.

Now we can see that name is always legal and reference is the default for all but simple types. Do not worry about the meaning of those types which are new. We shall consider their use when we encounter them.

Value parameters

A value parameter to a procedure acts as if it were a variable of that type declared in the body of the procedure. The value passed to it when the procedure is called is copied into it as part of the call

Table 6.1 Modes of transmission for parameter types

| | Mode | | |
Type	Value	Reference	Name
Simple type	Default	Illegal	Legal
text	Legal	Default	Legal
Object reference	Illegal	Default	Legal
Simple type array	Legal	Default	Legal
Reference type array	Illegal	Default	Legal
procedure	Illegal	Default	Legal
type procedure	Illegal	Default	Legal
label	Illegal	Default	Legal
switch	Illegal	Default	Legal

statement. Since values declared inside a block cannot be used outside that block, the value of this mode of parameter is lost on returning from the procedure.

When calling a procedure, any value of the correct type may be passed to a value mode parameter. Thus constants, expressions and variables are all allowed.

To see the effect of passing a parameter by value, consider example 6.6.

```
begin

    procedure P(Val); integer Val;
    begin
       OutInt(Val);
       OutImage;
       Val := Val - 1;
       OutInt(Val);
       OutImage
    end..of..P;

    integer OuterVal;
    OuterVal := 4;
    P(OuterVal);
    OutInt(OuterVal);
    OutImage
end
```

Example 6.6 Passing parameters by value

The value in OuterVal, 4, is copied into the parameter Val's location when P is called. Thus the first number printed will be 4.

When 1 is subtracted from Val, OuterVal is not changed. Thus the second number printed is 3, but the third is 4.

When a text is passed by value to a procedure (NB this is not the default) it has the effect of creating a reference to a local text frame with the same length as the text passed, into which the characters from the latter text are copied. Consider example 6.7.

```
begin
  text OuterT;

  procedure OutLine(T); value(T); text(T);
  begin
    OutText(T.Strip);
    OutImage
  end..of..OutLine;

  OuterT:-"Here's a line";
  OutLine(OuterT)
end
```

Example 6.7 Text parameter passed by value

OutLine is actually quite a useful procedure. Note that in order to pass our text parameter by value we have to give a mode specification for it, using the keyword *value*.

When the procedure is called, the parameter T is initialized as if the following statements had been executed:

```
T:- Blanks(OuterT.Length);
T:= OuterT
```

Reference parameters

When a parameter is passed by reference, the local parameter points at the location holding the object passed, rather as if the :− reference-assignment operator had been used. No local copy is made of the contents of the object.

For every reference-parameter type except text, this explanation is sufficient and should be reconsidered for its meaning when those types are encountered.

As we have seen, when a text is assigned by reference new copies of Pos, Length etc., are made, but the same actual text frame is referenced. Pos, Length etc., will have the same values as those for the original reference, but will not change if the originals do.

As far as the passing of text parameters by reference is concerned, the following effects occur:

1 The characters in the frame referenced by the parameter may be changed by the procedure. Since this is the same actual location as the frame of the reference which was copied, the contents of the frame remain changed when execution of the procedure is complete.

2 The other attributes have local versions created, with the same values as those current for the parameter. When those other attributes are changed for the parameter, they remain unchanged for the original. Thus, any changes to these are lost when execution of the procedure is complete.

Try rewriting the Concatenate procedure with all the parameters passed by reference. What would be the effect on running the program using it now?

You should find that it fails since the Length of Text3 cannot be changed by manipulating T3 inside the procedure. The only way to get this program to work would be to set the length of Text3 before calling the procedure, as shown in example 6.8.

Note that as reference mode is the default for all types where it is legal, it is never necessary to give a mode specification for reference parameters. Thus there is no keyword *reference* to match *value* and *name*.

Name parameters

Name parameters are very powerful, but complex. It is sometimes possible to make serious errors using them, through failing to consider all possible outcomes of their use.

When a variable is passed by name, its use within the procedure has the same effect as when that variable is used outside the procedure. Thus any actions on the parameter inside the procedure directly affect the variable passed in the call. This is obviously a suitable mode for getting values back from a procedure, as we have seen.

This contrasts with the use of reference mode, where the contents of what a variable points at are changed, but the variable still points at

```
begin

    procedure Concatenate(T1, T2, T3); text T1, T2, T3;
    begin
       T3 := T1;
       T3.SetPos(T1.Length + 1);
       while T2.More do T3.PutChar(T2.GetChar);
    end**of**Concatenate**by**reference;

    text Text1, Text2, Text3;

    Text1 :- "Fred";
    Text2 :- " Smith";
    Text3 :- Blanks(Text1.Length+Text2.Length);
    Concatenate(Text1,Text2,Text3);
    OutText(Text3);
    OutImage
end
```

Example 6.8 Concatenate using only reference-mode parameters

the same location. If a reference assignment is made to a name parameter, it is actually made to the variable passed originally, not a local
copy.

Example 6.5 returned the concatenated texts in the name parameter T3. When the procedure was called, the variable Text3 was
passed as this parameter and when the statement following the call was
executed, Text3 contained the combined texts. There is one statement
missing from this Concatenate. It is needed because the Pos, Length
and other attributes of Text3 will be changed by the procedure, when
it manipulates T3.

What is this missing line? See if you can work out what it is before
reading the polished version below.

Example 6.9 is the version of Concatenate which we can use in all
our programs. The missing statement must reset the position within T3
to the start of the characters it now contains, since it is left pointing to
their end.

Note that, since name mode is never a default for any type, the
mode specifier *name* must be used in a mode specification for any
parameters which are to be used in this way.

```
begin

    procedure Concatenate(T1, T2, T3);
    name T3; text T1, T2, T3;
    begin
       T3 :- Blanks(T1.Length + T2.Length);
       T3 := T1;
       T3.SetPos(T1.Length + 1);
       while T2.More do T3.PutChar(T2.GetChar);
       T3.SetPos(1); ! Did you get this right?;
    end**of**Concatenate;

    text Text1, Text2, Text3;

    Text1 :- "Fred";
    Text2 :- " Smith";
    Concatenate(Text1,Text2,Text3);
    OutText(Text3);
    OutImage
end
```

Example 6.9 Finished version of Concatenate

```
begin
  procedure Use_Name(Val1, Val2); name Val2; integer Val1, Val2;
  begin
    OuterVal := 3;
    OutInt(Val1,4);
    OutInt(Val2,4);
    OutImage
  end..of..Use_Name;

  integer OuterVal;
  OuterVal := 5;

  Use_Name(OuterVal+3,OuterVal+3)
end++of++program
```

Example 6.10 Expressions by name and by value

It is worth mentioning that all parameters passed by name are re-evaluated each time they are used inside the procedure. This is important in some cases since actions inside the procedure may change the value of an expression passed in this way, while expressions passed by value or reference are evaluated and their values copied into the local variables specifying those parameters, once and for all, at the call. Try compiling and running example 6.10 to see the difference.

Note also that while it is legal to pass expressions by name in this way, an attempt to assign to a name parameter when an arithmetic expression like those in example 6.10 or anything else which is not a valid left-hand side had been passed will cause a runtime error. The general rule is that the exact text of what is passed replaces each occurrence of the name parameter within the procedure.

Exercises

6.1 Write a program which uses a procedure to find the larger of two numbers and returns it in a name parameter.

6.2 Write a program which uses our multiple-space-removal program as a procedure. Devise a series of tests to cover all the cases you can think of which this procedure might have to cope with and try them. Do not use lots of tests which all check the same thing, but try to use one good test for each possibility.

6.3 Write and test a procedure which takes two text parameters and Concatenates them, returning the result in the first one.

6.4 Write and test a procedure which takes two characters and moves the value in the first into the second and the value in the second into the first.

6.5 Write and test a procedure which counts the number of non-space characters in a text.

Functions

There is another way to return values from procedures to the calling block. We have already seen examples of system procedures which use this mechanism in GetChar and InInt. Now let us see how to write such procedures for ourselves.

Example 6.11 is an example of such a procedure which adds two numbers together and returns the result. Such a procedure is usually referred to as a 'type procedure' or, most commonly, a 'function'.

This is a very simple example, but it shows how to declare and use such a procedure. The declaration is just like that of any non-type

```
begin

    integer procedure Add(Val1, Val2);
              integer Val1, Val2;
       Add := Val1 + Val2;

    integer Result;

    Result := Add(2,3);
    OutInt(Result);
    OutImage
end
```

Example 6.11 A simple type procedure or function

procedure, except that a type specifier, *integer* in this case, is given before the keyword *procedure*. This is the type of the value that is to be returned by a call on this procedure.

Within the procedure body, the name of the procedure may be used as a variable of the type specified for the procedure, but only on the left-hand side of assignment statements. If you use it anywhere else it is regarded as a further call on the procedure by itself. This idea of 'recursive' calling is looked at later in this chapter. When the program returns from a call to the procedure, the last value assigned to the procedure identifier is the value returned. This value may be assigned to a variable (as in example 6.11), used as a parameter or used as a value in an expression.

In example 6.11 there is only one statement in the procedure body and this assigns the total of the two parameters to the procedure identifier. The normal type rules apply. The result of the procedure call will be this value, which is here assigned to the variable Result as part of the calling statement in the main program.

If no assignment is made to the procedure identifier, the initial value for the type of the procedure, as defined in Chapter 3, is returned.

A type procedure may be called as if it was a typeless procedure and its returned value ignored. This is often the case with Open, a system procedure described later.

Example 6.12 is Concatenate as a text procedure and used as a parameter to OutText.

```
begin

    text procedure Concatenate(T1, T2); text T1, T2;
    begin
       text LocalText;
       LocalText :- Blanks(T1.Length+T2.Length);
       LocalText:= T1;
       LocalText.SetPos(T1.Length + 1);
       while LocalText.More do
          LocalText.PutChar(T2.GetChar);
       LocalText.SetPos(1);
       Concatenate :- LocalText; ! Now assign text as the result;
    end--of--Concatenate--as--a--function;

    OutText(Concatenate("PART ONE"," PART TWO"));
    OutImage
end
```

Example 6.12 Concatenate as a text procedure

Exercises

6.6 Write and test a function which returns the amount of tax payable on an income and which takes three parameters — the tax-free allowance, the rate of taxation and the amount earned.

6.7 Use the function to write a program which calculates the tax on a person's income, assuming the following rates:

> Tax-free allowance for single person = £2000
> Tax-free allowance for married person = £3500
> Tax rate for first £10000 = 30%
> Tax rate for next £5000 = 45%
> Tax rate for next £5000 = 60%
> Tax rate above this = 75%

What is the smallest set of test data needed to test this fully?

6.8 Write and test a program to find the occurrence of the sequence 'and' in a text. Extend this to provide a function to search for any given sequence, returning the position in the text where it is found.

6.9 Using the procedure from exercise 6.8, write a program to replace the next occurrence of a sequence with any other given sequence.

6.10 Using exercises 6.8 and 6.9 to provide procedures to locate and replace sequences in texts, write a simple editor which does the following:

(a) Reads in a text.

(b) Reads in and performs the following commands:

F/sequence/ — find a sequence in the text and report success or failure.

R/sequence2/ — replace the sequence just located with a new one.

S — move back to the start of the text.

E — end further command processing and print the final text.

Recursive procedures

A procedure must be declared inside a block. Like any other declared item, it may be used anywhere within that block. This includes using it within blocks and procedures which are also within that block. In a block which has more than one procedure declared within it, any one of these procedures may be called inside any or all of the others, even those which are declared before itself. This is known as the scope of such a declaration.

This has one rather important implication: a procedure may make a call on itself. This is known as a 'recursive' call. Example 6.12 is a program which uses a recursive procedure call.

When this happens each call creates a new incarnation of the procedure. Thus each has its own versions of the parameters and declared items for that procedure. In each, these items start with the value passed to them, for parameters, or at the initialization value for their type (see Chapter 3), not the value of their equivalent in the calling procedure.

Example 6.13 shows the use of recursion and emphasizes why the procedure identifier of a function has a different meaning when used as the left-hand side of an assignment than in any other use. This program removes the blanks at the start of a text, but uses recursion instead of a *while* loop. Here is a quick 'walkthrough' of Non__Blank.

First, note that this is an integer procedure. It will return the position of the first non-space character in the text passed to it as a parameter. Next, note that the parameter is passed by reference, the

```
begin

    integer procedure Non_Blank(Text1); text Text1;
    begin
        if Text1.GetChar NE ' ' then Non_Blank := Text1.POS - 1
                          else Non_Blank := Non_Blank(Text1);
    end OF Non_Blank;

    integer New_Start;

    InImage;
    T :- SysIn.Image;
    New_Start := Non_Blank(T);
    T :- T.Sub(New_Start, T.Length-New_Start);
    OutText(T);
    OutImage
end
```

Example 6.13 A recursive procedure call

default for text. These are the things to check in any procedure when you are trying to work out its use.

When Non__Blank is called it reads the next character of the text and compares it with the space character. If it is not a space then the first non-space character is the one just read. Thus the required result is the current Pos of the text parameter minus one, since we have gone one character past it by calling GetChar.

If the character read is a space, Non__Blank is called again and the text is passed again. Since the mode is reference, the current Pos, Length etc. are passed on, so that on this call Non__Blank starts from the character after that just read. Thus Non__Blank calls itself, updating the position in the text by one each time, until a call finds a non-space character. This call returns the position of this character, as we have seen. Each preceding call passes the value returned back as its result through the assignment

Non__Blank:= Non__Blank(Text1)

showing clearly the two uses of Non__Blank as left side of an assignment, returning the value for the function, and as recursive call, with parameter.

Try working through for yourself using texts with various numbers of spaces at their start. Once you have seen how it works for a couple of examples you should get the idea.

Text function results and recursion

A text procedure returns a text reference. Thus only reference assignments to the procedure identifier, within the procedure body, assign a new result. Value assignments merely alter the contents of the text frame of the currently assigned reference.

When the procedure identifier occurs on the right-hand side of an assignment the effect is independent of whether it is a reference or value assignment. Such an occurrence is always taken as a recursive call.

Dangers of recursion

It is not necessary to have a type procedure to use recursion. There are many instances when non-type procedures can use recursion. It is a very powerful device. Example 6.14 uses a non-type procedure and shows the power of recursion and the possible problems of using it without proper thought.

```
begin

    procedure Numbr(Tex, Num); Text TEX; integer Num;
    begin
       OutText(TEX);
       OutInt(Num);
       OutImage;
       Numbr(Tex, Num + 1)
    end OF Numbr;

    Numbr("Line no ",1)
end
```

Example 6.14 The danger of non-terminating recursion

Can you spot the problem? For once I am not going to suggest that you try running the program, especially if you are running on a batch machine. This sort of mistake can cost a lot of paper.

If you are not sure what is wrong, look carefully at the call on

Numbr inside the body of Numbr. Now try following through the working of the program. When will recursive calls stop being made? In the Non—Blank procedure in example 6.13, recursive calls stopped when a non-space character was found. More importantly they only happened when a space was found. Just like *while* loops, recursive calls must stop at the right point. They must not go on for ever.

In general, recursive calls must only be made as part of an *if* statement or an *if—then—else* statement and the condition for their being called must become false at some point. This requires some care, but is no more of a problem than writing *while* loops which stop at the desired point. In fact recursive calls and *while* loops are very similar.

Summary

- We have seen how to declare and call simple procedures, with and without parameters.
- We have seen how to specify the types of any parameters to a procedure.
- We have seen the meaning of the modes of parameter transmission and how to specify these.
- We have learned the default modes for all the possible types of parameters to procedures.
- We have learned how to declare and use type procedures or functions.
- We have learned how to use simple recursion.

Exercises

6.11   Use a recursive procedure to write a program which scans a text for occurrences of a sequence of characters and replaces them with another.

6.12   Use a recursive procedure to write a program which reads in lines of text and prints them out with a line number. Set the program to stop when the line

       .end

is found.

Chapter 7

Basic file handling

Storing and retrieving information

So far we have been limited in what our programs can do by the need to read everything in from the terminal or batch input stream and write everything out to the terminal or batch printer. This means that our SIMULA programs have not been able to use information already held on the computer or to leave information on the computer for other programs to use. This chapter will show how SIMULA provides very powerful mechanisms for this purpose.

You are probably used to the fact that computers keep permanent information in collections called files. Some systems use other names such as data sets, but they are essentially the same thing. These files have names by which you can identify them to the computer. Programs can read from these collections of information and write to them.

SIMULA has objects called Files as well. When you want to read from, or write to, a file on your computer, you must use a SIMULA ,File object to stand for the external file and tell the computer which external file you want. The exact way that this works may vary slightly from one computer to another, but the important points are the same.

In fact a SIMULA File can stand for any source of, or destination for, information. A printer can also be written to by using a File object to represent it in your programs. A magnetic tape reader can be used as a source of input in the same way.

In fact you have already been using two File objects without being told that that was what you were doing. These are the standard input File, SysIn, and the standard output File, SysOut. Whenever you have used InInt, OutImage and any other input/output instructions you have been using File attributes.

Simple input

To read information from the computer we normally use a type of File object known as an InFile. In fact InFile is a sub-class of the object type or class called File. This means that all the properties of File are properties of InFile or are redefined in InFile, but that InFile has some extra ones of its own. In fact all types of File objects are sub-classes of File. InFile is not a direct sub-class of File, however; there is another level between them, called ImageFile.

Put more simply, class File defines a type of object with a number of attributes used to access sources of and destinations for information on a computer, such as files, printers, terminals and tape readers.

File class ImageFile is a sub-class of File. It has all the attributes of its parent class File, some of which it redefines, and in addition some extra attributes used to handle information in certain ways.

ImageFile class InFile is a sub-class of ImageFile. It has all the attributes of both File and ImageFile plus extra ones for reading information using the ways suited to ImageFile's attributes.

This probably sounds far from simple on first reading, but the idea of thinking of objects as classes and sub-classes is central to SIMULA and so we use it to describe formally the relationships of the various sub-types of File.

Example 7.1 is a program using an InFile to provide its information. Notice the familiar names used for the same purposes, but now prefixed with a File name.

```
begin

    ref (InFile) Inf;
    text T1;

    Inf :- new InFile("MYRECORDS");
    Inf.Open(Blanks(80));
    Inf.InImage;
    T :- Inf.Image;
    OutText(T);
    OutImage;
    OutInt(Inf.InInt);
    OutImage;
    Inf.Close
end
```

Example 7.1 Simple input using InFile

There are a few new concepts in this program. Let us look at them one by one.

Firstly, we have a new type of declaration. It declares Inf to be a *ref* variable, but has the word InFile in parentheses between the keyword *ref* and the identifier Inf. A *ref* variable is a pointer to an object of a complex type. The class which defines that type is given in parentheses after the keyword *ref*. Thus Inf is a location which can be used to hold a pointer to an object which is of type InFile. It is initially pointed at an imaginary object called None, just as text variables initially reference NoText.

Inf is pointed at a real object by making a reference assignment to it, using the reference-assignment operator, :−. Value assignments are not possible since Inf can only hold a pointer to an object, not the object itself.

In our program, Inf is pointed at a new object of the required type by using an object generator as the right-hand side of a reference assignment to it. The statement

Inf:− new InFile("MYRECORDS")

thus creates a new InFile type object and points Inf at it. When an object is created in this way one or more parameters may be passed to it, depending on its type.

InFile demands a text-value parameter. In fact this parameter is demanded by the grandparent class File and must be given to all new objects whose type is a sub-class of File. This parameter provides the link between the SIMULA InFile object and the file or device on the actual computer which it will represent inside the program. The exact way in which this text is interpreted on any particular computer and its meaning to that computer varies considerably and you should consult the user's guide or programmer's reference manual for the system you are using.

In principle, the statement is saying that an InFile object which is initially pointed at (or referenced) by Inf will be used in this program to represent some source of input on the computer where the program is to run. The string "MYRECORDS" identifies to that computer the actual source to be used in a way which that computer can understand.

Having created the InFile object the program then prepares it for use by calling the procedure Open, which is an attribute of InFile and so is specified by the prefix 'Inf.'. This also takes a parameter, in this case a text-reference parameter, which must reference a variable text frame. This text frame will be used to hold the input read from the source. The parameter is reference assigned to a text attribute of ImageFile called Image.

Most of the rest of the program should be familiar, except for the prefixing of InImage and InInt by Inf. This tells the SIMULA system to read from the source associated with Inf rather than the standard input, as in our previous programs.

The final statement calls the procedure Close, to tell the SIMULA system that this File is not required until Open is called for it again.

Simple output

Corresponding to InFile, but used for output of information, is the class OutFile. This is also a sub-class of ImageFile.

Example 7.2 is a simple example of the use of OutFile. It corresponds fairly closely to the InFile example and so no further explanation is given yet.

```
begin

    ref (OutFile) Outf;

    Outf :- new OutFile("MYSTORAGE");
    Outf.Open(Blanks(132));

    Outf.OutText("This goes to a File");
    Outf.OutImage;
    Outf.OutInt(43,3);
    Outf.OutImage;
    Outf.Close
end
```

Example 7.2 Simple output using OutFile

Exercises

The information you have about files should now be sufficient to allow some simple attempts at reading and writing to files. This is mainly intended to familiarize you with the way in which your particular computer and SIMULA system treat the File objects in SIMULA programs. You should read the documentation for your system carefully at this point.

7.1 Write a program which prints the integer values 1, 2, 3 and 4 to an OutFile. Check what sort of File your system has created on the computer. See if you are able to examine its contents and list them to a printer.

7.2 Write a program which reads the contents of the File produced in exercise 7.1, using an InFile, and writes it to the terminal or batch output stream.

ImageFile class InFile

Having seen informally how input and output are handled in SIMULA, let us now consider three of the four sub-classes of ImageFile and what they do, starting with InFile. We shall not consider all the attributes of class InFile here. Some will be dealt with in Chapter 8. The remaining sub-class will be dealt with in Chapter 15.

Image

All ImageFile-derived File objects use a text in their reading or writing. This represents the current input/output line or record. Files using this mechanism are called 'record oriented'. This means that a whole record is read into the Image text or written from it at a time. Most attributes of an ImageFile object operate on the copy in Image, not the actual File or device it stands for.

Image is a text variable within the ImageFile object. In an InFile, the parameter passed to Open is used initially as its Image, i.e. is assigned by reference to Image. This is usually an anonymous text created by giving the text generator Blanks as the parameter to Open. The number given as parameter to Blanks determines the length of Image and should match the record or line length of the external file or device. Where the external record length is not fixed, the length of Image should be the maximum record length possible or expected.

Open

Open is actually a Boolean procedure. If the attempt by the SIMULA runtime system to find and access the external file specified is unsuccessful, Open will return the value False. This can happen if the external file does not exist, is not permitted to you, or for a number of reasons which are system dependent. Any attempt to read from the File subsequently will result in a runtime error.

Older systems will have Open as a type-less procedure and attempting to open a file which is not available will cause a runtime error on these systems.

If Open succeeds it will reserve the file or device for future use as a source of input by the program. It is not possible to write to an InFile.

Open also assigns its text-reference parameter to Image, creating a 'buffer' text into which all records from the external file or device will be read. It is possible to assign a new text as Image later in the program.

A successful call on Open will return the value True.

IsOpen

IsOpen is a Boolean procedure. It returns False if the File is not currently open, i.e. no call of Open has yet been made or the File has been closed. Open sets IsOpen to True. Close sets IsOpen to False.

Older systems may not have IsOpen as a File attribute.

SetAccess

Modern SIMULA systems allow programs to specify certain modes for open files. The exact meaning of these will depend on the physical file system of the computer. Each file used will have initial properties, some of which are defined in the SIMULA standard. These will be found in the documentation for the system you are using. A summary is given in Table 7.1.

All SIMULA systems which meet the current standard will allow files with the following properties.

Shared. Values can be: shared/noshared. Decides whether use of the file by this program excludes its use by others.

Append. Values can be: append/noappend. Decides whether output to this file will overwrite its existing contents or be appended to it.

Create. Values can be: create/anycreate/nocreate. At call of Open physical file must not exist/will be created if it does not exist/must already exist.

Readwrite. Values can be: readonly/writeonly/readwrite. Decides whether reading or writing is allowed for this File. Only relevant for DirectFiles. (See Chapter 15.)

Table 7.1 Default modes for file types

Mode	In-	Out-	Direct	Affects
		File type		
Shared	shared	noshared	noshared	Open
Append	N/A	noappend	noappend	Open
Create	N/A	anycreate	nocreate	Open
Readwrite	N/A	N/A	readwrite	Open
Bytesize:n	*	*	*	Open
Rewind	norewind	norewind	N/A	Open/Close
Purge	nopurge	nopurge	nopurge	Close

Bytesize. Values can be: any positive integer within a range allowed by that system. Tells the system how many bits are in a byte on this machine. Only relevant for ByteFiles. (See Chapter 15.)

Rewind. Values can be: rewind/norewind. Decides whether the file is to be reset in some way when Close is called.

Purge. Values can be: purge/nopurge. Decides whether the physical file is to be deleted when Close is called.

SetAccess is a Boolean procedure with a single text parameter, which must be one of the values given above or bytesize: followed by an integer. This is used to reset the appropriate mode value in the File. Where the mode is unrecognized or inappropriate for the type of file, SetAccess returns False. Otherwise it returns True.

InImage

The procedure InImage copies the next record from the external file or device into Image. This is equivalent to a text-value assignment. If the external record is shorter than Image.Length then it is copied into the leftmost character locations in Image and the remaining character positions are filled with spaces. If the external record is longer than Image.Length, calling InImage causes a runtime error to be reported.

InRecord

Newer SIMULA systems will also have Boolean procedure InRecord. This works in the same way as InImage, except where the record being read is either shorter or longer than Image.Length.

In the first case InRecord copies it into the start of Image, but leaves the rest of Image's text frame unchanged. Image.Pos will be set to point to the first unchanged character. In this case InRecord returns False.

Where the external record is longer than Image, only enough is read in to fill Image. In this case InRecord returns True, indicating that a further call will read in the missing part of the current Image, not a new record.

Where the lengths are the same InRecord acts exactly as InImage, but returns False.

Close

Boolean procedure Close tells the SIMULA system that the external file or device represented by this File object is no longer required by it. This means that it can be used by another File object. Thus, once an InFile has been closed, it can be reopened as an OutFile. Once an external file or device has been released in this way it may also be claimed by other programs and users. If an attempt is then made to reopen it using the original File object, a runtime error may result.

If Close is unable to perform its task, it returns False. Otherwise it returns True. Older systems will only have Close as a type-less procedure.

If a File is left open at the end of a program, it will be closed by the runtime system, with a warning in most systems. It is safer to close files in the program.

SetPos

This procedure is equivalent to Image.SetPos.

Pos

This integer procedure returns Image.Pos.

More

This integer procedure returns Image.More.

Length

This integer procedure returns Image.Length.

EndFile

This is a Boolean procedure. When the last character of the last record in the external file has been read it returns the value True, otherwise it returns the value False.

Example 7.3 shows of the use of EndFile to read and print the whole of a record-structured File.

Once the last record of the real file is read in by InImage, a further call will assign the ISO end of file character, !25!, as the first character of Image. EndFile now returns the value True. Example 7.3 uses the new keyword *not*, which reverses the condition being tested. Thus the *while* loop is performed as long as Inf.EndFile is not True.

```
begin

   ref (InFile) Inf;

   Inf :- new InFile("Source");
   if Inf.Open(Blanks(80)) then ! Assumes no records longer than 80;
   begin   ! Use Open as a Boolean procedure in case File not there;
      while not Inf.EndFile do
      begin
         Inf.InImage;
         OutText(Inf.Image);
         OutImage
      end;
      Inf.Close
   end

end
```

Example 7.3 Use of EndFile

LastItem

LastItem is a Boolean procedure, rather like EndFile. It returns False as long as there are any non-space characters left in the File. It will skip any spaces, updating Image and Pos, until it finds a non-space or the end of the File. If it has reached the end, it returns True; if it finds non-space characters, it returns False.

Example 7.4 is a word-counting program which uses LastItem.

```
begin

    ref (InFile) Words;
    integer WordCount;
    text ThisWord;
    Boolean ThisisFirstSpace;
    character Item;

    Words :- new InFile("LATESTPAPER");
    Words.Open(Blanks(132)); ! Assume line length of 132;
    ThisisFirstSpace := True;
    ThisWord :- Blanks(132);

    while not Words.LastItem do
    begin
      while Words.More do
      begin
        Item := Words.Image.GetChar;
        if Item ne ' ' then
        begin
          ThisisFirstSpace := True;
          ThisWord.PutChar(Item);
        end else
        if ThisisFirstSpace then
        begin
          ThisisFirstSpace := False;
          OutText(ThisWord.Strip);
          ThisWord :- Blanks(132);
          OutText(" ");
          WordCount := WordCount + 1
        end--of--a--word;
      end--of--a--line;
      if ThisisFirstSpace then
      begin
        WordCount := WordCount + 1;
        OutText(ThisWord);
        ThisWord :- Blanks(132)
      end;
      OutImage;
      OutText("   £££ Words so far = ");
      OutInt(WordCount,6);
      OutImage;
```

```
        end--of--word--counting--loop;
        OutText("Total word count is ");
        OutInt(WordCount,6);
        OutImage;
        Words.Close
    end
    begin
```

Example 7.4 Use of LastItem in word counting

Item-oriented input

Some procedures read in the sequence of characters in the real file as an item of a certain type. Most are described in Chapter 8, but here are two useful ones.

InChar

InChar is almost the same as Image.GetChar. It is a character procedure which returns the next character in the File. If the end of the current Image has been reached, i.e. Image.More returns False, InImage will be called and the first character in the new Image read.

Since SIMULA specifies that a call on InImage once the last record of the real File has been read will place the ISO end of file character, !25!, as the first in Image. A call on InChar once the last character of the real file has been read will return this non-printing character and EndFile will then return True. If the end of the File has been reached, i.e. EndFile returns True, a call on InImage will cause a runtime error. We can rewrite our word-counting program, using InChar to replace Image.GetChar, as shown in example 7.5.

```
    begin

        ref (InFile) Words;
        integer WordCount;
        text ThisWord;
        Boolean ThisisFirstSpace;
        character Item;

        Words :- new InFile("LATESTPAPER");
        Words.Open(Blanks(132)); ! Assume line length of 132;
        ThisisFirstSpace := True;
        ThisWord :- Blanks(132);
```

```
      while not Words.LastItem do
      begin
        while Words.More do
        begin
          Item := Words.InChar;
          if Item ne ' ' then
          begin
            ThisisFirstSpace := True;
            ThisWord.PutChar(Item);
          end else
          if ThisisFirstSpace then
          begin
            ThisisFirstSpace := False;
            OutText(ThisWord.Strip);
            ThisWord :- Blanks(132);
            OutText(" ");
            WordCount := WordCount + 1
          end--of--a--word;
        end--of--a--line;
        if ThisisFirstSpace then
        begin
          WordCount := WordCount + 1;
          OutText(ThisWord);
          ThisWord :- Blanks(132)
        end;
        OutImage;
        OutText("   £££ Words so far = ");
        OutInt(WordCount,6);
        OutImage;
      end--of--word--counting--loop;
      OutText("Total word count is ");
      OutInt(WordCount,6);
      OutImage;
      Words.Close
    end
    begin
```

Example 7.5 LastItem and InChar in word counting

InText

InText is a text procedure, with a single, integer value parameter. Its result is a text containing the next N characters in the real file, where N is the value of its integer parameter. It may include characters from more than one record in the real file, calling InImage as necessary.

Example 7.6 is a new line-splitting program, using InText. Note that it assumes an input file with lines 132 characters long. Note also that it does not deal with blanks at the end of Image.

```
begin
  ref(InFile) OldLines;
  OldLines:- new InFile("MANUSCRIPT");
  OldLines.Open(Blanks (132));
  while not OldLines.EndFile do
  begin
    OutText (OldLines.InText (80));
    OutImage
  end;
  OldLines.Close
end
```

Example 7.6 Line splitting with InText

ImageFile class OutFile

OutFile is the output equivalent of InFile and so has some similar attributes and some which are the output equivalents of InFile's input attributes. Again, some will be left until Chapter 8. EndFile and LastItem do not exist for OutFile, since they would have no meaning.

Image

The Image text of an OutFile is set up in the same way as that of an InFile. It is used to accumulate items which are to be output, until a call of OutImage or OutRecord writes the current line or record to the real file or device.

Open

Boolean procedure Open works in approximately the same way as for InFile, except that the real file or device is reserved for output, not input, and the real file may be created if it does not exist already. The text-reference parameter is used as the initial Image, as in InFile.

IsOpen

IsOpen works in exactly the same way as it does in InFile.

SetAccess

SetAccess works in exactly the way as it does in InFile.

OutImage

When OutImage is called either, explicitly, from the program or, implicitly, by one of the item output routines like OutChar, the current contents of Image are written as a new record to the file or device connected to this OutFile.

Image is then filled with spaces as if by

Image:− Blanks (Image.Length);

OutRecord

Procedure OutRecord works in a similar way to OutImage, but only writes out those characters preceding Pos in Image. Thus OutRecord can be used to create files with variable-length records, where the operating system supports this.

Older systems will not have OutRecord.

BreakOutImage

Procedure BreakOutImage writes out the contents of Image in the same way as OutRecord, except that it does not produce any implicit line terminator. Thus successive calls of BreakOutImage will write a series of Images to the same line.

It is intended to allow prompts to be displayed on interactive terminals, in a manner that allows input to be typed on the same line.

Where an operating system does not support output without line terminators, BreakOutImage is exactly equivalent to OutRecord.

Older systems will not have BreakOutImage.

Close

This procedure is the same as for InFile, except that, if the Image is non-empty at close, i.e. Image.Pos is not 1, there remain some un-written characters. In this case, Open calls OutImage to write out the remaining record.

Again, files will be closed automatically at the end of the program, although it is tidier and safer to close them in the program. This means that the programs in example 7.7 (a), (b) and (c) are equivalent.

It is much safer to call OutImage and Close explicitly, when they are needed. Consider the effect of extending the program to do further writing to Out1, if you are depending on the end of the program to output the Image containing "SUCCESS".

(a)

```
begin
  ref(OutFile) Out1;
  Out1:- new OutFile ("DESTINATION");
  if Out1.Open (Blanks (132)) then
  begin
    Out1.OutText ("SUCCESS");
    Out1.OutImage;
    Out1.Close
  end else
  begin
    OutText ("File DESTINATION could not be opened");
    OutImage
  end
end
```

(b)

```
begin
  ref(OutFile)Out1;
  Out1:-new OutFile("DESTINATION");
  if Out1.Open(Blanks (132)) then
  begin
    Out1.OutText("SUCCESS");
    Out1.OutImage  ;
    COMMENT do not call Out1.Close;
  end else
  begin
    OutText("File DESTINATION could not be opened");
    OutImage
  end
end
```

(c)

```
begin
ref(OutFile)Out1;
   Out1:-new OutFile("DESTINATION");
   if Out1.Open(Blanks (132)) then
   begin
      Out1.OutText("SUCCESS");
      COMMENT do not call Out1.OutImage
      or Out1.Close;
   end else
   begin
      OutText("File DESTINATION could not be opened");
      COMMENT do not call OutImage;
   end
end
```

Example 7.7 Use of Open and Close

CheckPoint

Boolean procedure CheckPoint is used to safeguard any output done so far. If it is called, the operating system is requested to complete all writing to the external file which may have been buffered or delayed before returning. If this is successful, CheckPoint returns True. If it fails, or the operating system does not allow checkpointing, False is returned.

SetPos, Pos, More and Length

These are all exactly as for InFile, i.e. equivalent to Image.SetPos, Image.Pos, Image.More and Image.Length.

Item-oriented output

Several attributes of OutFile are procedures which write out items of various types. Most are dealt with in Chapter 8, but here are the two which match those given for InFile.

OutChar

This procedure takes a single character-value parameter. It writes this to the File. If there is space in the current Image, i.e. Image.More returns True, it is written by Image.PutChar, otherwise OutImage is first called and the character is then written as the first in the next record.

OutText

This takes a single text-value parameter. As with OutChar, if there is insufficient space in Image, OutImage is first called. The characters of the text are copied into Image as if by successive OutChar calls. Pos is thus increased. If the length of the text is greater than Image.Length a runtime error occurs.

Exercises

7.3 Write a program to remove double spaces from a whole file, producing a new file. Extend this to place a double space after each full stop.

7.4 Write a program to remove blank lines from a file, producing a new file.

7.5 Write a program which reads a file with no blank lines and produces a double-spaced copy, i.e. a file with a blank line between each line of its contents.

7.6 Write a program which asks for the following information

> input file;
> output file;
> line spacing (double/single);
> multiple-space-removal required?;
> word count wanted?;
> number of spaces after full stop;
> number of spaces after comma;

and then copies the input file to the output file in the required format.

OutFile class PrintFile

The third sub-class of ImageFile is actually a sub-sub-class, being an extension of OutFile. A PrintFile has all the attributes of an OutFile, plus some extra facilities. It is designed for use when output is to go to a printer.

The attributes of PrintFile are designed for output with a maximum number of lines on each page. The length of each line will depend on Image.Length. Printing of lines can be set to be double or multiple spaced.

Some of the attributes of OutFile are redefined to allow for this page-oriented output. It is a feature of classes in SIMULA that an attribute of a class can be redeclared with a different meaning in a sub-class. The meaning in the sub-class is then used for objects which are referred to as being of the sub-class.

Only those attributes of PrintFile which are not in OutFile or which are redefined in PrintFile are listed here. All the other attributes of OutFile exist for PrintFile.

Open

Open operates exactly as for OutFile, but also instructs the printer to move to the start of the first line of a new page.

Close

Close also performs all the tasks of Close in OutFile. In addition it moves the printer to the end of the page and resets the Spacing, LinesPerPage and Line attributes to 1, system default and zero respectively.

OutImage and OutRecord

OutImage and OutRecord operate exactly as for OutFile, but in addition:

1   Before Image is printed, check to ensure that the last line on the current page, defined by LinesPerPage, has not been passed. If it has, the printer is instructed to move to the start of the next page.

2   Skip one or more lines if Spacing has been set to produce double or multiple spaced output.

3   Update a counter indicating how many lines have been output to the current page.

LinesPerPage

The PrintFile initially assumes that some standard number of lines are allowed on a page. This number is different for different systems and you should consult the user's guide or programmer's reference manual for your system to find what it is.

During execution of a program, this number can be reset to fit the printer or paper being used, by calling the procedure LinesPerPage, which has a single integer-value parameter. The value of the parameter sets a new maximum number of lines per page.

A value of zero resets the default. A negative value indicates continuous printing without page breaks. A positive value is the new number of lines per page.

Example 7.8 writes pages containing only ten lines. Try it and see the effect when you list the output to a printer. (Not all terminals behave like printers and so the effect may not show up if you use one as your output device.) In recent SIMULA systems LinesPerPage is an integer procedure returning the value prior to this call. Older systems will have it as a type-less procedure.

```
begin
   ref(PrintFile) Printer;
   ref(InFile) Source;
   Printer:- new PrintFile ("LP23");
   Source:- new InFile ("MYTEXT");

   Printer.Open (Blanks (80)); ! Sets line length;
   Source.Open (Blanks (80));
   Printer.LinesPerPage (10);
   while not Source.EndFile do
   begin
      Source.InImage;
      Printer.OutText (SOURCE.Image);
      Printer.OutImage
   end;
   Printer.Close;
   Source.Close
end
```

Example 7.8 Small pages using a PrintFile

Line

The PrintFile keeps a count of how many lines it has printed on the current page. Line is an integer procedure with no parameters which returns the number of the next line on the page. When the last

OutImage has filled the current page, Line will return a value greater than that set by LinesPerPage. When the File is not open, Line returns zero.

Spacing

The procedure Spacing has a single integer-value parameter. This controls the number of blank lines output after each OutImage, i.e. the amount by which Line will have increased. Spacing is called by the system with 1 as a parameter when the PrintFile object is generated and again by Close.

Example 7.9 shows the effect of Spacing.

```
begin
  ref(PrintFile) Prnt1;

  Prnt1:- new PrintFile ("Out1");
  Prnt1.Open (Blanks (132));

  Prnt1.OutText ("LINE 1");
  Prnt1.OutImage;
  Prnt1.OutText ("LINE 2");
  Prnt1.OutImage;
  Prnt1.Spacing (2);
  Prnt1.OutText ("LINE 3");
  Prnt1.OutImage;
  Prnt1.Spacing (3);
  Prnt1.OutText ("LINE 4");
  Prnt1.OutImage;
  Prnt1.OutText ("LINE 5");
  Prnt1.OutImage;
  Prnt1.Close
end
```

Example 7.9 The effect of Spacing in PrintFile

Eject

Procedure Eject has a single integer-value parameter. It moves the printer to a line determined by the value of this parameter, as follows:
- Value zero or negative, report a runtime error.
- Value greater than number of lines allowed per page, move to first line of next page.

- Value greater than current value returned by Line, but less than maximum allowed per page, move forward on current page to that line number.
- Value less than or equal to current value returned by Line, move to that line number on next page.

Try the program in example 7.10 which demonstrates the legal alternatives described above.

```
begin
  ref(PrintFile) Prnt2;

  Prnt2:- new PrintFile ("OUT2");
  Prnt2.Open (Blanks (132));
  Prnt2.LinesPerPage (20);
  Prnt2.OutText ("LINE 1");
  Prnt2.OutImage;
  Prnt2.Eject (10); ! Greater than current Line;
  Prnt2.OutText ("LINE 2");
  Prnt2.OutImage;
  Prnt2.Eject (6); ! Less than current Line;
  Prnt2.OutText ("LINE 3");
  Prnt2.OutImage;
  Prnt2.Eject (7); ! Equal to current line;
  Prnt2.OutText ("LINE 4");
  Prnt2.OutImage;
  Prnt2.Eject (30); ! Greater than LinesPerPage;
  Prnt2.OutText ("LINE 5");
  Prnt2.OutImage;
  Prnt2.Close
end
```

Example 7.10 Legal variations of Eject in PrintFile

A useful shorthand

It is rather tedious writing

```
Prnt2.OutImage;
Prnt2.Eject(30)
```

etc., when the prefixing name is always Prnt2. SIMULA allows a shorthand, known as an *inspect* statement. This may not be used for prefixes which are text identifiers, however, since text is not defined as a class, but is a special type on its own.

The following statements are equivalent for the purposes described here.

> Prnt2.OutImage
> inspect Prnt2 do OutImage

Obviously, the new form is longer for this simple case, but consider the syntax of this *inspect* statement. There is the keyword *inspect*, followed by an identifier referencing an object, followed by the keyword *do*, followed by a statement.

The semantic rule for an *inspect* statement is that any use of an attribute of the referenced object (i.e. the one whose identifier appears between *inspect* and *do*) inside the statement following *do* is not required to be prefixed by the identifier and a dot.

If we use a compound statement or block as the statement following *do*, we can save a lot of tedious writing. Thus, the programs in examples 7.11 (a) and (b) are exactly equivalent.

```
(a)    begin
           ref (PrintFile) P1;

           P1:- new PrintFile ("OUT");

           P1.Open (Blanks (80));
           P1.OutText ("Message");
           P1.OutInt (2,3);
           P1.OutImage;
           P1.Close
       end
```

```
(b)    begin
           ref (PrintFile) P1;

           P1:- new PrintFile ("OUT");

           inspect P1 do
           begin
              Open (Blanks (80));
              OutText ("Message");
              OutInt (2,3);
              OutImage;
              Close
           end
       end
```

Example 7.11 Use of simple inspect

Where we want to use more than one object we are allowed to use nested inspect statements. In other words we can use another *inspect* statement as the statement following the *do*. This is shown by example 7.12.

```
begin
    ref(PrintFile) P1;
    ref(InFile) I1;

    P1:-new PrintFile ("OUT");
    I1:-new InFile ("IN1");

    inspect P1 do
        inspect I1 do
        begin
            P1.Open (Blanks (132)); ! Needs P1;
            Open (Blanks (80)); ! refers to I1;
            InImage; ! Can only refer to I1;
            OutText (Image); ! OutText is P1, Image is I1;
            OutImage; ! Can only be P1;
            Close; ! refers to I1;
            P1.Close; ! Needs P1;
        end*of*inspect*I1;
end
```

Example 7.12 Nested *inspect* statements

Notice that all attributes are taken to be of I1, which is the inner-most object inspected, if they might be of P1 as well. Thus, when P1 is opened, we must use P1.Open explicitly, whereas I1 only requires Open, with no prefix. Where an attribute only exists in one of the objects there is no ambiguity. For instance, OutImage does not exist for the InFile, I1, but does exist for the PrintFile, P1.

SysIn and SysOut

If no prefixing object is used for OutText, InImage etc., we have seen that the SIMULA system assumes that they refer to the standard input and output devices for the system. These may be the screen and the keyboard of a terminal, the job stream and journal of a batch system or whatever is appropriate for the particular computer.

The default input device is accessed through a system InFile referred to as SysIn. The default output device is accessed through a system PrintFile referred to as SysOut.

The program block of a SIMULA program acts as if it were inside a nested *inspect* statement. This would look as follows:

```
inspect SysIn do
    Inspect SysOut do
    begin
        . . .
        . . .
        . . .
        . . .
    end
```

SysOut is defined, not as a ref(PrintFile) variable, but as a ref(PrintFile) procedure. This means that you cannot assign another File to be SysOut during your programs. Similarly, SysIn is defined as a ref(InFile) procedure.

This is not as complex as it may sound. The implications are roughly as follows:

1   The real devices referred to by SysIn and SysOut are determined by the SIMULA system and cannot be changed during a program.

2   Any use of an attribute of InFile or PrintFile in a SIMULA program, which does not have an appropriate object defined for it by the dot notation or by an enclosing *inspect* statement, is assumed to refer to SysIn or SysOut.

3   Since SysOut is the inner object inspected, any attribute found in both InFile and PrintFile is assumed to belong to SysOut. Others are assumed to belong to the appropriate one of SysIn and SysOut.

4   To refer to attributes of SysIn which also occur in PrintFile, the attributes must be prefixed by SysIn or inside an *inspect* SysIn statement, as we saw in several earlier examples.

Summary

- We have seen how sub-classes of File are used by SIMULA to allow programs to access real files or input/output devices on a computer.
- We have looked especially at 'record oriented' input and output, based on File class ImageFile.
- We have seen the idea of a class and a sub-class.
- We have looked at the attributes of three sub-classes of ImageFile, namely InFile, OutFile and PrintFile.

- We have seen the use of *inspect* statements as an alternative to dot notation for accessing attributes of objects, when the object is not a text.
- We have seen the way in which SysIn and SysOut provide default input and output devices.

Chapter 8

Item-oriented text and file manipulation

Reading and writing numbers

This chapter will consider the mechanisms in SIMULA for translating numbers into sequences of characters within texts and for translating sequences of characters within texts into numbers. This is clearly a useful thing to be able to do. In fact, we have already used some of these features to make our programs possible. Now we will look in detail at the attributes of text and File which are used for this purpose.

Essentially, this is an extension of the 'item oriented' concept used in describing InChar, OutChar, InText and OutText. Instead of considering a sequence of characters as just part of the text in which they occur, we are going to interpret them as integers or reals. Instead of adding to a text some sequence of characters from another text, we are going to write an integer or a real value as such a sequence.

Adding numbers to a text

There are four procedures which are attributes of text and can be used to add sequences of characters to the text, which represent numbers. In each the number is converted to a sequence of characters, representing its value as the appropriate type. There are no spaces, commas or other separators in such sequences, except in PutFrac. If the number is negative, a minus sign precedes the first digit, with no intervening space.

This sequence of characters is added to the text, starting at the current position returned by Pos. The current position in the text is updated to the position following the last character added.

If the text refers to NoText, the attempt to add the sequence causes a runtime error. If the number of characters in the text to the right of the current Pos is smaller than the length of the sequence to be added, the value is not written. Instead the remainder of the text is filled with asterisk characters and the current position moved to the end of the text.

116

PutInt

PutInt has a single integer-value parameter. It converts this value to a sequence of digits representing it as a whole number and adds it to the text as described above. See example 8.1.

```
begin
  text T1;
  T1 :- Copy("1234");
  OutText(T1);
  OutImage;
  T1.PutInt(4321);
  OutText(T1);
  OutImage
end
```

Example 8.1 Use of PutInt

PutFix

Oddly, SIMULA uses the name PutFix for the more natural of the two procedures in text which add numbers as reals in texts. As we have seen earlier with OutFix, numbers which are represented as fixed-point real numbers consist of a sequence of digits, representing the integer part of the number, followed, if necessary, by a decimal point and a sequence of digits, representing the fractional part of the number.

PutFix has two parameters, a real value one, which holds the value to be added to the text, and an integer value one, which contains the number of places of decimals to be printed. When the value is converted to a sequence of characters, it is rounded to give the required number of digits after the decimal point. If the required number of decimal places is zero, no decimal point is printed and PutFix acts like PutInt. If the number of significant digits after the decimal point is too small, zeros are added to give the required number. See example 8.2.

PutReal

PutReal represents real values in floating-point form. This is useful to scientists, engineers and mathematicians, since it allows very large or very small numbers to be represented. PutReal is described in appendix B.

```
begin
  text T2;
  T2 :- Blanks(80);
  T2.PutFix(3.2438,4); ! Prints all the significant figures;
  T2.PutChar(' ');
  T2.PutFix(432.45678,3); ! Prints rounded to 3 places;
  T2.PutChar(' ');
  T2.PutFix(21.93,4); ! Prints with two trailing zeros;
  T2.PutChar(' ');
  T2.PutFix(367.487,0); ! Prints as a whole number;
  OutText(T2);
  OutImage
end
```

Example 8.2 Use of PutFix

PutFrac

SIMULA allows integers to be represented as 'grouped items'. This is occasionally useful, when representing such things as amounts of money. It also allows orders of magnitude to be assessed at a glance.

A grouped item is a string of digits, separated into groups of three by spaces. There may also be a decimal point as a separator, somewhere in the sequence.

Where there is no decimal point, the sequence is broken into groups starting at the right, as shown in example 8.3. Where the number of digits is not an exact multiple of three, the leftmost group will have less than three digits.

```
416 379 408
 16 063
9 327 524
```

Example 8.3 Grouped items without a decimal point

Where there is a decimal point, the sequence to the left of the decimal point is as described above. The sequence to the right is divided into groups working from the decimal point towards the right. Thus the rightmost group after a decimal point may contain less than three digits (see example 8.4).

287 901.386 974 203
 12 592.769 23
 32 006.641 974 05

Example 8.4 Grouped items with a decimal point

PutFrac has two integer-value parameters. The first of these is the number to be represented as a grouped item. The second is the number of places which it should occupy after the decimal point. See example 8.5.

```
begin
    text T5;
    T5 :- Blanks(80);
    T5.PutFrac(23478912,4); ! Should give 2 347.891 2;
    OutText(T5);
    OutImage
end
```

Example 8.5 Use of PutFrac

Exercises

8.1 Use PutFrac in a program to calculate a weekly wage, where the first forty hours are paid at £2.30 per hour and subsequent overtime at the normal rate plus half. The program should read in the hours worked and print out the wages for normal working, overtime and as a total.

8.2 What would the representation of the following calls be? Write a program to check your answers.

(a) PutInt(965)
(b) PutFix(43.2,2)
(c) PutFrac(492871409217,5)
(d) PutFix(43.2056,2)
(e) PutFrac(492871409217,6)
(f) PutFix(43.2049,2)
(g) PutFrac(492871409217,4)
(h) PutInt(96.7)
(i) T:- Blanks(4); T.PutInt(721964)

Reading numbers from texts

Corresponding to the procedures for adding numbers to texts as sequences of characters, there are attributes of text which are procedures for interpreting the next sequence of characters, which must have the format used to represent the type required, as a number of that type.

Any spaces at the start of the sequence are skipped. Any other characters before the start of the numeric item cause a runtime error to be reported. The sequence translated is the longest one that fits the format for the appropriate type. If the sequence ends without fully matching the required format, a runtime error is reported.

The current position in the text is moved one character past the item read.

GetInt

GetInt is an integer procedure. It takes a sequence of digits and interprets them as an integer value, returning this value. The sequence is deemed to end at the first non-digit or at the end of the text. Only spaces at the start of the sequence are skipped. See example 8.6.

```
begin
  text T6;
  T6 :- Copy("12 345.678 12");
  OutText("FIRST ITEM");
  OutInt(T6.GetInt,4);        ! 12;
  OutText("SECOND ITEM");
  OutInt(T6.GetInt,4);        ! 345;
  OutText("THIRD ITEM");
  OutChar(T6.GetChar);        ! . ;
  OutText("FOURTH ITEM");
  OutInt(T6.GetInt,4);        ! 678;
  OutText("FIFTH ITEM");
  OutInt(T6.GetInt,4);        ! 12;
  OutImage
end
```

Example 8.6 Use of GetInt

GetReal

Real procedure GetReal is the only way of reading items as reals. It accepts either the format used by PutFix or that used by PutReal. In either case the sequence must be complete. For the fixed-point format, which we are considering here, this means that the sequence must be:

1 a simple sequence of digits, as for an integer;
2 a sequence of digits, followed by a decimal point and a further sequence of digits;
3 a decimal point followed by a sequence of digits.

See example 8.7. A sequence of digits, followed by a decimal point, but with no further digits is not legal.

For floating-point representations allowed, see appendix B.

```
begin
  text T7;
  real R1;
  T7 :- Copy("12 345.678 12");
  OutText("FIRST ITEM");
  R1 := T7.GetReal;
  OutFix(R1,3,8);        ! 12;
  OutText("SECOND ITEM");
  R1 := T7.GetReal;
  OutFix(R1,3,8);        ! 345.678;
  OutText("THIRD ITEM");
  R1 := T7.GetReal;
  OutFix(R1,3,8);        ! 12;
  OutImage
end
```

Example 8.7 Use of GetReal

GetFrac

Grouped items, as described for PutFrac, are read in by GetFrac. This is an integer procedure, which returns the value of the grouped item as if it were an integer, ignoring any spaces or the decimal point if it is present. See example 8.8.

Exercises

8.3 Write a program to read a sequence of real numbers, ending with a negative number, and write them as suitably grouped items. The decimal point should be in the correct place.

8.4 Write a program to read the marks obtained in examinations in English, Mathematics, History and French, in that order, for a class of

```
begin
   text T8;
   integer I8;
   T8 :- Copy("12 345.678 12");
   I8 := T8.GetFrac;
   OutText("ONLY ITEM");
   OutInt(I8,12);              ! 1234567812;
   OutImage;
   OutFrac(I8,5,20);
   OutImage
end
```

Example 8.8 Use of GetFrac

thirty students. The marks will be given as integers, separated with commas between each subject and with full stops at the end of each student's marks. You may assume that each student's marks are on a new line. Extend your program to write out the results in six columns, with appropriate headings. The first four should give the marks for each subject. The fifth should contain the student's total. The last should contain the student's average, to two decimal places.

Fixed repetition

The problem in exercise 8.4 shows a different type of loop to those that we have used before. Your solution will probably have used the *while* loop that we learned in Chapter 5. The *while* loop is very powerful, allowing us to write loops which continue for as many repetitions as are necessary to complete the task. Yet in exercise 8.4 we usually knew the number of times that we wanted to repeat the loop. This meant using a counter to keep track of how many times the loop had been performed.

There is nothing wrong with such a solution, but SIMULA allows us to write the same loops more concisely, using the *for* loop. Example 8.9 is the reading part of exercise 8.4, using a *while* loop, and example 8.10, using a *for* loop.

Note the structure of the *for* loop. The keyword *for* is followed by a sequence known as a *for* clause, which is in turn followed by the keyword *do* and a statement. Thus, the *while* and condition of the *while* loop statement are replaced by a *for* and a *for* clause.

```
begin
  character Char1;
  integer C1, C2, Val;
  C1 := 1;
  inspect SysIn do
    while C1 le 30 do
    begin
      InImage;
      C2 := 1;
      while C2 < 4 do
      begin
        Val := Image.GetInt;
        Char1 := ' ';
        while Char1 ne ',' do Char1 := Image.GetChar;
        C2 := C2 + 1;
      end;
      Val := Image.GetInt;
      C1 := C1 + 1;
    end
end
```

Example 8.9 Fixed repetitions using *while*

```
begin
  integer C1,C2,Val;
  character Char1;
  for C1:=1 step 1 until 30 do
  begin
    InImage;
    inspect SysIn do
    begin
      for C2:=1 step 1 until 3 do
      begin
        Val:=Image.GetInt;
        Char1:=Image.GetChar;
        while Char1 ne ',' do Char1:=Image.GetChar;
      end;
      Val := Image.GetInt
    end
  end
end
```

Example 8.10 Fixed repetitions using *for*

The *for* clause specifies a variable and a series of values which are to be assigned to it. The values are assigned in turn and the statement following the *do* is performed once after each of these assignments.

There are two commonly used forms of the *for* clause. Example 8.10 uses the *step—until* form. This specifies:

- a starting value, which follows the assignment operator, :=,
- an amount to be added to the variable next and each succeeding time, which follows the keyword *step*,
- and the upper (or lower) limit for the value of the variable, which follows the keyword *until*.

The variable to which the values are assigned is known as the 'controlled variable'. Its value, compared to the limit value, controls the number of times that the loop will be executed.

Consider what will happen in the outer *for* loop in example 8.10. When the line containing

for C1:=1 step 1 until 30 do

is first reached, the value 1 is assigned to the controlled variable, integer C1. The statement following the keyword *do*, which is a compound statement in this example, is then performed.

The value in C1 is then compared with the limit value, and if C1 is the greater, the *for* loop is complete and the statement following *for* is skipped.

When all the actions of the compound statement are complete, the program comes back to the keyword *for* and adds the value following *step*, 1 in this example, to the value in the controlled variable, C1. C1 now contains the value 2. If this is now greater than the limit, the rest of the *for* loop is skipped and the program moves to the next statement or, in this case, the end of the block or compound statement containing the *for* loop.

In this example the program will cause the value of C1 to be set to 1 and increased by 1 twenty-nine times, reaching 30. After each change in C1, the statement following *do* will be performed. Thus this statement will be performed thirty times.

The first value does not have to be 1, neither does the step value. They may even be negative. The statement in example 8.11 uses a negative step to copy the characters from one text to another in reverse.

When the step value is negative, the controlled variable decreases each time round the loop and the check made is that it is not yet less than the limit value.

```
begin
  integer C1;
  text T1,T2;
  T2:-Blanks (12);
  T1:-Copy ("ABCDEFGHIJKL");
  for C1:=12 step -1 until 1 do
  begin
    T1.SetPos(C1);
    T2.PutChar (T1.GetChar)
  end;
  OutText (T1);
  OutImage;
  OutText (T2);
  OutImage
end
```

Example 8.11 Negative steps in a *for* loop

It is also possible to use a real variable as the controlled variable and to use variables or expressions of the appropriate type for any of the values. Example 8.12 gives some of the many possible variations.

(a) Using real values

```
begin
  real R1;
  for R1:=0.1 step 0.3 until 1.0 do OutFix(R1, 2, 4);
  OutImage
end
```

(b) Using variables as step and limit values

```
begin
  integer I1, I2, I3, I4;
  I2:=4;
  I3:=6;
  I4:=28;
  for I1:=I2 step I3 until I4 do OutInt (I1, 3);
  OutImage
end
```

Example 8.12 Variations on the *for* clause

A word of caution

The three values obtained from the expressions in the *step−until* sort of *for* clause are checked each time round the loop. It is possible to assign to them inside the loop, which will disturb the normal sequence of values. In fact some very 'clever' programs have been written to exploit this. It is, however, a very unsafe practice and you should normally be very careful not to change the values except in the *for* clause itself. If you use type procedures in these expressions you may produce unexpected side-effects too. Keep your programs simple if you want them to work.

for clauses using lists of values

The *step−until for* clause is very useful when we want to increase or decrease the value of the controlled variable by some constant amount. By using a variable as the *step* value and altering the value of this during the statement following the *do*, the change in the controlled variable can be varied, but this is rather dangerous and rarely useful. A simpler means of assigning a series of values, which are not obtainable by repeated additions or subtractions of a *step* value, is to use a list as the *for* clause. Consider example 8.13.

```
begin
   text T;
   character C;
   T:-Blanks(5);
   for C:='B', 'E', 'G', 'I', 'N' do
   begin
      T.PutChar(C);
      OutText(T);
      OutImage
   end
end
```

Example 8.13 for clause with a simple list

This program will assign the characters in the list to C in the order they are given. After each assignment the compound statement following *do* will be performed. If you compile and run the program your output should be

```
B
BE
BEG
BEGI
BEGIN
```

which is fairly self-explanatory. One important point is that non-arithmetic values may be used, such as characters and texts. This is not possible in the *step−until* form.

Steps in lists

The permutations allowed in the *for* clause are often only of academic interest. We do not need to consider most of them here. If you are really keen to explore them, I suggest that you refer to the *1986 SIMULA Standard*. It may be useful to note that a *step−until* construction may be used as one element in a list in a *for* clause. This is shown in example 8.14. Try it and see the effect.

```
begin
   integer I;
   for I:=4 step 1 until 6, 3, 8 step 2 until 20 do
   begin
      OutInt (I,3);
      OutImage
   end
end
```

Example 8.14 Mixing steps and lists

Exercises

8.5 Rewrite exercise 8.4 using *for* loops where possible.

8.6 Write a program to print out the multiplication tables from two to twelve, in the following format:

2	3	4	5	etc.
$1 \times 2 = 2$	$1 \times 3 = 3$	$1 \times 4 = 4$	$1 \times 5 = 5$	
$2 \times 2 = 4$	$2 \times 3 = 6$	$2 \times 4 = 8$	$2 \times 5 = 10$	

etc.

8.7 Write a program which reads in a series of words and prints them five to a line, with a blank line after every six lines.

8.8 Extend your answer to exercise 8.7 to print successively the letters a, b, c, d, e, f before the lines in each block and to number the blocks.

Item-oriented I/O with Files

Matching the item-oriented procedures for reading and writing in a text are procedures for reading and writing sequences of characters which represent numbers in Files. Those for output are local to OutFile, and thus PrintFile, while those for input are local to InFile.

Output of numeric items

The numeric-item procedures in OutFile output are OutInt, OutFix, OutReal and OutFrac. Each has the same parameters as its Put equivalent, plus an additional width parameter, which is an integer and comes after the others.

Basically each procedure creates a sequence of characters in the Image of the OutFile, starting at the current position. These are of the same forms as for the corresponding Put procedures, but their positioning is controlled by the width parameter.

The meaning of the width parameter

The width parameter specifies how many characters in the Image will be used by the numeric item. If the actual item is shorter than this width, space characters are added on the left of the item to achieve the required length. Thus the items are said to be 'right aligned' within the length of text specified by their width fields, since their last character always fills the rightmost space specified by the width parameter.

If the actual item is longer than the width specified, it is not output. Instead a sequence of asterisks of the specified length is printed. This is known as an editing overflow and many SIMULA systems will report the number of such overflows at the end of the program. By not allowing more than the specified number of characters to be output, the alignment of columns of figures is preserved. By printing asterisks, the user is warned that insufficient space was allowed for printing the required values.

Before writing an item, the SIMULA runtime system will check that there is sufficient space left in the current Image. If not, an OutImage is performed to copy the current Image to the actual File or output device, and the item is written at the start of the new Image. If the item is longer than Image.Length, a runtime error is reported.

Example 8.15 shows the use of some of the output procedures. It shows an overflow and an implicit OutImage.

```
begin
   ref (OutFile) OutPut;

   OutPut:-new OutFile ("TABLES");

   inspect OutPut do
   begin
      Open(Blanks(40));
      OutInt(203, 10); !3 characters in 10 spaces;
      OutFix(283.42, 5, 10); !8 characters in 10 spaces;
      OutFrac(10348215, 3, 10); !10 characters in 10 spaces;
      OutInt(9654, 5); !4 characters in 5 spaces;
      OutInt(103694, 4); !6 characters in 4 spaces->overflow;
      OutInt(3, 2); !Not enough space left in Image->implicit OutImage;
      OutImage;
      Close
   end*of*inspect
end
```

Example 8.15 Item-oriented output to a File

Exercises

8.9 Rewrite your answer from exercise 8.6 using OutInt.

8.10 Write a program which reads and prints the name, age in years and weight of a given number of people. The program should:
- (a) ask for and read the number of people to be dealt with,
- (b) ask for each item in turn for each person,
- (c) print out each person's details on a separate line, with the columns correctly aligned.

Input of numeric items

The input of numeric items is done by InInt, InReal and InFrac. No parameters are required. Each is a procedure of the appropriate type.

Thus InInt reads the next sequence in the current Image as an integer, returning its value. InReal reads it as a real, returning its value. InFrac reads it as a grouped item, returning the corresponding integer value.

As with the Get procedures in a text, any spaces are skipped. If the first sequence of non-spaces encountered is not in the correct form for the required type, a runtime error is reported.

The end of the current Image ends the item. If no non-space character is found before the end of the current Image, an InImage is performed and the search continues. Example 8.16 shows the input procedures in use.

```
begin
    ref (InFile) InPut;
    real R1; integer I1;
    InPut:-new InFile ("SOURCE");

    inspect InPut do
    begin
        Open(Blanks(80));
        OutInt (InInt, 4);    ! Output goes to SysOut;
        R1:=InReal;
        I1:=InFrac;
        Close
    end*of*inspect*input;
    OutImage
end
```

Example 8.16 Item-oriented input from a File

If a number is read which is larger than the largest positive value or smaller than the smallest negative value of the appropriate type which can be held on a particular computer, a runtime error, either integer overflow or floating-point overflow, should be reported. If a real value which is too near to zero is read a runtime error, floating-point underflow, should be reported. The limits for each SIMULA system are given in the appropriate programmer's reference manual or user's guide.

Text concatenation

As we have now completed the attributes of text, a word on the recently introduced text-concatenation operator is perhaps appropriate. This operator, &, combines two text frames, producing a reference to a new text frame.

The combined text has a frame consisting of a copy of the characters from the text to the left of the operator, followed by a copy of the characters from the text to the right. Example 8.17 shows the use of the concatenation operator. Only up-to-date SIMULA systems will have this feature.

```
begin
    text T1, T2, T3;
    T1 :- "Left";
    T2 :- "Right";
    T3 :- T1&T2;
    OutText(T3);
    OutImage
end
```

Example 8.17 Text-concatenation operator

Exercise

8.11 Rewrite the exam result question using all the new features which are appropriate.

Summary

- We have extended the idea of item-oriented input and output to cover the reading and writing of sequences of characters which represent arithmetic values in texts.
- We have seen the attributes of text which allow such operations on integer, real and grouped items.
- We have seen how to write *for* loops, which allow us to perform a task a certain number of times or once for each member of a list of values. We have also noted certain dangers with this.
- We have seen the equivalents of the text-item-oriented attributes which exist for InFile and OutFile.
- The text concatenation operator has been described.

Chapter 9

Classes as complex data types

A simple example

One very common use for computers in offices today is for printing self-adhesive labels for envelopes. Consider a program which reads in a name and address followed by the number of labels required. We will simplify things by printing our labels underneath one another, one at a time.

Using our knowledge of SIMULA so far, we might write the program shown in example 9.1.

```
begin
    integer NumLabs,I;
    text Nam, Street, Town, County, Code;

    procedure OutLine(T); text T;
    begin
        OutText(T);
        OutImage
    end*of*OutLine;

    text procedure InLine;
    begin
        InImage;
        inspect SysIn do InLine:-Copy(Image.Strip)
    end*of*InLine;

    OutLine("Name?");
    Nam:-InLine;
    OutLine("Street?");
    Street:- InLine;
    OutLine("Town?");
    Town:- InLine;
    OutLine("County?");
    County:- InLine;
    OutLine("Code?");
    Code:- InLine;
    OutLine("How many copies?");
    InImage;
```

```
    NumLabs:=InInt;
    Eject(1);
    for I:=1 step 1 until NumLabs do
    begin
      OutLine(Nam);
      OutLine(Street);
      OutLine(Town);
      OutLine(County);
      OutLine(Code)
    end
end
```

Example 9.1 Simple labels program without classes

This example may not be the neatest SIMULA writeable with our current knowledge, but it does the job. It also shows that, within the program, a label is a sequence of five text values, which are first read in and then printed out. What we are really doing, in a clumsy way, is using an object which has five text variables as attributes.

SIMULA allows us to use complex objects, made up of attributes which are already defined. These attributes may be of the standard SIMULA types or may be reference types defined by the user, i.e. one user-defined type may use others as attributes.

The construction in SIMULA which can be used to declare a complex type is the class. We have already seen predefined system classes when we looked at File and its sub-classes. Now let us declare a class Lab for use in our program. Example 9.2 shows 9.1 reworked using such a class.

```
begin
  integer NumLabs, I;

  procedure OutLine(T); text T;
  begin
    OutText(T);
    OutImage
  end;

  text procedure InLine;
  begin
    InImage;
    inspect SysIn do InLine:- Copy(Image.Strip)
  end;
```

```
class Lab;
begin
   text Nam, Street, Town, County, Code;
end--of--class--Lab;

ref(Lab) Label1;! Declare a pointer to a Lab object;
Label1:- new Lab;! Create a Lab object and point Label1 at it;
comment Remote access through dot notation;
Label1.Nam:- InLine;
Label1.Street:- InLine;
Label1.Town:-InLine;
Label1.County:- InLine;
Label1.Code:- InLine;
InImage;
NumLabs:= InInt;
comment Now connected access through inspect;
inspect Label1 do
begin
   for I:=1 step 1 until NumLabs do
   begin
      OutLine(Nam);
      OutLine(Street);
      OutLine(Town);
      OutLine(County);
      OutLine(Code)
   end
 end
end
```

Example 9.2 Simple labels program with classes

This example may seem longer and more complicated than example 9.1. It is certainly true that, for very simple purposes, using classes may offer little advantage. For any but the simplest programs, however, classes can make things much simpler. By the end of this chapter, we shall see this with our labels program.

Let us look at the new features used here. First there is the class declaration. This provides a description for a class of objects which all have the same attributes. In this case we define Lab (*label* is a SIMULA keyword and may not be used as an identifier). In general, a class declaration is very like a procedure declaration, with the keyword *class* instead of *procedure*. We shall look at the precise syntax later.

The declaration of Lab specifies the name of the complex type being defined as the identifier following the keyword *class*. This identifier is followed by a semi-colon. The attributes of the class are defined in a statement, known as the class body, which follows. Thus Lab has five attributes, all of type text.

Having defined the attributes of our new type, we can now create an object, or as many objects as we like, with those attributes. This is done by using an object generator.

An object generator can be used as a statement on its own or as a reference expression, i.e. on the right-hand side of a reference assignment or as a reference parameter. Examples of all these are shown in 9.3.

(a) As a complete statement

    new Printer

(b) As the right-hand side of a class-reference assignment

    OutF:− new OutFile

(c) As a class-reference parameter

    Queue__Up (new Passenger)

Example 9.3 Valid occurrences of object generators

Other cases are also possible, as we shall see shortly, but these are the main ones.

Our labels program uses the commonest and most easily grasped of these, the reference assignment. A variable is first declared, whose type is *ref*(Lab). This means that it identifies a location where a pointer to an object of the type defined by class Lab may be stored. This variable is used first as the left-hand side (destination) of a reference-assignment statement.

The effect of this statement is that a new object containing the attributes of Lab is created. Since Label1 is assigned a pointer to this object (references it), the object's attributes can be accessed through the variable Label1. As we have seen with objects which were of types InFile and OutFile, there are two ways of doing this. Both are shown in example 9.2.

'Remote accessing' of a class object is done by using the identifier of a reference variable which currently contains a pointer to the object,

Label1 in our example. A *ref*(Lab) procedure could also be used, as we have seen with SysIn and SysOut. This reference is followed by a dot, followed by the name of a visible attribute of the class which defines the type of the object being accessed.

This method of accessing attributes may be used for both text objects and class objects. This distinction is important, since the type 'text' is not defined by a class.

The other way of accessing the attributes of an object is by 'connecting' it first. To connect an object we must use an *inspect* statement. The syntax of a simple *inspect* statement was described in Chapter 8. In the statement which follows the keyword *do*, the use of any identifier which has a declaration in the class defining the type of the connected object is assumed to refer to this attribute. If no matching declaration is found in this class or its prefixes, the identifier is assumed to belong outside the object.

Thus, within the *inspect* statement in example 9.2, the occurrences of Nam, Street, Town, County and Code are taken to refer to attributes of the object Label1, since declarations for them are found in class Lab.

A full description of remote accessing is given in Chapter 13.

Exercises

9.1 Rewrite the labels program, adding an integer attribute to class Lab. Extend the program so that it will:
  (a) read a label from SysIn, prompting for each attribute in turn, including the integer attribute;
  (b) copy labels from an InFile, holding any number of labels, to a PrintFile;
  (c) insert the new label in the correct place as it writes them, assuming the labels to be in numerical order, defined by the integer attribute.

Devise suitable test data and check that your program copes with all possible cases.

9.2 A company wishes to computerize its personnel records. Each record contains the following information:

Name
Age
Date of birth

Works number
Job
Salary
Marital status

Devise a program which will:

  (a) read in a new record, prompting for input, and add this record to the existing file of records, held in order of works number;
  (b) request the user to type in the service required and then perform it, initially only performing (a) above;
  (c) add an additional service to find a record according to its works number;
  (d) add another service to print out all records where a specified attribute has a specified value, e.g. Name=F.Jones;
  (e) add another service to find a record and update any or all of its attributes and write an updated file.

Making classes work for themselves

Classes are objects containing attributes. These may be of any type visible in the block where the class is declared. As we have seen, this can allow us to create objects which match the natural groupings of data that we wish to process in our program. This approach is usually called 'object oriented' programming.

We also saw, when we considered class File and its sub-classes, that it is not just data attributes that a class object can contain. The power of the class concept as a way of representing objects in our programs is considerably increased by the ability to define procedures as attributes of classes.

Consider our labels program. In example 9.2 we read in each attribute, one at a time, and wrote it out in the same piecemeal way. In the extended version of exercise 9.1, which inserts a new label in the correct place in a file of labels, all with the same structure, this piecemeal reading will have to occur in several places in the program. We have used the action of copying a single line into a text, repeated five times, to read five lines of label data into the five text attributes of a Lab object. This is really one action on an object of type Lab, so far as our object-oriented view of labels is concerned, just as addition is an action on two arithmetic objects.

Example 9.4 shows the labels program again, but this time the reading and writing of the contents of a Lab object are made into procedures local to class Lab. The actions allowed on the object are now included in its definition.

Note how indentation and the use of comments after each *end* makes the structure of the program much easier to follow.

```
begin
  integer NumLabs, I;

  procedure OutLine(T); text T;
  begin
    OutText(T);
    OutImage
  end--of--OutLine;

  text procedure InLine;
  begin
    InImage;
    inspect SysIn do InLine :- Copy(Image.Strip)
  end--of--InLine;

  class Lab;
  begin
    text Nam, Street, Town, County, Code;

    procedure ReadLabel;
    begin
      Nam :- InLine;
      Street :- InLine;
      Town :- InLine;
      County :- InLine;
      Code :- InLine
    end++of++ReadLabel;

    procedure  WriteLabel;
    begin
      OutLine(Nam);
      OutLine(Street);
      OutLine(Town);
      OutLine(County);
      OutLine(Code)
    end++of++WriteLabel;

  end--of--Lab;

  ref(Lab) Label1;
```

```
Label1 :- new Lab;
Label1.ReadLabel;
InImage;
NumLabs := InInt;
for I := 1 step 1 until NumLabs do Label1.WriteLabel
```

end..of..program

Example 9.4 Labels program using procedures as attributes of a
class

One major advantage of this approach is that, given a sensible
choice of names, we will have a much more readable program. Complicated detail is moved from the main part of the program to the
procedure attributes of the class and replaced by meaningful procedure
names.

By designing the data structure and the operations to be performed
on that structure together, as a class declaration, we make the writing
of the main program much simpler. We are freed from detail and can
think in high-level terms. The essence of object-oriented programming
is to use good design of class declarations to make the rest of our task
easier. Once we had defined ReadLabel as an attribute of Lab, for
instance, we no longer had to worry how to read in the data each time it
was needed. Any program using our Lab class objects can rely on a
standard-reading procedure call.

Example 9.4 shows a solution to exercise 9.1 using procedures as
attributes of Lab. I think it is much clearer than any solution without
them.

You will probably have noticed that in these examples the procedures InLine and OutLine have not been declared inside the class
body of Lab, although they are used only there. This is because they
do not refer directly to the data structure which Lab represents.
They refer to the more general data structure defined by text and
so are declared at the most general level, the program block. This
leaves them free for use anywhere in the program that they are useful.
ReadLabel and WriteLabel are only useful as part of Lab.

Example 9.5 uses File objects to allow label lists to be accessed and
created. Note carefully the use of MyInput and MyOutput, which
allows input and output to be switched between the default Files, SysIn
and SysOut, and the user-defined ones, using the same procedures.

```
begin
  comment*****************************************
  * MyInput and MyOutput replace SysIn and SysOut. *
  * They can be redefined as necessary.           *
  *************************************************,

  ref(InFile) MyInput;
  ref(OutFile) MyOutput;

  comment***************************
  * Variables used by main program *
  *********************************,

  text Request, Source, Output;
  Boolean Unwritten;
  integer Count;
  ref(Lab) NewLabel, NextLabel;

  comment***********************************************
  * Utility procedures, used throughout the program *
  ***************************************************,

  procedure OutLine(T); text T;
  begin
    inspect MyOutput do
    begin
      OutText(T);
      OutImage
    end
  end--of--OutLine;

  text procedure InLine;
  begin
    text Tem;
    inspect MyInput do
    begin
      InImage;
      InLine :- Copy(Image.Strip)
    end
  end--of--InLine;

  comment******************************
  * Basic label class definition - Lab *
  ************************************,
```

```
class Lab;
begin

   comment * Data attributes of Lab * ;

   text Nam, Street, Town, County, Code;
   integer Sequence_No;

   comment * procedures operating on objects of type Lab * ;

   procedure WriteLabel;
   begin
      MyOutput.OutInt(Sequence_No,10);
      MyOutput.OutImage;
      OutLine(Nam);
      OutLine(Street);
      OutLine(Town);
      OutLine(County);
      OutLine(Code)
   end++of++WriteLabel;

   Boolean procedure ReadLabel;
   begin
      text First;
      First :- InLine;
      if First ne ".end" then
      begin
         Sequence_No := First.GetInt;
         Nam :- InLine;
         Street :- InLine;
         Town :- InLine;
         County :- InLine;
         Code :- InLine;
         ReadLabel := True;
      end
   end++of++ReadLabel;

end--of--Lab;

comment********************
* Main program starts here *
**************************.
                          ;

MyInput :- SysIn;
MyOutput :- SysOut;
```

```
OutLine("Please type name of file holding labels");
Source :- InLine;    ! Read old label file from SysIn;
Output :- Blanks(Source.Length+1);
Output := Source;
Output.PutInt(Count);    ! New list in file Output;
OutLine("Do you wish to add another label? Please type Yes or No");
Request :- InLine;
while Request="Yes" do
begin
   UnWritten := True;
   NewLabel :- new Lab;
   OutLine("Type the new label, using a new line for each item");
   if not NewLabel.ReadLabel then OutLine("No new label?");
   MyInput :- new InFile(Source);    ! Read old list from Source;
   MyOutput :- new OutFile(Output);  ! Write new list to Output;
   MyInput.Open(Blanks(80));
   MyOutput.Open(Blanks(80));
   NextLabel :- new Lab;
   while NextLabel.ReadLabel do
   begin
      comment Copy old to new, checking sequence nos.;
      if NextLabel.Sequence_No>NewLabel.Sequence_No then
      begin
         if Unwritten then
         begin
            NewLabel.WriteLabel;
            Unwritten := False; ! Prevent further copies;
         end
      end;
      NextLabel.WriteLabel
   end*of*copying*file*to*file;
   OutLine(".end");
   MyInput.Close;
   MyOutput.Close;
   Count := Count + 1;
   Source :- Copy(Output); ! Use Output as input for next addition;
   Output.SetPos(Output.Length-1);
   Output.PutInt(Count); ! Name of next Output file;
   MyInput :- SysIn;
   MyOutput :- SysOut;
   OutLine("Do you wish to add another label? Type Yes or No.");
   Request :- InLine
end*of*while*"Yes";
MyOutput.OutText("New label list written in file ");
OutLine(Source);      ! Name of last Output file used;
end*of*program
```

Example 9.5 Inserting a numbered label using procedure attributes

Making classes work even harder

Procedures as attributes make it possible to embed sequences of actions inside classes. This removes the need for tedious reprogramming of these sequences every time they are used in the main program. Having designed and implemented the class attributes, their internal details can be forgotten. Another mechanism can save even more tedious work.

Often the first actions performed on a new object of a particular class follow the same pattern each time one is created. Typically they involve setting the initial values of the data attributes of the object. In class Lab we made this much easier by writing ReadLabel in the definition of the class. This meant that creating and initializing the data in a Lab object required only two statements. By using a simple extension of the class declaration of Lab, we can do it in one.

Consider example 9.6. Here we have a sequence of statements at the end of the class body of Lab. These read in the values of its various attributes. Such a sequence will be executed whenever a new object of this class is generated by *new*.

```
begin

   procedure OutLine(T); text T;
   begin
     OutText(T);
     OutImage
   end--of--OutLine;

   text procedure InLine;
   begin
     InImage;
     inspect SysIn do InLine :- Copy(Image.Strip);
   end--of--InLine;

   class Lab(Prompt); Boolean Prompt;
   begin
     integer Sequence_No;
     text Nam, Street, Town, County, Code;

     procedure WriteLabel;
     begin
       OutInt(Sequence_No,10);
       OutImage;
       OutLine(Nam);
```

```
    OutLine(Street);
    OutLine(Town);
    OutLine(County);
    OutLine(Code)
end++of++WriteLabel;

procedure ReadLabel;
begin
    Sequence_No := InInt;
    Nam :- InLine;
    Street :- InLine;
    Town :- InLine;
    County :- InLine;
    Code :- InLine
end++of++ReadLabel;
```

comment These actions are performed each time a Lab object
            is generated;

```
if Prompt then
begin
    OutLine("Type, on separate lines, sequence number, Name, "
"Street, Town, County and Code.")
    end**of**prompting**if**requested;

    ReadLabel
    end--of--Lab;

ref(Lab) Label1;

Label1 :- new Lab(True);   ! Use prompting;
Label1.WriteLabel
end..of..program
```

Example 9.6 Parameters and initialization Code in classes

Another novel feature is the use of a parameter in the class declaration. Here it is a Boolean, used to indicate whether the new
object should prompt for input or merely read without prompting.
This can allow interactive input to be treated differently from input
from a file. The value of the parameter must be supplied in the object
generator.

For the moment we shall treat parameters to classes rather informally, but the following points are important:

Table 9.1 Modes of transmission to classes for parameter types

		Mode	
Type	Value	Reference	Name
Simple type	Default	Illegal	Illegal
text	Illegal	Default	Illegal
Object reference	Illegal	Default	Illegal
Simple type array	Illegal	Default	Illegal
Reference type array	Illegal	Default	Illegal
procedure	Illegal	Illegal	Illegal
type procedure	Illegal	Illegal	Illegal
label	Illegal	Illegal	Illegal
switch	Illegal	Illegal	Illegal

1   Parameters may not be in Name mode. Only the default mode for the type may be used with classes (see Table 9.1).

2   Once an object has been generated by *new*, at which point matches for all the parameters in the declaration must be supplied, these parameters can be treated as normal attributes of the object. They may be accessed by remote accessing via dot notation or connection.

3   Procedures and labels may not be used as parameters to classes.

The value of Prompt in example 9.6 is set to True, so that input is prompted for. If we rewrote example 9.5 using this version of Lab, the value given would be True for NewLabel and False for NextLabel, to avoid prompting when reading from a file.

Summary

- In this chapter we have seen how a programmer can define his or her own complex object types, using structures composed of simpler types. The SIMULA feature which is used for this is the class.
- We have seen that procedures may also be attributes of classes.
- The means of creating an object of a type defined by a class using the object generator *new* has been explained.
- The two methods of remote accessing of attributes of a class object, dot notation and connection by *inspect*, have been revised.
- The concepts of object-oriented programming have been explained and we have seen some of the benefits of this approach. We have

noted particularly how the use of procedure attributes to manipulate data attributes can simplify the rest of a program.

- The inclusion of actions in the definition of classes has been described. Their use in setting initial values for the data attributes has been shown.

- Lastly we have seen the use of parameters to classes. The types and modes allowed have been listed and the need to specify them in the object generator has been explained.

Exercises

9.3 Extend the definition of a label object to describe a letter to someone. Data should include name and address of both sender and recipient, text of the letter, date and method of sending, e.g. surface or air mail. You may assume any suitable maximum number of lines for the text. Write a program which reads in a letter and prints it along with a label for mailing it.

What problems would occur if the letter had to be able to contain a large and unspecified number of lines?

9.4 Rewrite your answers to exercises 9.1 and 9.2 using the new features introduced since then. What are the problems when adding several new records, which cannot be assumed to be in order themselves, to an ordered set like those in our labels file? Think especially of a system where the amount of storage space on the computer is limited. What extra features in SIMULA can you think of to help?

Chapter 10

Arrays and simple linked lists

Storing lists

In setting exercises 9.3 and 9.4, I hoped to focus your attention on the need to hold lists in ways which are easy to access. Many programs need to read, update and write out long series of data items. These items are the objects which we wish to manipulate. It is rarely worthwhile to use a computer to process one or two items. Even our program which wrote only a few copies of one label used an object with a list of data items within it.

The use of files allows us to read lists from outside the program and to store them at its end. Unfortunately, as our updating programs show, it is not a good idea to create a new file, external to the program, each time we add, delete or modify an item in a list. We soon end up with a multitude of out-of-date files.

The use of objects defined by classes allows us to hide a number of basic items inside larger, more complex items. It does not solve the problem of how to refer conveniently to a long list of items in succession. The need to declare and use a separate identifier for each possible line of a letter, for instance, makes long letters unwieldy to process and those of indefinite length almost impossible.

This chapter is the first of three dealing with the handling of lists. It provides simple but elegant mechanisms for solving most of the problems mentioned above. Let us start with the problem of holding a long list of items, which are all of the same type.

The letter program revisited

The text of a letter can be represented as a list of SIMULA text objects, with a maximum number of characters in each. So far, the only way we have seen to hold them is as a list of text declarations, one for each line. This leads to a very long-winded program and you probably confined your answer to exercise 9.3 to letters with only a few lines. A much simpler and more concise way of representing the same thing is to declare a single identifier, representing a numbered list of text references. Such an identifier represents an object known as an array of texts.

Example 10.1 shows the use of an array in a much simplified letter program, where no addresses are allowed for, only the text and the name of the sender.

First look at the array declaration in class Leter. (The misspelling is deliberate since there is a system Boolean procedure called Letter, which we might well wish to use in the same program. This is described in Chapter 12.)

```
begin
  class Leter;
  begin
    text Sender;
    text array Line(1:60);
    integer Len;

    procedure ReadLetter;
    begin
      InImage;
      inspect SysIn do
        while Image.Strip ne ".end" do
        begin
          Len := Len + 1;
          Line(Len) :- Copy(Image.Strip);
          InImage
        end
    end++of++ReadLetter;

    procedure WriteLetter;
    begin
      integer Current;
      for  Current := 1 step 1 until Len do
      begin
        OutText(Line(Current));
        OutImage
      end;
      OutText("         Yours faithfully,");
      OutImage;
      OutText("            ");
      OutText(Sender);
      OutImage
    end++of++WriteLetter;
```

```
      OutText("Type your letter, ending with '.end' on a line by itself");
      OutImage;
      ReadLetter;
      OutText("Now type your name on a single line");
      OutImage;
      InImage;
      inspect SysIn do Sender :- Copy(Image.Strip)

   end--of--class--Leter;

   new Leter.WriteLetter

end**of**program
```

Example 10.1 Letter program using a text array

Simple array declarations

The syntax of an array declaration is the type specifier of the items in the list (*integer*, *ref*(Leter) etc.), followed by the keyword *array*, followed by an identifier, followed by the 'bounds' of the list, enclosed in parentheses. Spaces (or ends of line) are used to separate keywords and identifiers as usual. They are not required between the identifier and the left parenthesis, but may be used if you wish.

It is legal to omit the type specifier, in which case the array is assumed to be of type real.

The syntax has not included the form of the bounds. In the commonest case we wish to declare a simple numbered list. The bounds then are two arithmetic values, which are converted to integers if necessary, separated by a colon. In example 10.1 the constant integers 1 and 60 are the bounds. This definition is only the simplest variant, but it covers most uses of arrays for the moment.

The semantics of such a declaration produce information telling the system to reserve space for a list of items of the specified type. This list is to be numbered consecutively, starting with the value before the colon and ending with the value after the colon. This also defines the number of elements in the list.

This list as a whole is referred to by its identifier. Thus a whole array can be passed as a parameter to a class or procedure, by giving just the identifier. Individual items in the list can be referred to by the identifier followed by an arithmetic value enclosed in parentheses, giving the number of the element to be accessed, within the list.

Thus the declaration in example 10.1 tells the SIMULA system to reserve space for a list of sixty text variables. These are to be numbered from one to sixty. The list will be referred to in the program by the identifier Line.

Note that the value of the first bound does not have to be 1. The bounds can have any values, even negative ones, as long as the first bound is less than the second or equal to it. The first bound is usually referred to as the lower bound and the second as the upper bound.

Note also that the values of the bounds may be given as real values. In this case they are converted to integers in the same way as for assignments. The values can be arithmetic expressions as well as constants. The normal rules for evaluating expressions apply.

Using array elements

The items in an array list are often called its 'elements'. Example 10.1 shows how an individual element of Line can be accessed. This is known as a subscripted variable. The value within the parentheses is called the subscript or the index.

Item number Len of the list is accessed in ReadLetter. It is referred to as Line(Len). Since Len is increased by one before each Image is copied to Line(Len) the effect is to copy successive lines of input into successive elements of the text array Line.

The syntax of a simple subscripted variable is an identifier followed by an arithmetic value enclosed in parentheses. The arithmetic value may be a constant, a variable or a more complicated expression, including a call on an arithmetic type procedure. Where necessary the value will be converted to an integer, following the normal rules.

The semantics are also simple. The value of the subscript gives the number used as an index to the elements of the array.

Note that the value of the lower bound is important in determining which element this refers to. A subscript of six will only refer to the sixth element if the lower bound was one. If the lower bound was four, indexing by six gives the third element.

A subscripted variable may be used wherever a simple variable of the same type may be used.

The value of the subscript, converted to an integer if necessary, must lie between the values of the lower and upper bounds, inclusive. If it is outside this range a runtime error will be reported.

Notes on differences amongst SIMULA systems

Some older SIMULA systems may require square brackets, [and], instead of parentheses, (and). Programs written for such machines may require changes to compile on up-to-date systems and vice versa. Some compilers will accept either form, which requires even greater care when moving programs.

The lowest permitted value for the lower bound, the highest permitted value for the upper bound and the maximum total number of items permitted in an array are all likely to be different on different systems. The maximum number of elements in an array of one type may also be different from that of another type, even on the same system. Check the programmer's reference manual or user's guide for the system you are using.

Variable length lists

Clearly the use of arrays allows large amounts of data to be held in locations declared within our programs, without the continual need to access files and without declaring long lists of identifiers. The use of loops, especially *for* loops, allows us to handle arrays in concise and clear ways.

One problem with the use of arrays is that we must tell the system in their declarations how many elements they contain and what their bounds are. Often this may not be known until runtime. This means that example 10.1 can only cope with letters of up to sixty lines. If someone wanted to use the program for a longer letter, they would have to alter the source and recompile it.

Although the array is not always the best solution when there is no way of knowing in advance how long the list will be, it can be made more generally useful by specifying the bounds in other ways.

We have defined the bounds as any expressions giving arithmetic values. This includes constants, as used in example 10.1, but also variables and expressions involving operators and type procedures. The only restriction is that any variables used must already have their values fixed before entering the block in which the array is declared.

This means that the bounds can be changed each time a block is entered.

This idea is not necessarily obvious at first, so take a while to get it straight in your mind. The SIMULA system allocates the space used by each block only when that block is entered. Thus it does not need to know how big an array is until then. If a variable used in the bounds of an array has been declared in an outer block, this variable can have its value set in that outer block before the array's space is allocated in the inner block. The variable must not be declared in the same block as the array, since the system may allocate the block's arrays before its other variables and, anyway, these variables could only have their initial zero values, since no statements may come in front of declarations in a block.

As a consequence, the only block which cannot use variables in array bounds is the program block. This is the outermost block and must use constants in all its array bounds.

All sub-blocks, procedures and classes used in a program are free to use variables in array bounds so long as these are declared in an enclosing block or, for classes and procedures, are parameters. Remotely accessed variables may also be used.

The simple examples in 10.2, 10.3 and 10.4 show how 'dynamic bounds', as this mechanism is known, may be used for sub-blocks, procedures and classes respectively. These trival examples demonstrate a very powerful facility.

```
begin
    integer I1,I2;   ! Declared at the outermost block level;
    I1 := 2;         ! Sets a non-zero value in I1;
    I2 := 3;         ! Sets a non-zero value in I2;
    begin

        comment Start a sub-block which can only be entered after
                I1 and I2 have had their values set;

        integer array A1(I1:I2);   ! Declare with I1 and I2 as bounds;
        A1(2) := 6;
    end--of--sub-block;
    comment Array no longer accessible;
end
```

Example 10.2 Dynamic-array bounds in a sub-block

```
begin

    procedure Bounder(Lowest); integer Lowest;
    begin
        comment Parameters may be used as bounds inside a procedure body;

        character array C1(Lowest:4*Lowest); ! Use an expression containing
                                                    Lowest as upper bound;
        C1(Lowest*2+1) := '&';    ! Use an expression in the subscript too;
        OutChar(C1(5));           ! Null unless Lowest is 2;
        OutImage
    end--of--procedure--Bounder;

    Bounder(2);                   ! Should print &;
end**of**program
```

Example 10.3 Dynamic-array bounds in a procedure

```
begin
    integer Lower;
    class Cl1(Upper); integer Upper;
    begin
        Boolean array BoolArr(Lower:Upper); ! Use a mixture of enclosing
                            block's declarations and parameters to set
                                        bounds;
        BoolArr(Lower+3) := True
    end--of--class--Cl1;

    ref(Cl1) Cl1Ref;
    Lower := 4;        ! Sets lower bound before object generation;
    Cl1Ref :- new Cl1(7);      ! Passes upper bound as a parameter;
    if Cl1Ref.BoolArr(5) then OutText("True") else OutText("False");
    OutImage
end**of**program
```

Example 10.4 Dynamic-array bounds in a class

One important point to note is that when the parameters of a procedure or class are used in bounds for arrays declared in that procedure or class body, they are treated as outside that body. This is the only case where any distinction is made between parameters and other locally declared variables inside the procedure or class body. It is very important that this be allowed.

A more practical use of dynamic arrays

Let us return to our general text-processing system. It has been some
time since we looked at it, but I hope the features introduced since
then have been suggesting solutions to the problems we were facing. In
particular, I hope the use of classes and object-oriented programming
has seemed relevant.

This section shows how the combination of class objects and arrays
can help the design of the Book level of our program. What we are
going to try to do is design a class Book, with the necessary data
structures and procedures for manipulating them. Consider example
10.5.

```
begin

   class Book(Num_of_Chaps); integer Num_Of_Chaps;
   begin
      text Title, Author;
      ref(chapter) array Chaps(1:Num_Of_Chaps);
      ref(Contents) Cont;
      ref(Preface) Pref;
      ref(Index) Ind;
      integer Count;

      procedure Title_Page;
      begin
         Eject(10);
         OutText(Title);
         OutImage;
         OutText("   by");
         OutImage;
         OutText(Author);
         OutImage;
         Eject(0);
      end++of++Title++Page;

      Pref :- new Preface;
      for Count := 1 step 1 until Num_Of_Chaps do
              Chaps(Count) :- new Chapter(Count);
      Cont :- new Contents(Pref,Chaps);
      Ind :- new Index(Chaps);
      Cont.PrintContents;
      Pref.PrintPreface;
```

```
   for Count := 1 step 1 until Num_Of_Chaps do
         Chaps(Count).PrintChap;
   Ind.PrintIndex
end--of--Book;

class Chapter(Numbr); integer Numbr;
begin
   procedure PrintChap;
   begin comment Print out this chapter in appropriate format;
      ...
      ...
   end++of++PrintChap;
   ...
   ...
end--of-Chapter;

class Contents(Pref,Chaps); ref(Preface) Pref; ref(Chapter) array Chaps;
begin
   procedure PrintContents;
   begin comment Print a contents page for Pref and Chaps;
      ...
      ...
   end++of++PrintContents;
   ...
   ...
end--of--Contents;

class Preface;
begin
   procedure PrintPreface;
   begin comment Print a preface in appropriate format;
      ...
      ...
   end++of++PrintPreface;
   ...
   ...
end--of--Preface;

class Index(Chaps,Num_Chaps); ref(Chapter) array Chaps;
                            integer Num_Chaps;
begin
   procedure PrintIndex;
   begin comment Print an index for Chaps;
      ...
```

```
    ...
  end++of++PrintIndex;
    ...
    ...
  end--of--Index;

  comment This is the main program;
  OutText("How many chapters?");
  OutImage;
  new Book(InInt)
end**of**main**program
```

Example 10.5 Class Book and the accompanying program block

The Book is represented as a class. It is assumed to have a title page, a contents, a preface, a sequence of chapters and an index. The different data structures of each of these are represented in turn by classes. Since each may only exist as a part of a book, they are declared inside the body of Book (or 'local to' Book).

A single ref variable is declared for each of these classes, except for Chapter. The number of chapters in a book can vary considerably and so an array of *ref*(Chapter) variables is declared. Its lower bound is 1 and its upper bound is a parameter of Book. The actual number of chapters can be specified when the Book object is generated in the main program block. We use

  new Book(InInt)

so that the number is read in and passed, in one statement.

Top down again

Example 10.5 shows how object-oriented programming makes top-down design easier. Only the skeletons of the components of Book are provided, yet its own actions can be fully defined in terms of these. Actions to be performed on one component can be made into local procedures within the class corresponding to that component. The detail of how such procedures will work can be left until that class is itself considered in detail.

This leads to the following description of top-down, object-oriented design.

The visible properties of each component are defined by the operation of the object of which it forms part. Properties which are not externally visible can be left undefined until the component itself is implemented in detail.

Even simpler is:

Don't clutter up your program with unnecessary detail until you need it.

Exercises

10.1   Write a program which reads the names of a group of students and creates an array of pupil records, holding name, age, address and marks in maths, English and physics. Allow student details to be filled in in any order, copying the details into the correct entry in the array. Print out the contents in the order in which the list of names was first given.

10.2   Extend 10.1 to sort the names into alphabetical order as it first reads them and to print the records in this order.

10.3   Further extend your program to calculate each student's average mark and to print separate lists ordered alphabetically, by order of marks in each subject and by overall average mark.

Rearranging lists

An array is an ordered list. Each item in the list is numbered and can be accessed by this number combined with the name of the array. This is very useful where the order is fixed or is irrelevant.

Exercise 10.2 shows that it is often useful to be able to rearrange the order in which the items of a list are held. Exercise 10.3 takes this further and shows that the same items may need to be thought of as being on several different lists, held in different orders. The array can only do this by clumsy rearrangement of its elements or by copying the same elements into a number of different arrays.

Even an apparently trivial operation, like adding a new item to a list which is already in order is not easy. Consider example 10.6.

Once the correct position in the list has been found, it is necessary to move all the labels after this up by one in the array, unless the new

```
begin

  ref(InFile) MyInput;

  class Lab;
  begin
    procedure ReadLabel;
    begin
      integer I;
      inspect MyInput do
      begin
        SeqNo := InInt;
        InImage;
        for I := 1 step 1 until 5 do
        begin
          Address(I) :- Copy(Image.Strip);
          InImage
        end
      end
    end--of--ReadLabel;

    text array Address(1:6);
    integer SeqNo;
  end++of++Lab;

  integer Count1, Count2, I;
  ref(InFile) Source;
  ref(Lab) array Labs(1:100);
  ref(Lab) NewLab;

  Source :- new InFile("Labels");
  inspect Source do
  begin
    Open(Blanks(20));
    MyInput :- Source;
    while not EndFile do
    begin
      comment Assume labels in Source already in order of SeqNo;
      Count1 := Count1 + 1;
      Labs(Count1) :- new Lab;    ! Read in successive labels;
      Labs(Count1).ReadLabel
    end..of..reading ..source..into..Labs;
    Close
  end%%of%%inspecting%%Source;
```

```
MyInput :- SysIn;
NewLab :- new Lab;
NewLab.ReadLabel;
Count2 := 1;
while Count2<=Count1 do
begin
   if Labs(Count2).SeqNo>NewLab.SeqNo then
   begin
      comment New label goes before Labs(Count2) so make room;
      for I := Count1 step -1 until Count2 do Labs(I+1) :- Labs(I);
      Labs(Count2) :- NewLab;
      Count2 := Count1 + 2;   ! Force end of while loop;

   end--of--adding--new--label;
   Count2 := Count2 + 1;
end..of..while..loop;

if Count2=Count1+1 then Labs(Count2) :- NewLab; ! Goes at the end;

comment Check the sequence;
for I := 1 step 1 until Count1 + 1 do OutInt(Labs(I).SeqNo,3)

end**of**program
```

Example 10.6 Adding an item to an ordered list in an array

label happens to belong at the end. This is potentially very time consuming. Another problem is that the array may not be large enough. If we want to allow for a list of unknown length, with any number of new labels, arrays are not likely to be useful.

Fortunately, SIMULA allows us to create much more flexible lists, tailored to the needs of a program. These use the ability of class objects to contain pointers or links, in the form of reference variables, to other objects. Lists can be formed in this way, known as 'linked lists'.

Reading into a linked list

Figure 10.1 shows how a new object is added to a linked list. Each object of class Linked__Lab contains an attribute called Next, which is of type *ref*(Linked__Lab). The corresponding program is shown in example 10.7.

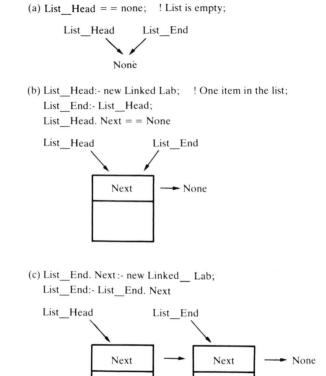

(a) List__Head = = none;   ! List is empty;

(b) List__Head:- new Linked Lab;   ! One item in the list;
    List__End:- List__Head;
    List__Head. Next = = None

(c) List__End. Next:- new Linked__ Lab;
    List__End:- List__End. Next

Fig. 10.1 Building a single linked list.

New objects are added to the end of this list. Pointers to the current first and last members of the list are held in the *ref*(Linked__Lab) variables List__Head and List__End.

The concept of adding to a list by manipulating pointers is very powerful. It is worth spending some time getting example 10.7 clear in your mind.

Class reference comparison

The final *while* loop of example 10.7 contained a class-object-reference comparison. This used the operator =/=, which means 'does not reference' or 'does not point at'. Formally, it tests for reference inequality. It is similar to the text-reference comparator.

```
begin
  class Linked_Lab;
  begin
    ref(Linked_Lab) Next;
    integer SeqNo;
    comment Simplified version of Lab;
    SeqNo := Inint;
  end--of--Linked--Lab;

  ref(Linked_Lab) List_Head, List_End, Temp;

  ! a)  List_Head and List_End are both None;

  ! b); List_Head :- List_End :- new Linked_Lab;

  ! c); List_End.Next :- new Linked_Lab;
        List_End :- List_End.Next;

  comment Now print the SeqNo of each item in the list;

  Temp :- List_Head;
  while Temp=/=None do
  begin
    OutInt(Temp.SeqNo,3);
    Temp :- Temp.Next
  end..of..printing..list

end**of**program
```

Example 10.7 Building the linked list in Fig. 10.1

There is also a positive equivalent, $==$, meaning 'does reference', which tests for reference equality. Thus

> if $P1==P2$ then OutInt(3,3)

would print 3 if the class-object-reference variables P1 and P2 pointed to the same object.

None

The same comparison also used None as one of the reference variables. None is a reference to no object. Any reference variable initially references None. Any reference variable can be pointed back to None.

Exercises

10.4   Extend example 10.7 to build a list of five objects.

10.5   Write a program to add items to the start of a linked list, rather than the end, and which builds a list of four such items.

Generalizing simple linked lists

In exercises 10.4 and 10.5 you will have noticed that for all items except the first, adding a new item to a linked list requires the same sequence of statements. There is a clear case for using procedures for such tasks.

   If we think further, a linked list is a data structure with attributes unique to itself. Each list has a head and a tail (although it is possible to use just a head). Furthermore, our proposed procedures for adding items at the beginning and end of a list operate only on attributes of a list object. It is sensible to define a class embodying these attributes for use in processing linked lists. Example 10.8 shows how this might be implemented.

   Example 10.8 also shows how a new item can be added to the middle of a list without needing to update all the items which follow. The mechanism used is illustrated in Fig. 10.2. Only two reference assignments are needed to achieve it.

```
begin
  class Linked_Label;
  begin
    ref(Linked_Label) Next;
    integer SeqNo;
    SeqNo := InInt
  end--of--Linked--Label;

  class Label_List;
  begin
    ref(Linked_Label) Head, Tail;

    procedure AddtoEnd(Lab);ref(Linked_Label) Lab;
    begin
      if Head==None then
      begin
        comment Special case when list is empty;
        Head :- Tail :- Lab
      end else begin
        comment Normal case;
```

```
        Tail.Next :- Lab;
        Tail :- Lab
      end
    end++of++AddtoEnd;

    procedure AddtoFront(Lab);ref(Linked_Label) Lab;
    begin
      if Head==None then
      begin
        comment Special case when list is empty;
        Head :- Tail :- Lab
      end else begin
        comment Normal case;
        Lab.Next :- Head;
        Head :- Lab
      end
    end++of++AddtoFront;

end--of--Label--List;

ref(Label_List) Labs;
ref(Linked_Label) New_Lab, Temp;
integer Count;

comment Create an initial list of 4 items;
Labs :- new Label_List;
for Count := 1 step 1 until 4 do Labs.AddtoEnd(new Linked_Label);

comment Add a new label to the front;
Labs.AddtoFront(New Linked_Label);
comment Add a new label between existing nos. 2 and 3;
New_Lab :- new Linked_Label;
Temp :- Labs.Head;
Temp :- Temp.Next;
comment Temp now points to item 2 on list;
New_Lab.Next :- Temp.Next;    ! Step b) in diagram 10.2;
Temp.Next :- New_Lab;         ! Step c) in diagram 10.2;
Temp :- Labs.Head;
while Temp=/=None do
begin
  OutInt(Temp.SeqNo,3);
  Temp :- Temp.Next
end;
OutImage
end**of**program
```

Example 10.8 Class Label__List

(a)

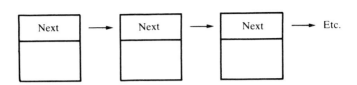

(b)

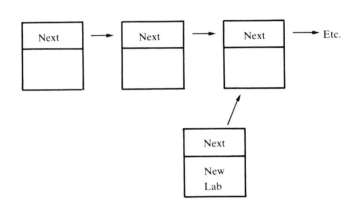

(c)

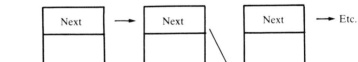

Fig. 10.2 Inserting a new item in the middle of a linked list.

Exercises

10.6 Write a program which locates and removes an item in a linked list.

10.7 Add local procedures to class Linked__Lab, one of which inserts a label object after a given member of the list and one of which removes a label from the list.

10.8 Rewrite your answers to exercises 10.2 and 10.3 using linked lists instead of arrays. Remember that an object can have as many ref attributes as you like and so can be on as many linked lists simultaneously as you wish.

Arrays versus linked lists

We have seen that arrays are a very convenient way of storing simple values and references to more complex class objects in an ordered list. We have seen that rearranging such lists is very inconvenient. Although the use of dynamic bounds allows greater flexibility, the need to specify the overall size and bounds of an array at the start of the block in which it is declared still imposes quite strict limits to the usefulness of arrays.

Linked lists are much easier to rearrange and to extend. We do not need to fix an upper limit to the number of elements in them. The same object can exist on several such lists at once. On the other hand, if we wish to find item number six, say, on a linked list, we must chain through, counting as we go. In an array, accessing item number six is trivial.

There are strengths and weaknesses in both these list structures. It is a question of picking the more appropriate one for your purposes. As we shall see later, linked lists can be even more flexible than those we have used so far and some of their limitations can be reduced. For certain very common purposes, however, arrays remain the best choice.

Summary

- We have seen how simple, ordered lists can be held in arrays. The means for declaring and accessing arrays have been learned, especially how to use subscripted variables to treat any item of an array as a simple variable of the same type.

- The use of dynamic bounds to allow variable-sized arrays has been shown.
- We have considered briefly the use of simple linked lists and noted their advantages over arrays.
- Finally we have compared the merits of arrays and linked lists and concluded that each structure is better suited to certain applications.

Chapter 11

Sub-classes and more complex Boolean expressions

Building on what you have

One of the important ways we have of making sense of the world is to classify things. We put them into categories or classes. SIMULA allows us to reflect this very natural way of thinking in the way we write programs.

When classifying things we first group them either very generally, e.g. as animal, vegetable or mineral, or very specifically, e.g. as bees or roses, depending on circumstances. These approaches correspond to the programming techniques known as 'top down' and 'bottom up' design, respectively.

In practice, it is fairly easy to classify things in general terms, but appearances can be deceptive when it comes to detail. Things which look alike may actually have very different origins. Thus the hedgehog and the spiny ant-eater look remarkably similar and live very similar lives, yet, genetically, they are not closely related at all.

SIMULA takes the top-down approach as the safest, just as natural science has tended to. It allows us to define a Class, as we have seen, to represent a general type of object. This may then be extended, to reflect the special characteristics of sub-types by defining sub-classes of the original. These retain some or all of the characteristics of the parent type, but include characteristics which are only found in certain objects of this type.

It is important to notice that sub-types in SIMULA extend and refine the range of characteristics of the parent type. The more general the class of objects described, the fewer characteristics that are given to it.

One example of the use of such sub-types, that we have already seen, is the class File and its sub-classes. If you look back at Chapter 7, you will see that special purpose files are represented by adding to the attributes of first File, then ImageFile and, for PrintFile, Outfile. We can show this as a tree — a family tree. Figure 11.1 is the File family tree as we have seen it so far.

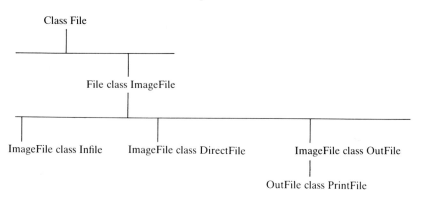

Fig. 11.1 Family tree of class File.

The syntax of a sub-class declaration is very simple. The keyword *class* is preceded by the name of the parent class. Otherwise the declaration is the same as for a simple class. The new class is said to be 'prefixed' by the parent.

A word-processing example

We can consider a chapter in a book as a sequence of pages. This sequence can, as we have seen, be represented as an array or as a linked list. In either case we want all the pages to be of the same type. If they are not, they cannot be held together. All items in an array must be of the same type. All items in a linked list are joined by pointers declared as *ref*(type) variables, with type the same for all. Thus we need a basic class Page.

Each Page will contain printed blocks. The first Page in each Chapter will have a title block, followed by a sequence of other blocks. The other blocks could contain text or diagrams. A linked list of Print__Block objects can represent the contents of a Page.

Example 11.1 shows the outline of such a set of classes. The parent class for blocks on a page is Print__Block. It contains a link in the form of *ref*(Print__Block) Next. It also contains an array of text variables, Contents, representing the lines in the block. Parameters Width and Length are integers representing line length and number of lines in the block, respectively. Each member of the text array is filled with blanks, initially.

```
begin
  class Page;
  begin
    class Print_Block(Width,Length);integer Width, Length;
    begin
      ref(Print_Block)Next;
      text array Contents(1:Length);
      integer Count;
      for Count:=1 step 1 until Length
      do Contents(Count):-Blanks(Width)
    end--of--Print_Block;

    Print_Block class Title_Block(Title);text Title;
    begin
      Contents(Length//2):=Title
    end--of--Title_Block;

    Print_Block class Text_Block;
    begin
      for Count:=1 step 1 until Length do
      begin
        InImage;
        Contents(Count):=Intext(Width)
      end
    end--of--Text_Block;

    Print_Block class Diagram(Title); text Title;
    begin
      Contents(1):=Title
    end--of--Diagram;

    ref(Print_Block) Head, Tail, New_Block;
    text Directive;
    integer Len;

    procedure Add(NewBlock); ref(Print_Block) NewBlock;
    begin
      if Head==None then Head :- NewBlock;
      if Tail=/=None then Tail.Next :- NewBlock;
      Tail :- NewBlock
    end++of++Add;

    Directive :- InText(2);
    while Directive NE "$E" do
    begin
      if Directive= "$B" then
```

```
        begin
          Len := InInt;
          InImage;
          Add(new Title_Block(80,Len,InText(80)))
        end
        else if Directive="$C" then
          Add(new Text_Block(80,InInt))
        else begin
          Len := InInt;
          InImage;
          Add(new Diagram(80,Len,InText(80)))
        end;
        Directive :- InText(2)
      end
    end..of..Page;
    new Page;
end
```

Example 11.1 Representing pages as Print—Block objects

This parent class is used to prefix the three classes representing different types of block on a page. Each contains additional attributes, actions or both. Two contain parameters. Note that these also are additional to those in the parent class.

A few properties of sub-classes

The program shows some important features of sub-classes.

1   The attributes of the prefixing class are normally visible in its sub-classes. As we shall see later there is a way of 'hiding' the parent's attributes. Note that this visibility of local quantities is unlike any other type of block, such as a sub-block or procedure body.

2   The parameters of the prefixing class must still be given when generating a new object of one of its sub-classes. Thus, the generation of a new Title—Block requires three parameters, the two declared for parent Print—Block followed by the additional one for Title—Block. The prefixing-class parameters always come before the sub-class parameters.

3   The actions specified for the prefixing class are performed, before those of the sub-class, when a new sub-class object is generated. Thus the for-loop which sets the elements of Contents to blank-filled texts of

the desired Width, takes place before any of the actions of Title—Block, Text—Block or Diagram.

4   A reference variable which points to objects of the prefixing class can also point to objects of its sub-classes. Variables which are declared as ref to a sub-class cannot point to a parent object, however. Thus the use of *ref*(Print—Block) variables for all the links in the list of blocks means that objects of type Print—Block, Title—Block, Text—Block and Diagram can all fit onto the same list. They are all 'qualified' by the type Print—Block. On the other hand, objects created by the generator new Print—Block, would not be allowed on a list linked by pointers declared as *ref*(Text—Block).

What the program does

The program reads text from SysIn. This text is assumed to end with a line starting with the characters '$E', meaning end of page. The character '$' followed by a sequence of letters and numbers is assumed to be a directive, telling the program what the next sequence represents. Lines of 80 characters are assumed.

The directive '$B' means that a Title—Block is required. The number of, mostly blank, lines to be used, is given as an integer following the $B directive. The text for the title parameter is on the following line. The title is copied into the middle line of the block by the actions of a new Title—Block.

The directive '$C' means that a new Text—Block is required. The number of eighty-character lines in this block is given as an integer following the directive and is used as a dynamic upper bound to Contents. The contents of the block are on the following lines. The actions of a new Text—Block copy this into Contents.

The directive '$D' means that a space for a diagram should be left. Again the number of lines to be left follows and the next line is the text to be used for the title of the diagram. This is copied into the first text element of Contents by the actions of a new Diagram object.

Exercises

11.1 Add a printing procedure to class Print—Block and use the program to process a source in the required format.

11.2 By using a linked list to hold lines, remove the need to specify the number of lines in a Text__Block. Use a line breaker to avoid splitting words at the ends of a line.

Sub-sub-classes

As is clear from the File family tree, a sub-class can prefix its own extensions. The rules given above still apply, except that the parameters, local variables and actions of all three classes are combined in the grandchild, in the order grandparent, parent, grandchild. Example 11.2 shows this in a trivial example. Try compiling and running it to see the effects for yourself.

```
begin
  class OuterMost(First); text First;
  begin
    text OuterText;
    OuterText :- Copy("Outermost=first on prefix chain");
    OutText(OuterText);
    OutImage;
    OutText(First);
    OutImage
  end--of--OuterMost;

  OuterMost class Middle(Second); text Second;
  begin
    text MiddleText;
    MiddleText :- Copy("Middle=second on prefix chain");
    OutText(MiddleText);
    OutImage;
    OutText(First);
    OutText(Second);
    OutImage
  end--of--Middle;

  Middle class InnerMost(Third); text Third;
  begin
    text InnerText;
    InnerText :- Copy("Inner=last on prefix chain");
    OutText(InnerText);
    Outimage;
    OutText(First);
    OutText(Second);
    OutText(Third);
    OutImage
  end--of--InnerMost;
```

```
new OuterMost("One");
new Middle("One","Two");
new InnerMost("One","Two","Three")
```

end**of**program

Example 11.2 Concatenation...sub-sub-classes

There is no limit to the number of levels of such prefixing which you may use. The same rules apply with each extension. The combining of attributes and actions in the correct order is called the 'concatenation' of the prefixing classes and the final extension.

The sequence class, sub-class, sub-sub-class, etc. is called a 'prefix chain'. In more technical descriptions the first class on the prefix chain is called the 'outermost' and the final one the 'innermost'. A sub-class is 'inner' to its parent, grandparent, etc. A class is 'outer' to its sub-classes, their sub-classes, etc.

Name conflicts in sub-classes

It is quite legal to declare identifiers in a sub-class with the same name as those declared in its parent or another outer class. This is shown in example 11.3. The effects are simple to describe, but can sometimes be confusing to grasp. It is perhaps worth running example 11.3 before reading on, to give you a practical experience of the concepts.

```
begin
  class Grandad;
  begin
    text T;
    T :- Copy("Grandad"); ! Always refers to the preceding declaration;
    OutText(T);          ! Should always print Grandad;
    OutImage
  end--of--Grandad;

  Grandad class No1Son;
  begin
    text T;              ! Conflicts with declaration in Grandad;
    T :- Copy("No1Son");  ! Refers to T immediately above;
    OutText(T);          ! Should always print No1Son;
    OutImage
  end--of--No1Son;
```

```
Grandad class No2Son;
begin
   OutText(T);        ! Should always print Grandad, no conflict;
   OutImage
end--of--No2Son;

No1Son class GrandDaughter;
begin
   OutText(T);        ! Should use T from No1Son, print No1Son;
   OutImage
end--of--GrandDaughter;

new Grandad;          ! Prints   Grandad;

new No1Son;           ! Prints   Grandad
                                 No1Son;

new No2Son;           ! Prints   Grandad
                                 Grandad;

new GrandDaughter;     ! Prints  Grandad
                                 No1Son
                                 No1Son;
end**of**program
```

Example 11.3 Name conflicts in prefix chains

In a parent class the use of the identifier always refers to the declaration of that identifier inside that class.

In a sub-class the use of the identifier always refers to the declaration of that identifier inside the sub-class.

That is fairly straightforward. The formal description is that the use of an identifier within the class body where a declaration exists for it, always refers to the location associated with that declaration. If no declaration exists for it inside the class body where it is used, it is said to be 'uncommitted' at that prefix level. It is then assumed to refer to the innermost prefixing class containing such a declaration. If there is no class on the prefix chain outer to the class in which the identifier is used which contains a declaration for it, the identifier is looked for outside the class and is not an attribute of it.

Top and tailing — the use of *inner*

The use of actions within classes should be familiar by now. The ability to build on these in suitably different ways in sub-classes is used in the three sub-classes of Print—Block in example 11.1. This is a very powerful feature of SIMULA.

The usefulness of sub-class actions is increased still further by the *inner* statement. This allows a parent class to specify one set of actions to be performed before those of its sub-classes and another to be performed after them. Consider example 11.4.

```
begin
   class Parent;
   begin
      OutText("Before inner");
      OutImage;
      Inner;
      OutText("After inner");
      OutImage
   end--of--Parent;

   Parent class Child;
   begin
      OutText("In the inner class");
      OutImage
   end--of--Child;

   new Parent;
   new Child
end**of**program
```

Example 11.4 The use of *inner*

The class Parent contains a statement consisting of the keyword *inner* and nothing else. When an object is generated from Parent itself, this statement is ignored.

The class Child is prefixed by Parent. If the *inner* statement was not in Parent all the actions of Parent would be performed before any actions of Child, whenever an object was generated from Child. The effect of the *inner* statement is to alter this sequence.

The two statements of Parent before the *inner* are executed first.

The actions of sub-class Child are performed when the *inner* is reached. The remaining statements of Parent are only performed when those of Child are complete.

This allows the outer class to define both a prologue and an epilogue to the actions of the inner one. When an object of such an outer class is generated rather than of the inner class, the *inner* statement is ignored.

Only one *inner* statement can appear in a class body, since it can only have one inner class whose statements it will perform.

A sub-class may contain an *inner* statement, in which the actions of any sub-sub-classes will be performed when it is reached, and so on along the prefix chain. Practical uses of this feature, especially in conjunction with prefixed blocks, will be demonstrated later in this book.

Exercises

11.3 Use an *inner* statement in class Print—Block to write the number of lines created for that block when processing of it is complete. Write it to a different file from the one used for the actual text.

11.4 Study the following program. What would its output be? Try running it to check your answer.

```
begin
  class Outer;
  begin
    text T;
    T :- Copy("ABC");
    OutText(T);
    inner;
    OutImage
  end--of--Outer;

  Outer class Middle;
  begin
    text T;
    T :- Copy("DEF");
    OutText(T);
    inner;
    OutText(T);
    OutImage
  end--of--Middle;
```

```
        Outer class Centre;
        begin
           text T1;
           T1 :- Copy("DEF");
           OutText(T);
           OutImage
        end--of--Centre;

        Middle class Inner;
        begin
           text T1;
           T1 :- Copy("GHI");
           OutText(T);
           T := T1;
        end--of--Inner;

        new Outer;
        new Middle;
        new Centre;
        new Inner
     end**of**program
```

The types of class objects

We have seen in example 11.1 some of the rules governing the types or qualifications of class objects. Here we will consider these further and more systematically. We shall also see how to check the qualification of a class object.

When a class object is generated it possesses all the attributes of the class whose name is given in the object generator. This includes any visible attributes from classes on its prefix chain, following the rules given above concerning name clashes.

The type of such an object is the class specified and this is called its qualification. It can also be thought of as being qualified by the classes on its prefix chain, except that not all the attributes of these may be visible.

A variable which is declared as a *ref* to a class which is the qualification of an object or is on the prefix chain of its qualifying class may be used to access that object. The type of the reference variable used controls how much of the prefix chain may be so accessed.

It is only legal to treat an object which is being remotely accessed as if it was qualified by the class of the referencing variable. Thus, in example 11.1, when New__Block is set to denote a new Text__Block only the attributes declared in Print—Block, which prefixes Text—Block, may be accessed through New—Block. This is because New —Block is declared as a *ref*(Print—Block) not a *ref*(Text—Block) variable. This means that the statement

>   NewBlock.Count:= 3

would be illegal.

Breaking any of these rules will cause the SIMULA system to report an error, either during compilation or at runtime. Some extra features of SIMULA can be used to circumvent these restrictions, as we shall see later, but these checks provide an important safeguard against serious errors which could occur otherwise.

Checking the qualification of an object

In addition to checking whether or not two reference variables point to the same object (reference equality and inequality), SIMULA also allows us to check the qualification of any referenced object. To do this we use the reference comparators *is* and *in*.

The operator *is* checks whether an object is qualified by a particular class. It will only give the value True when the object's innermost class matches that with which it is compared. Thus

>   Obj is ThisClass

will only give True if the object referenced by Obj was generated by

>   new ThisClass.

The operator *in* makes a less strict check. It will give True if the object is either of the specified class or has that class on its prefix chain.

The use of *is* and *in* is shown in example 11.5

```
begin
  class A;
  begin
    integer I;
  end--of--A;

  A class A1;
  begin
    integer K;
  end--of--A1;
```

```
A class A2;
begin
   integer L;
end--of--A2;

ref(A) Obj1,Obj2,Obj3,Obj4;

Obj1 :- new A;
Obj2 :- new A1;
Obj3 :- new A2;

for Obj4 :- Obj1,Obj2,Obj3 do
begin
   if Obj4 is A then OutText("Object is A") else
   if Obj4 in A then
   begin
      OutText("Object in A");
      if Obj4 is A1 then OutText(" and is A1")
                    else OutText(" and is A2")
   end else OutText("Object is not A and is not in A");
   OutImage
end
end**of**program
```

Example 11.5 The use of *is* and *in*

Exercise

11.5 Rewrite the text-processing program so that it recognizes the directive $A. This is followed by a text sequence which is to be printed after all the other blocks. In every other way it is treated as a Text__Block. Use *is* to test the blocks and print them in the correct order.

Some extra features for Boolean expressions

As we have often seen, comparisons are what make it possible to write most of our useful programs. You will probably have begun to realize that making the right test in the right place is vital to success in programming. To help with this, SIMULA provides facilities for making more than one comparison in a single *if* statement, *while* loop or whatever. These facilities allow us to write neater, more compact code. At the same time they make it even more important to check when we use them that the right tests are being applied.

A comparison is more formally called a 'simple Boolean expression', giving the value True or False. The keywords True and False are themselves simple Boolean expressions, with a constant value. Boolean variables and Boolean procedures, like LastItem in a text, are also simple Boolean expressions.

Thus a Boolean expression is a sequence of SIMULA which can be evaluated to True or False.

Not

The simplest extension to a simple Boolean expression is the Boolean operator *not*. The keyword *not* reverses the value of the Boolean expression which follows immediately after it. The Boolean expression

    3 = 2

has the value False, and so the expression

    not 3 = 2

has the value True.

And

When two Boolean expressions are linked by the operator *and*, the value of the combined Boolean expression is False unless both the linked expressions have the value True.

The expression

    3 = 2 and 4 = 4

has the value False, since one of its sub-expressions has the value False. Example 11.6 shows the other possibilities.

```
a) 4=4 and 7=7;   ! Value is True
b) 2=2 and 6=8;   ! Value is False
c) 10=1 and 2<0;  ! Value is False
```

Example 11.6 The use of *and*

Or

Two Boolean expressions linked by the operator *or* form a combined

Boolean expression which has the value True if either of the sub-expressions has the value True. Only where both have the value False does the combined expression have the value False.

It is easy to confuse the operator *and* with the operator *or* in ordinary speech, since we often use these words very loosely. You should take great care to get your meanings precise in SIMULA.

Example 11.7 shows the possible combinations.

```
a) 3=2 or 4=4;    ! Value is True
b) 4=4 or 7=7;    ! Value is True
c) 2=2 or 6=8;    ! Value is True
d) 10=1 or 2<0;   ! Value is False
```

Example 11.7 The use of *or*

Eqv

Two Boolean expressions linked by the operator *eqv* form a combined Boolean expression which has the value True if both sub-expressions have the same value, and has the value False if the sub-expressions have different values. *Eqv* is an abbreviation for 'equivalent to'.

Example 11.8 shows the possible combinations.

```
a) 3=2 eqv 4=4;   ! Value is False
b) 4=4 eqv 7=7;   ! Value is True
c) 2=2 eqv 6=8;   ! Value is False
d) 10=1 eqv 2<0;  ! Value is True
```

Example 11.8 The use of *eqv*

Imp

Imp is also used to link two Boolean expressions to form a combined expression. Its meaning is only of interest to formal mathematicians, but I include it for completeness. The possible combinations using it are given in example 11.9. (*Imp* is an abbreviation for 'implies'.)

```
a) 3=2 imp 4=4;   ! Value is True
b) 4=4 imp 7=7;   ! Value is True
c) 2=2 imp 6=8;   ! Value is False
d) 10=2 imp 2<0;  ! Value is True
```

Example 11.9 The use of *imp*

Summarizing Boolean operators

Table 11.1 shows a summary of the effects of the various Boolean operators. B1 represents the first Boolean sub-expression, B2 the second. This sort of table is often called a 'truth table'.

Table 11.1 Effects of Boolean operators

B1	= TRUE	TRUE	FALSE	FALSE
B2	= TRUE	FALSE	TRUE	FALSE
B1 AND B2	= TRUE	FALSE	FALSE	FALSE
B1 AND THEN B2	= TRUE	FALSE	FALSE	FALSE
B1 OR B2	= TRUE	TRUE	TRUE	FALSE
B1 OR ELSE B2	= TRUE	TRUE	TRUE	FALSE
B1 EQV B2	= TRUE	FALSE	TRUE	FALSE
B1 IMP B2	= TRUE	FALSE	TRUE	TRUE
NOT B1	= FALSE	FALSE	TRUE	TRUE
NOT B2	= FALSE	TRUE	FALSE	TRUE

Combining Boolean operators

Boolean operators can be combined to form more complicated expressions. The rules for evaluating Boolean expressions are then as follows. All working out is done from left to right.

1 All the comparisons are performed and the values True or False put in their places.

2 All *not* operations are carried out.

3 All *and* operations are carried out.

4 All *or* operations are carried out.

5 All *imp* operations are carried out.

6 All *eqv* operations are carried out.

Example 11.10 shows this sequence for an unusually complicated sequence.

Bracketing

Parentheses may be placed around any sub-expression. This has the effect of forcing the value of that sub-expression to be fully evaluated

3=2 or 7=7 and 9<10 eqv 7>4 imp not 23=23

1) False or True and True eqv True imp not True
2) False or True and True eqv True imp False
3) False or True eqv True imp False
4) True eqv True imp False
5) True eqv False
6) False

Example 11.10 Evaluation of complex Boolean expressions

before the rest of the main expression and so can override the order given above. This is equivalent to the use of parentheses in arithmetic expressions.

Example 11.11 shows the effects of bracketing on parts of example 11.10. Note that the innermost brackets' contents are evaluated first and so on.

3=2 or (7=7 and (9<10 eqv 7>4)) imp not 23=23

1) False or (True and (True eqv True)) imp not 23=23
2) False or (True and (True)) imp not True
3) False or (True) imp not True
4) False or True imp False
5) True imp False
6) False

Example 11.11 Evaluation of complex Boolean expressions with bracketing

Hints on using Boolean operators

The use of *and* and *or* in particular can make programs shorter and easier to read. The sequence

    if I=J then
    begin
        if K>L then

can nearly always be replaced by

    if (I=J) and (K>L) then

which seems a lot clearer, to me at least. (The reason for saying 'nearly always' will be explained below.)

The use of parentheses, even when, as above, they are not strictly necessary, can also make it easier to see which sub-expressions are linked by which operators. It is not always easy to remember which of *and* and *or* will be evaluated first, but it is easy to remember that bracketed expressions are evaluated before others. The expressions

I=J and K<L or I<L and K=J

and

(I=J and K<L) or (I<L and K=J)

have exactly the same value, but the second is much clearer.

Finally, by way of warning, do not try to be 'clever' in your use of Boolean expressions. Keep them as straightforward and clear as possible. Sometimes it may be better to use two nested *if* statements rather than a convoluted Boolean expression, keeping the program's meaning clear at the cost of making it slightly longer.

Side-effects and how to avoid them

I hope I am not over emphasizing Boolean expressions. They are often the key to a successful program. They are certainly the cause of many errors in programs which may be very difficult to locate if we do not take great care to use them sensibly. Most of us will find *and*, *or* and *not* very useful and it is worth looking at one problem with the first two which is rare, but very hard to find when it does occur.

In addition to *or* and *and*, SIMULA has operators *or else* and *and then*. These produce the same value as their simpler counterparts, as Table 11.1 shows. They are included to allow programs to be written which run faster, at the expense of introducing the possibility of unpredictable side-effects from procedure calls. In most cases *and then* is interchangeable with *and*, while *or else* is interchangeable with *or*.

The difference is that when two sub-expressions are linked by *and* or by *or*, both are evaluated, regardless of the value of the first. Yet, with *and*, when the value of the first sub-expression is False, we know without having to evaluate the second that the value of the two added together must be False. Similarly with *or*, if the first sub-expression gives True, the overall value will always be True. The evaluation of the second sub-expression is unnecessary in these cases.

The use of *and then* prevents the evaluation of the second sub-expression if the first is False. The use of *or else* prevents it if the first is True. This may make the program run faster. It also prevents any procedures which form part of the second sub-expression being called.

It is the second effect which can cause problems. If the calling of a type procedure in the second sub-expression affects values which are used elsewhere in the program, the effect of skipping its evaluation could be disastrous. If you must write such programs, you must use the simpler forms, even though they will result in slower running.

Example 11.12 shows a program with side-effects. Running it and supplying first a sequence not containing 99 and then one which does contain it demonstrates the problem. It may seem 'smart' to write like this. It is certainly an interesting technique. It is even more certainly a very unsafe one.

```
begin
   integer I,J,K;

   Boolean procedure SideSwipe;
   begin
      J := J + 1;   ! J is updated here;
      SideSwipe := I>0
   end..of..SideSwipe;

   K := InInt;
   while J<K do
   begin
      I := InInt;
      comment The first test could interfere with the updating of J;
      if I NE 99 and then SideSwipe then OutText("Greater")
                           else OutText("Less")
   end;

   OutImage
end**of**program
```

Example 11.12 Unsafe side-effects in a complex Boolean expression

Exercise

11.6   What are the values of the following expressions?

   (a) 4=3 or 0>2 and 3=3
   (b) (4=3 or 0>2) and 3=3
   (c) 4=3 or (0>2 and 3=3)

Summary

- This chapter has dealt with sub-classes, qualification and Boolean operators.
- We have seen how to use classes as prefixes to form families of sub-classes, which extend their parent's attributes.
- We have learned the rules governing this concatenation, including the order of execution of actions.
- We have seen how the qualification of a class object and its prefix chain control both the objects which may be pointed to by references of particular class types and the attributes which may be accessed remotely using such references.
- The use of *inner* to allow epilogues of actions in prefixing classes has been demonstrated.
- The use of Boolean operators to extend the power of Boolean expressions has been shown, along with some dangers associated with their use.

Chapter 12

Character handling

Working with texts

Most of our examples have been concerned with some sort of manipulation of characters in the form of texts. Occasionally we have used GetChar and PutChar to manipulate the individual characters in them. At other times we have used GetInt, PutFix, etc. to manipulate groups of characters within texts. Any text processing or editing programs are heavily dependent on the manipulation of individual characters as well as their combinations. This chapter shows those features of SIMULA designed to help in this.

Most of these features are system procedures. We start with two simple ones, shown in example 12.1. This shows a program which finds all the numbers in a text containing a mixture of digits and letters. It is assumed that no other characters will be present.

```
begin
    text Input, LettersOut, NumbersOut;
    character Next;
    InImage;
    Input:-SysIn.Image;
    LettersOut :- Blanks(80);
    NumbersOut :- Blanks(80);
    while Input.More do
    begin
        Next:=Input.GetChar;
        if Letter(Next) then LettersOut.PutChar(Next) else
            if Digit(Next) then NumbersOut.PutChar(Next)
    end;
    OutText(Input);
    OutImage;
    OutText(LettersOut);
    OutImage;
    OutText(NumbersOut);
    OutImage

end
```

Example 12.1 Sorting letters and numbers

Procedures Letter and Digit

SIMULA provides two Boolean procedures, Letter and Digit, both taking a single, character parameter. If this parameter is one of a−z or A−Z the procedure Letter will return the value True, otherwise it will return the value False. If its parameter is one of 0−9, Digit will return True, otherwise False. See Example 12.1.

Representing characters

Computers store characters in their memory as numbers. Each character is represented by a different integer value.

Unfortunately there is no single system for this. The numbers representing each character can vary from machine to machine. In practice most machines use either the EBCDIC system or the International Standards Organization (ISO) system. The ISO system is often called by its earlier name, ASCII. The two systems are shown in Tables 12.1 and 12.2. These tables are known as the collating sequences for the two systems.

Using the internal values

It is sometimes useful to be able to find the internal number representing a *character* or to be able to convert a number into the corresponding *character*. SIMULA provides procedures for both of these.

Example 12.2 shows a program which converts characters in a *text* which uses ISO characters into an equivalent *text* containing EBCDIC characters. This is often necessary when reading files transferred from another computer.

Rank

System integer procedure Rank takes a single character-value parameter and returns the number representing the character.

In example 12.2, the characters inside ISOText are in the ISO form and so the call

Rank(ISOText.GetChar)

Table 12.1 ISO character set — printing characters

0	nul	1	soh	2	stx	3	etx	4	eot	5	enq
6	ack	7	bel	8	bs	9	ht	10	lf	11	vt
12	ff	13	cr	14	so	15	si	16	dle	17	dc1
18	dc2	19	dc3	20	dc4	21	nak	22	syn	23	etb
24	can	25	em	26	sub	27	esc	28	fs	29	gs
30	rs	31	us	32	space	33	!	34	"	35	£
36	$	37	%	38	&	39	'	40	(| 41 |)
42	*	43	+	44	,	45	–	46	.	47	/
48	0	49	1	50	2	51	3	52	4	53	5
54	6	55	7	56	8	57	9	58	:	59	;
60	<	61	=	62	>	63	?	64	@	65	A
66	B	67	C	68	D	69	E	70	F	71	G
72	H	73	I	74	J	75	K	76	L	77	M
78	N	79	O	80	P	81	Q	82	R	83	S
84	T	85	U	86	V	87	W	88	X	89	Y
90	Z	91	[	92	\	93	]	94	^	95	_
96	`	97	a	98	b	99	c	100	d	101	e
102	f	103	g	104	h	105	i	106	j	107	k
108	l	109	m	110	n	111	o	112	p	113	q
114	r	115	s	116	t	117	u	118	v	119	w
120	x	121	y	122	z	123	{	124	|	125	}
126	~	127	del	128	ctl	129	ctl	130	ctl	131	ctl
132	ctl	133	ctl	134	ctl	135	ctl	136	ctl	137	ctl
138	ctl	139	ctl	140	ctl	141	ctl	142	ctl	143	ctl
144	ctl	145	ctl	146	ctl	147	ctl	148	ctl	149	ctl
150	ctl	151	ctl	152	ctl	153	ctl	154	ctl	155	ctl
156	ctl	157	ctl	158	ctl	159	ctl	160	ctl	161	ctl
162	ctl	163	ctl	164	ctl	165	ctl	166	ctl	167	ctl
168	ctl	169	ctl	170	ctl	171	ctl	172	ctl	173	ctl
174	ctl	175	ctl	176	ctl	177	ctl	178	ctl	179	ctl
180	ctl	181	ctl	182	ctl	183	ctl	184	ctl	185	ctl
186	ctl	187	ctl	188	ctl	189	ctl	190	ctl	191	ctl
192	ctl	193	ctl	194	ctl	195	ctl	196	ctl	197	ctl
198	ctl	199	ctl	200	ctl	201	ctl	202	ctl	203	ctl
204	ctl	205	ctl	206	ctl	207	ctl	208	ctl	209	ctl
210	ctl	211	ctl	212	ctl	213	ctl	214	ctl	215	ctl
216	ctl	217	ctl	218	ctl	219	ctl	220	ctl	221	ctl
222	ctl	223	ctl	224	ctl	225	ctl	226	ctl	227	ctl
228	ctl	229	ctl	230	ctl	231	ctl	232	ctl	233	ctl
234	ctl	235	ctl	236	ctl	237	ctl	238	ctl	239	ctl
240	ctl	241	ctl	242	ctl	243	ctl	244	ctl	245	ctl
246	ctl	247	ctl	248	ctl	249	ctl	250	ctl	251	ctl

NB Ranks less than 32 and greater than 126 are not visible printing characters. Where appropriate the standard control meaning is supplied. Ranks greater than 127 are normally used for graphics or alternative character fonts.

```
begin
   integer Count, ISONumber, EBCDICNumber;
   character ISO, EBCDIC;
   text ISOText, EBCDICText;
   integer array EBCDICChar (0:255);
   for EBCDICNumber := 0,
     1,   2,   3,  55,  45,  46,  47,  22,   5,  37,
    11,  12,  13,  14,  15,  16,  17,  18,  19,  60,
    61,  50,  38,  24,  25,  63,  39,  28,  29,  30,
    31,  64,  79, 127, 123,  91, 108,  80, 125,  77,
    93,  92,  78, 107,  96,  75,  97, 240, 241, 242,
   243, 244, 245, 246, 247, 248, 249, 122,  94,  76,
   126, 110, 111, 124, 193, 194, 195, 196, 197, 198,
   199, 200, 201, 209, 210, 211, 212, 213, 214, 215,
   216, 217, 226, 227, 228, 229, 230, 231, 232, 233,
    74, 224,  90,  95, 109, 121, 129, 130, 131, 132,
   133, 134, 135, 136, 137, 145, 146, 147, 148, 149,
   150, 151, 152, 153, 162, 163, 164, 165, 166, 167,
   168, 169, 192, 106, 208, 161,   7,  32,  33,  34,
    35,  36,  21,   6,  23,  40,  41,  42,  43,  44,
     9,  10,  27,  48,  49,  26,  51,  52,  53,  54,
     8,  56,  57,  58,  59,   4,  20,  62, 225,  65,
    66,  67,  68,  69,  70,  71,  72,  73,  81,  82,
    83,  84,  85,  86,  87,  88,  89,  98,  99, 100,
   101, 102, 103, 104, 105, 112, 113, 114, 115, 116,
   117, 118, 119, 120, 128, 138, 139, 140, 141, 142,
   143, 144, 154, 155, 156, 157, 158, 159, 160, 170,
   171, 172, 173, 174, 175, 176, 177, 178, 179, 180,
   181, 182, 183, 184, 185, 186, 187, 188, 189, 190,
   191, 202, 203, 204, 205, 206, 207, 218, 219, 220,
   221, 222, 223, 234, 235, 236, 237, 238, 239, 250,
   251, 252, 253, 254, 255 do
   begin
      EBCDICChar(Count) := EBCDICNumber;
      Count := Count + 1
   end;
   InImage;
   ISOText:-SysIn.Image;
   EBCDICText:-Blanks (Image.Length);
   while ISOText.More do
   begin
      ISO:=ISOText.GetChar;
      ISONumber:=Rank(ISO);
      EBCDICNumber:=EBCDICChar(ISONumber);
      EBCDIC:=Char(EBCDICNumber);
      EBCDICText.PutChar(EBCDIC)
   end
end
```

Example 12.2 Character-set conversion

Table 12.2 EBCDIC character set — printing characters

0	nul	1	soh	2	stx	3	etx	4		5	ht
6		7	del	8		9		10		11	vt
12	ff	13	cr	14	so	15	si	16	dle	17	dc1
18	dc2	19	dc2	20		21		22	bsp	23	
24	can	25	em	26		27		28	fs	29	gs
30	rs	31	vs	32		33		34		35	
36		37	lf	38	etb	39	esc	40		41	
42		43		44		45	enq	46	ack	47	bel
48		49		50	syn	51		52		53	
54		55	eot	56		57		58		59	
60	dc4	61	nak	62		63	sub	64	space	65	
66		67		68		69		70		71	
72		73		74		75	.	76	<	77	(
78	+	79	|	80	&	81		82		83	
84		85		86		87		88		89	
90	!	91	$	92	*	93	)	94	;	95	~
96	−	97	/	98		99		100		101	
102		103		104		105		106	|	107	,
108	%	109	_	110	>	111	?	112		113	
114		115		116		117		118		119	
120		121	‘	122	:	123	£	124	@	125	’
126	=	127	"	128		129	a	130	b	131	c
132	d	133	e	134	f	135	g	136	h	137	i
138		139		140		141		142		143	
144		145	j	146	k	147	l	148	m	149	n
150	o	151	p	152	q	153	r	154	⌢	155	
156		157		158		159		160		161	~
162	s	163	t	164	u	165	v	166	w	167	x
168	y	169	z	170		171		172		173	[
174		175		176		177		178		179	
180		181		182	⌢	183		184		185	
186		187		188		189	]	190		191	
192	{	193	A	194	B	195	C	196	D	197	E
198	F	199	G	200	H	201	I	202		203	
204		205		206		207		208	}	209	J
210	K	211	L	212	M	213	N	214	O	215	P
216	Q	217	R	218		219		220		221	
222		223		224	\	225		226	S	227	T
228	U	229	V	230	W	231	X	232	Y	233	Z
234		235		236		237		238		239	
240	0	241	1	242	2	243	3	244	4	245	5
246	6	247	7	248	8	249	9	250		251	
252		253		254		255					

NB EBCDIC character sets vary from machine to machine. This table is only one variant; example 12.2 uses an alternative mapping between EBCDIC and ISO to allow a complete conversion.

will return the internal number of the next ISO character in the text, following Table 12.1.

The integer array EBCDICChar has 127 characters, corresponding to the ordinary control and printing characters in the two character sets used. Each element of the array is set so that its value is the internal EBCDIC representation of the character whose ISO representation is the number of the index to that element.

As an example, the internal representation of a space character is 64 in EBCDIC and 32 in ISO. Thus element 32 of the array is set to 64.

To convert the ISO values returned by Rank above into EBCDIC, the value returned is used to index the array in a subscripted variable and the value of this will be the EBCDIC representation of the same character.

Using the same example, if Rank(ISOText.GetChar) returns 32, having found a space in the text, this is used to index EBCDICChar, i.e. EBCDICChar(32). The value of element 32 is 64, the EBCDIC representation of a space.

Thus the use of GetChar, Rank and indexing of the array EBCDICChar has found the value of the EBCDIC representation of an ISO character in our text. Now we need to convert this into a character.

Char

System character procedure Char takes a single integer-value parameter, whose value must be legal as the internal representation of a character on that system. (This range should be specified in the documentation for the SIMULA system you are using.) Char returns a character whose internal representation is the number passed as a parameter.

It is important to note that Rank and Char do not concern themselves with which character set is being used, only with moving a number, held in some form such as a binary number, from a location reserved for a character to one reserved for an integer or vice versa. Char objects only if the integer is too large to fit into the, usually, smaller space used for a character. Interpreting characters according to ISO, EBCDIC or whatever, is only done by some reading and writing procedures.

Thus, in the example, the EBCDIC representation of the character obtained from ISOText, is passed to Char, which returns a character with this as its internal representation. This can then be written as the EBCDIC translation into EBCDICText, using PutChar.

Avoiding character set problems

When writing character-handling programs to run on any computer, it is very inconvenient to have to allow for the possible character sets on each particular machine. This makes it nearly impossible, in fact, to write truly portable programs using the procedures Char and Rank. Fortunately SIMULA has a way of avoiding this.

On any but the oldest SIMULA systems, two more system procedures are supplied. They are called ISOChar and ISORank. They match Char and Rank exactly except that they work entirely in terms of the ISO character set.

For ISORank, this means that the value returned is converted from the internal representation of the character parameter in the machine's own character set, to the ISO internal representation.

For ISOChar, it means that when the integer parameter is converted into a character, it is first converted into the internal representation of the character that it would represent in the ISO set.

If we take our space character on a machine using EBCDIC as its internal character set, we would find the following results with ISOChar and ISORank.

If we call Rank (' '), we get 64 returned, which is the local, EDCDIC, internal representation of a space. A call of ISORank (' '), on the other hand, will return us 32, the ISO equivalent.

Conversely, to get Char to return a space, we need to call Char(64), but using ISOChar we must call ISOChar(32).

Using these procedures we can write totally portable character-handling programs. Example 12.3 shows how to write a portable program to convert all the lower-case characters in a text into upper case. This is sometimes called 'folding' the text into upper case.

The difference between ISORank('A') and ISORank('a') is the same as the difference between the internal representations of each upper-case character and its corresponding lower-case character, in the ISO character set. Thus the value assigned to Factor will enable us to convert any lower-case character's ISORank to that of its upper-case equivalent.

begin

```
   text Buffer, Update;
   integer Convert, Factor;
   character Next;
   Buffer:- Copy("This little piggy was Fred");
   Update:- Buffer;
   Factor := ISORank('A') - ISORank('a');
   while Buffer.More do
   begin
     Next:= Buffer.GetChar;
     Convert:= ISORank(Next);
     if Convert GE ISORank('a') and Convert LE ISORank('z') then
     begin
       Convert:= Convert + Factor;
       Next:= ISOChar(Convert)
     end;
     Update.PutChar(Next)
   end;
   OutText(Buffer);
   OutImage;
   OutText(Update);
   OutImage
```

end

Example 12.3 Lower to upper-case conversion using ISORank and
              ISOChar

The program checks each character to find if it is a lower-case letter. Lower-case letters in the ISO sequence are represented by consecutive numbers, starting with 'a' and ending with 'z'. This makes it easy to check whether the Rank of each character is within this range. (This would not work with EBCDIC. See Table 12.2.)

Note how useful *and* is in these checks. We can use a single *if* statement, instead of two nested ones. Checking that a number lies within a certain range is a very common use of *and*.

When the program finds a lower-case letter it adds Factor to its ISORank, putting the result in Convert.

The program uses the technique, seen earlier, of creating two references to the same text frame. By reading through one reference and writing through the other, at an equal rate and left to right, we update the text frame without the need to copy into another and back again.

Note that this program would not work for the EBCDIC character set, if Char and Rank replaced ISOChar and ISORank. This demonstrates the usefulness of the ISO procedures in writing portable programs rather neatly.

Exercises

12.1 Because of hardware problems, a file has been corrupted. It now contains a number of unprintable characters. Assuming that letters, digits, spaces, full stops, commas, colons and semi-colons are the only characters which should be present, write a program which will remove the others.

12.2 Write a program which converts all upper-case letters to lower and all lower to upper in a file.

12.3 Go back to exercise 7.8. Using this, add the capability to your editor to change the case of the next letter from its current position.

Making quick decisions

When writing our text-formatting program in Chapter 11, we were forced to use more and more deeply-nested *if* statements to check which directive was being read. This becomes rather clumsy and difficult to read when more than a few choices are possible. It is also slow to run when lots of checks must be made before a course of action is selected.

To help with this sort of situation, SIMULA contains a feature called a *switch*. To see how this works, consider example 12.4. This is example 11.1 rewritten with a *switch*.

The letters in the directives are in alphabetic sequence starting with 'B'. Thus they follow the ISO collating sequence. Thus, by subtracting ISORank ('A') from the ISORank of each directive's letter, we can obtain a value between one and three, inclusive. Each integer value so obtained represents one of the three directives.

Switch declarations

The switch declaration is unusual, in that it contains the value-assignment

```
begin
  class Page;
  begin

    class Print_Block(Width,Length);integer Width, Length;
    begin
      ref(Print_Block)Next;
      text array Contents(1:Length);
      integer Count;
      for Count:=1 step 1 until Length
      do Contents(Count):-Blanks(Width)
    end--of--Print_Block;

    Print_Block class Title_Block(Title);text Title;
    begin
      Contents(Length//2):=Title
    end--of--Title_Block;

    Print_Block class Text_Block;
    begin
      for Count:=1 step 1 until Length do
      begin
        InImage;
        Contents(Count):=InText(Width)
      end
    end--of--Text_Block;

    Print_Block class Diagram(Title); text Title;
    begin
      Contents(1):=Title
    end--of--Diagram;

    ref(Print_Block) Head, Tail, New_Block;
    text Directive;
    integer Len;

    procedure Add(NewBlock); ref(Print_Block) NewBlock;
    begin
      if Head==None then Head :- NewBlock;
      if Tail=/=None then Tail.Next :- NewBlock;
       Tail :- NewBlock
    end++of++Add;

    switch Action := TitleB, TextB, DiagB;
    Character ActionCode;
```

```
      Directive :- InText(2);
      while Directive ne "$E" do
      begin
         Directive.SetPos(2);
         ActionCode := Directive.GetChar;
         go to Action(ISORank(ActionCode) - ISORank('A'));
TitleB :    ! Directive = $B - New banner;
         Len := InInt;
         InImage;
         Add(New Title_Block(80,Len,InText(80)));
         go to Repeat;
TextB :     ! Directive = $C - New content;
         Add(new Text_Block (80,Inint));
         go to Repeat;
DiagB :     ! Directive = $D - New diagram;
         Len := InInt;
         InImage;
         Add(new Diagram(80,Len,InText(80)));
         go to Repeat;
Repeat:
         Directive :- InText(2)
      end.of.while.loop
   end--of--Page;
   new Page


end.of.program
```

Example 12.4 The use of a switch

operator, :=, as well as identifiers. The syntax of such a declaration is the keyword *switch*, followed by an identifier giving the name of the switch, followed by the value-assignment operator, followed by a list of so-called 'designational expressions'.

Designational expressions can take a number of forms. In the example they all have the commonest form, a simple identifier.

The identifiers used in such a list specify places in the program to which a 'jump' may be made. If you look at the example, three identifiers are listed. (The minimum is one and the maximum will be different on different SIMULA systems.) Further on in the program, each of these identifiers occurs again, followed by a colon. This second occurrence is called a label.

Label declarations

An identifier followed by a colon is a declaration of a label for the following statement. Such a declaration is different from those of any other type, since it can occur in the middle of a sequence of statements, rather than before any statements. The example contains four label declarations. The first three, TitleB, TextB and DiagB are used to label the next statement. The fourth, Repeat, appears to label the keyword, *end*. *end* is not a statement and so to preserve the rule that label declarations always precede statements, there is said to be an imaginary statement between the colon and *end*.

go to statements with switches

The switch, Action, is used in a statement starting with the keywords *go to*. In fact these can be written as a single keyword *goto*, if you prefer. This is the only combination of keywords where this is allowed.

A *go to* statement is the keyword(s) *goto* followed by a designational expression. In the example the switch identifier, Action, followed by an integer value in parentheses, is used. This is the other form of designational expression that we shall use. This integer value is an index to the list of designational expressions in the switch declaration above. Thus it can be used to identify a label declaration and through this the next statement to be executed.

In the example, we have seen that the value generated when we evaluate

ISORank(ActionCode) — ISORank('A')

should be an integer in the range $1-3$. The designational expressions in a switch declaration are assumed to be numbered consecutively starting with 1. Thus, if he directive $C is found, the index to Action in the *go to* statement will be 2, and so the second label in the declaration of Action, TextB, will mark the next instruction to be executed.

This leads us to the meaning of a *go to* statement. It causes the program to move to the statement whose label is identified by the designational expression in the *go to* statement. No other statements are executed before this jump. After the jump the program continues with the statement following the label. Such a jump may be forwards, as in all the cases shown, or backwards.

To see this, consider again the $C directive. The first *go to* is followed by

Action(ISORank(ActionCode) — ISORank('A'))

which, as we have seen, will equal 2. This means that the label to use is identified by the second item in the list of designational expressions in the declaration of Action. This is the identifier TextB, which is the name of a label. The label TextB is further on in the program. The program therefore misses the intervening statements and continues from the statement

New Text__Block (80,InInt)

If the directive $D is encountered, the program jumps to the third label in the switch declaration, DiagB. If $B is encountered it jumps to the first. Check the logic of this for yourself.

go to statements with labels

A *go to* statement makes the program jump to a label specified by a designational expression. A subscripted switch variable is one form of designational expression, but we have seen a simpler one. This is a simple label identifier.

In the example, three statements have the form of *go to* followed by an identifier. As it happens, the identifier is the same in each case. The effect is again to jump to the statement labelled with the identifier found from the designational expression. In the case of a simple identifier this is very straightforward.

These three statements all cause the program to jump to the statement labelled by Repeat. This takes the program to the InImage at the end of the compound statement of the *while* loop. In other words, once the actions for that directive are complete, the program jumps to start processing the next line, which is assumed to contain the next directive.

Exercises

12.4 By extending the list for the switch declaration, moving the position of Repeat and adding a new label declaration, rewrite example 12.4 without the *while* loop.

12.5 What would happen in example 12.4 if the *go to* Repeat statements were missing? Try removing them to check. Note the effect carefully.

Notes and warnings

Some people write very intricate programs, which use lots of *go to* statements. In certain, rather limited, programming languages this is necessary. In SIMULA it is almost never needed.

　　The use of too many *go to* statements makes programs very hard to read and understand. They should only be used when absolutely necessary or in the sort of situation shown in example 12.4, where a switch can simplify a program and make it easier to extend.

　　It is important in a program using a switch to provide label declarations to match all the designational expressions in the switch declaration. It is not illegal to declare a switch which leads to non-existent labels. It is a runtime error to try to jump to one. In fact it is often best to check before the *go to* statement that the value of the expression used in the subscripted switch variable is not too large for the list in the declaration and to print an error message or warning if necessary.

A very special jump

A rather new feature in SIMULA, which may not exist in some older systems, is the system procedure Terminate__Program. This causes a jump to the very end of the program, regardless of the current position. This can be useful in providing warnings of disastrous errors and then stopping the program.

　　Terminate__Program is the only way for a program using a pre-fixing, separately-compiled class containing an *inner* statement (see Chapter 16) to stop itself without executing the instructions following that *inner*. It is the only way to stop a program dead from anywhere within it and guarantee that no further actions will be carried out.

Switches and labels as parameters

It is possible to pass switches and labels as parameters to procedures. The default mode is reference and name is also legal.

Using such a parameter, or a switch or label from a block enclosing the one the program is currently in, it is possible to jump out of a block. The normal rules for ending the appropriate type of block will apply.

Summary

- We have looked at how characters are represented by numbers and seen the procedures which allow us to use this.
- We have seen the use of switches and labels, in *go to* statements and as parameters.
- We have learned the benefits and, most importantly, the dangers of *go to* statements.
- We have seen the system procedure Terminate_Program.

Chapter 13

Remote accessing of classes

Recap

So far we have treated inspection and dot-notation accessing as the same thing. In most simple cases they are. In other situations they may be used to do rather different things. In particular, the *inspect* statement can be used for much more than just a convenient shorthand.

Essentially we have seen that the dot-notation form of remote accessing allows us to use the attributes of a class object from outside it. It is also used to access the attributes of text objects, which are not class objects.

The *inspect* statement has allowed us to assume that any identifiers used in the statement following the keyword *do* are possibly attributes of the class object being inspected. Thus the programs in example 13.1 can be treated as identical. A text object may not be inspected in this way.

Example 13.1b shows the situation where an identifier inside the class is the same as an identifier in the main program. When Int is used inside the class, it refers to the declaration inside the class. When Int is used outside the class, it normally refers to the declaration in the main program block. When it is used inside an *inspect* statement it is always taken to refer to the declaration in the class inspected.

The rule is that the statement following the *do* in an *inspect* statement is treated as if it were inside the body of the class being inspected.

This can cause confusion when there is a name conflict, like the one in example 13.1b. It is often clearer to use dot notation in such cases. A better solution, of course, is to avoid name conflicts where possible.

Limitations of dot notation

The most important limitation on dot notation occurs with an object qualified by a class which itself has classes declared within its body or within the body of a prefixing class. This is shown in example 13.2a.

Class Outside contains a class declaration for Inside and other

(a) Dot notation

```
begin
   integer Int;

   class Example(Ch); character Ch;
   begin
      integer Int;
      text Txt;
      procedure Proc; OutText("Called");
   end--of--Example;

   ref(Example) Ex1;
   Ex1 :- new Example('?');
   OutChar(Ex1.Ch);
   Ex1.Proc;
   for Int := Ex1.Int step 2 until 6 do Ex1.Txt := "Txt"
end
```

(b) *inspect* statement

```
begin
   integer Int;

   class Example(Ch); character Ch;
   begin
      integer Int;
      text Txt;
      procedure Proc; OutText("Called");
   end--of--Example;

   ref(Example) Ex1;
   Ex1 :- new Example('?');
   inspect Ex1 do
   begin
      OutChar(Ch);
      Proc;
      comment Note that the first Int in the next statement now refers to
              the attribute of Ex1, not the declaration in the main program;
      for Int := Int step 2 until 6 do Txt := "Txt"
   end
end
```

Example 13.1 Remote accessing

(a) An illegal use of dot notation

```
begin

    class Outside;
    begin

        class Inside;
        begin
           text InsideText;
        end..of..Inside;

        integer Int1;
        text Text1;

    end--of--Outside;

    Outside class Outside2;
    begin
        integer Int2;
        text Text2;
    end;

    ref(Outside) Outsider;
    ref(Outside2) Outsider2;

    Outsider :- new Outside;
    Outsider2 :- new Outside2;
    Outsider.Text1 :- Copy("Illegal");
    Outsider2.Int2 := 4

end++of++program
```

(b) A legal version of the same program using *inspect*

```
begin

    class Outside;
    begin

        class Inside;
        begin
           text InsideText;
        end..of..Inside;

        integer Int1;
        text Text1;
```

```
end--of--Outside;

Outside class Outside2;

begin
    integer Int2;
    text Text2;
end;

ref(Outside) Outsider;
ref(Outside2) Outsider2;

Outsider :- new Outside;
Outsider2 :- new Outside2;
inspect Outsider do Text1 :- Copy("Legal");
inspect Outsider2 do Int2 := 4

end++of++program
```

Example 13.2 Limitations of dot notation

attributes. The main program contains a variable Outsider which references an object of class Outside. Using dot notation we cannot
access any of the attributes of Outsider from the main program block.

Similarly, the class Outside2 is a sub-class of Outside. The *ref*(Outside2)
object, Outsider2 has attributes in addition to those of Outside, but
none of these may be accessed by dot notation because the prefix
Outside has a local class declaration. (NB the restriction refers to class
declarations, not reference-variable declarations.)

In order to access these attributes from the main program block we
must use an *inspect* statement as shown in example 13.2b.

Extending *inspect*

The simple *inspect* statement that we have used so far is useful so long
as we know the type or qualification of the object being inspected. This
may not always be sufficient.

We saw in Chapter 11 that it is possible to reference all objects
which are sub-classes of one parent class using a variable declared as a
ref to the parent. This enabled us to form a linked list of objects of

different sub-classes, for instance. At the same time we saw the limitation of this, in that the sub-class attributes could not be accessed
through these variables, only the attributes of the parents. Neither dot
notation nor simple *inspect* statements can get around this problem.

Another problem with remote accessing is that it is clearly nonsense to use a reference variable before it has been pointed at an
object (assigned a reference). Such an attempt is in fact illegal and will
cause a runtime error to be signalled.

To get around these problems we can use extensions of the *inspect*
statement.

inspect plus *otherwise*

The simplest extension allows us to detect the use of references which
currently do not point to a class object. Such references are said to
point to an imaginary object, with no attributes, called None. This is
the only object that any reference, regardless of its type, can point at.

Consider example 13.3. The first program would simply ignore
some elements of the array References, since not all the reference
variables in this array have been pointed at objects of class Example.
The second program, on the other hand, will detect such variables and
report which they are. It does this by adding an *otherwise* clause to its
inspect statement.

The syntax of our extended *inspect* statement is now the keyword
inspect, followed by a reference to a class object, followed by the
keyword *do*, followed by a statement, optionally followed by an *otherwise* clause. The syntax of an *otherwise* clause is the keyword *otherwise*
followed by a statement.

The reason for choosing *inspect* as the keyword for this type of
statement is perhaps a little clearer now. The meaning of an *inspect*
statement makes it a suitable choice. The class object is first inspected
to see if it is None. If not, it is used to provide the class which is
assumed to be remotely accessed in the statement following the keyword *do*, which is then executed. If it is None, the statement following
the keyword *otherwise* is executed, where present. If there is no *otherwise* clause, the use of None will cause the statement following *do* to
be skipped.

Notice that we have used the phrase, 'reference to a class object',
for what comes between *inspect* and *do*. This is usually an identifier of

(a) A program which fails to check for None

```
begin

   class Example;
   begin
     text Message;
     Message :- Copy("Legal")
   end..of..Example;

   ref(Example) array References(0:10);
   integer Counter;

   comment Only every other element assigned to;
   for Counter := 0 step 2 until 10 do References(Counter) :- new Example;

   comment Every element inspected;
   for Counter := 0 step 1 until 10 do
      inspect References(Counter) do
      begin
        OutText(Message);
        OutImage
      end--of--inspecting--element

end++of++program
```

(b) The same program using *otherwise* to check for None

```
begin

   class Example;
   begin
     text Message;
     Message :- Copy("Legal")
   end..of..Example;

   ref(Example) array References(0:10);
   integer Counter;

   for Counter := 0 step 2 until 10 do References(Counter) :- new Example;

   comment Still inspect every element, but use otherwise to report nones;
   for Counter := 0 step 1 until 10 do
      inspect References(Counter) do
      begin
        OutText(Message);
        OutImage
```

```
end--of--the--connection--block
otherwise
begin
   OutText("Illegal");
   OutImage
end--of--the--othrwise--clause

end++of++program
```

(c) The same program without *inspect*

```
begin

   class Example;
   begin
     text Message;
     Message :- Copy("Legal")
   end..of..Example;

   ref(Example) array References(0:10);
   integer Counter;

   for Counter := 0 step 2 until 10 do References(Counter) :- new Example;

   comment Use direct checking and dot notation;
   for Counter := 0 step 1 until 10 do
   begin
     if References(Counter)=/=None then
     begin
       OutText(References(Counter).Message);
       OutImage
     end--of--legal--reference--case
     else
     begin
       OutText("Illegal");
       OutImage
     end--of--the--None--case
   end**of**for**loop

end++of++program
```

Example 13.3 Detecting None with *otherwise*

ref to class type, possibly subscripted, but could be any expression yielding a *ref* to class result. An example of an alternative could be a type procedure, whose type is ref to a class and which returns a reference to a class object, like SysIn and SysOut. Chapter 17 will make a lot of use of such type procedures.

The statement following *do* acts as if it were inside the class object being inspected. All identifiers are first matched against declarations within the class and its prefixing classes. In technical terms, the qualification of this statement is the same as the class inspected.

This extension to the *inspect* statement is quite useful, but it does not allow us to do anything that was not already possible. Example 13.3c shows the same program written without the *otherwise*, but still checking for None. To see the real power of the *inspect* concept, we must extend the definition still further.

The use of *inspect* plus *when*

The *inspect* statement used so far allows us to treat None and one particular type of class object differently. By adding a feature called the *when* clause, we can treat a class object according to its actual type, out of a range of possible alternatives.

Example 13.4 shows the use of an *inspect* statement with *when* clauses to process a linked list. All the objects on the list belong to classes sharing a common prefix. They are linked by variables declared as ref to this common prefix.

```
begin

  class A;
  begin
    ref(A) Link;
    procedure Print; OutText("Class A");
  end..of..A;

  A class B;
  begin
    procedure Print; OutText("Class B");
  end..of..B;

  A class C;
  begin
    procedure Print; OutText("Class C");
  end..of..C;
```

```
B class D;
begin
  procedure Print; OutText("Class D");
end;

C class E;
begin
  procedure Print; OutText("Class E");
end..of..E;

ref(A) Head, NextA;

for NextA :- new B, new C, new D, new E do
begin
  NextA.Link :- Head;
  Head :- NextA
end--of--building--mixed--list;

while NextA=/=None do
begin
  NextA.Print; ! Always prints "Class A";
  inspect NextA
    when E do Print
    when D do Print
    when C do Print
    when B do Print
    when A do Print
    otherwise OutText("Not a predicted subclass of A");
  OutImage;
  NextA :- NextA.Link
end--of--while--loop

end++of++program
```

Example 13.4 Mixed list processing using *when*

When we come to process each object, we wish to treat it differently according to its innermost type. In fact we need not select the innermost, but we are restricted to the level of qualification that we choose, so that attributes at inner levels would be invisible within the *when* clause.

This extension's syntax replaces the single keyword *do* with one or more *when* clauses. The *otherwise* clause remains optional, but its meaning changes slightly.

Each *when* clause consists of the keyword *when*, followed by the name of a class, followed by the keyword *do*, followed by a statement. Each occurrence of the keyword *when* marks the beginning of a new *when* clause.

The *when* clause contains an identifier matching a class declared in the program and visible to the *inspect* statement. The execution of an extended *inspect* statement tries to match the qualification of the inspected object or one of its prefixing classes to the class identifiers in each *when* clause in turn. Once a match is found, the statement following the *do* in that *when* clause is executed.

The statement following the *do* in a *when* clause is treated as if it were declared inside the class whose identifier is used in that clause. Thus, in example 13.4, when the objects on the list are inspected this determines which prefix level the declaration of procedure Print is taken from. Although the objects from the list can only be accessed as *ref*(A) objects, within each *when* clause the attributes of the appropriate sub-classes can be used.

Note the order of the *when* clauses. Inner classes must be tested for before outer, if we wish them to be distinguished. This is an important consequence of the rules given above.

If no match is found, the statement is skipped unless it contains an *otherwise* clause, in which case that is executed.

Within the extended *inspect* statement the *otherwise* clause, where present, is executed if the referenced object is None, as before, and also if its qualification fails to match any of the *when* clauses. In programs which are still being developed this can be used to handle currently missing cases, by printing out a suitable warning. It can also catch those cases which you have forgotten to deal with!

A practical example — simple sorting and merging

Example 13.5 shows the use of a *when* clause to help in processing records which are read in unsorted. The records are of four types and are marked by the contents of their first line. The first character of this line is 'M' for a male and 'F' for a female. The second character is 'A' for an accountant and 'D' for a dancer. Input is terminated by a line containing 'end' as its start.

The program first reads each record into an object of one of four classes designed to hold their particular data. All four of these classes are prefixed by class Linker, which contains pointers to allow linked lists to be built up. At first a single list of all the objects is constructed using the first pointer variable in Linker.

This list is then processed, with the aid of a *when* clause, and the objects placed on one from each of two pairs of lists, using the other two pointers in Linker. Finally these lists are written out separately.

The two complementary actions of sorting and merging lists are fundamental to many uses of computers. The addition of facilities to insert new items in a list and to modify existing items gives a powerful basic set of tools for manipulating data. We are now in a position to build such tools and extend them as the need arises.

Exercise

13.1 A theatrical agent has a file of records of different kinds of artists. He also has a file of records of requests for artists to be sent for audition. Assume that there are artists who are actors, musicians, singers and comedians and that requests may be for any of these. Further, assume that requests may specify the sex of the required artist and the age, with the age given as child, youth, mature or elderly. Write a program, based on the techniques used in example 13.5, to match requests and artists, and print lists of all suitable artists for each request and all suitable requests for each artist.

```
begin

    class Linker;
    begin
      ref(Linker) Next, Sex, Employment;
      text ID;
    end--of--Linker;

    Linker class Male_Dancer;
    begin

      ! Should contain full details;

    end--of--Male--Dancer;

    Linker class Female_Dancer;
    begin
```

```
   ! Should contain full details;

end--of--Female--Dancer;

Linker class Male_Accountant;
begin

   ! Should contain full details;

end--of--Male--Accountant;

Linker class Female_Accountant;
begin

   ! Should contain full details;

end--of--Female--Accountant;

procedure Onto_List(Entry,Gender,Occupation);
                name Gender,Occupation;
                ref(Linker) Entry,Gender,Occupation;
begin
   Entry.Sex :- Gender;
   Gender :- Entry;
   Entry.Employment :- Occupation;
   Occupation :- Entry
end--of--Onto--List;

procedure Write_List(Heading, ListHead); text Heading;
                                ref(Linker) ListHead;
begin
   Boolean SexList;
   SexList := (ListHead==Males or ListHead==Females);
   OutImage;
   OutText(Heading);
   OutImage;
   OutImage;
   while ListHead=/=None do
   begin
      OutText(ListHead.ID);
      OutImage;
      if SexList then ListHead :- ListHead.Sex
               else ListHead :- ListHead.Employment
   end
end--of--Write--List;
```

```
text Line;
ref(Linker) NextEntry,List,Males,Females,Dancers,Accountants;

comment First read the input onto a single list;

InImage;
Line :- Blanks(80);
while SysIn.Image.Strip ne ".end" do
begin
  Line.SetPos(1);
  Line := SysIn.Image;
  if Line.GetChar='F' then
  begin
    if Line.GetChar='D' then NextEntry :- new Female_Dancer
                   else NextEntry :- new Female_Accountant
  end else begin
    if Line.GetChar='A' then NextEntry :- new Male_Accountant
                   else NextEntry :- new Male_Dancer
  end;
  InImage;
  NextEntry.ID :- Copy(SysIn.Image);
  InImage;
  NextEntry.Next :- List;
  List :- NextEntry
end;

comment Now process the main list, forming threaded lists;

NextEntry :- List;
while NextEntry=/=None do
begin
  inspect NextEntry

    when Male_Dancer do Onto_List(NextEntry,Males,Dancers)

    when Female_Dancer do Onto_List(NextEntry,Females,Dancers)

    when Male_Accountant
    do Onto_List(NextEntry,Males,Accountants)

    when Female_Accountant
    do Onto_List(NextEntry,Females,Accountants);

  NextEntry :- NextEntry.Next
end;

comment Now write out by lists;
```

```
if Females=/=None then Write_List("Females",Females);
if Males=/=None then Write_List("Males",Males);
if Dancers=/=None then Write_List("Dancers",Dancers);
if Accountants=/=None then Write_List("Accountants",Accountants)
```

end++of++program

Example 13.5 Merging and sorting using *inspect*

Getting round the qualification rules

SIMULA goes to great lengths to force you to respect the type of a reference to a class object. In general a reference to such an object can only be used to access those attributes visible at the qualification level of the reference.

The restriction means that in a program containing declarations of class A, A class B and B class C, a variable declared as *ref*(B) can normally only be used as follows.

1   It cannot reference objects of class A.

2   It can reference objects of class B. Through it all the attributes declared in B and all the attributes declared in A whose names are not re-used in declarations in B can be accessed remotely.

3   It can reference objects of class C, but only attributes declared in A or B can be accessed. Even if the name of an attribute declared in A or B is redeclared in C, the use of a reference whose qualification is B prevents the use of the meaning given in C.

One method of overcoming these restrictions is the use of the *when* clause form of *inspect* statement. We have seen that this can allow us to identify inner classes and access their attributes.

An alternative to this is known as 'instantaneous' qualification. It does not allow a series of choices, like the full *inspect* statement with *when* clauses. Nor does it allow us to avoid references pointing to None. In these ways it is less powerful than inspection. On the other hand, it can be used to restrict as well as extend the levels of attributes which may be used.

The feature used is based on the keyword *qua* and example 13.6 shows two ways of using it.

13.6a shows it used rather like a *when* clause. It allows legal access to a class object at a level inner to that at which it is being referenced.

13.6b shows its power in the reverse direction. It is used to access

```
begin

  class A;
  begin
    integer I,J;
  end--of--A;

  A class B;
  begin
    text I,J;
  end--of--B;

  ref(A) ARef1, ARef2;
  ref(B) BRef;

  ARef1 :- new B;
  BRef  :- new B;
  ARef2 :- new A;


! a);  ARef1 qua B.I :- Copy("Getting inside");


! b);  BRef qua A.I := 4;


! c);  ARef2 qua B.I :- Copy("No inside to get to")

  end++of++program
```

Example 13.6 Uses of *qua*

the procedure POuter declared in class A, through a reference to A class B, even though POuter is redeclared as an integer inside B.

13.6c shows an illegal use of *qua*. An attempt is made to access an inner level when the object referenced is not of the inner type. This would produce a runtime error.

Syntax and semantics of reference expressions using *qua*

The use of *qua* is in expressions giving a reference to a class object. Its syntax is any reference to a class object, followed by the keyword *qua*, followed by the name of a class.

This group is still a reference to the class object, but it is accessed at the prefix level defined by the class specified. Only the attributes of this class and any prefixes to it may be accessed.

Referencing yourself

This chapter has introduced some very powerful concepts, but the usefulness of them is not always immediately apparent. It is only when you have to write quite complex programs that you may appreciate *qua*, for instance.

One very useful but much simpler feature in SIMULA is the ability of an object to reference itself. It is achieved by using the keyword *this*. Example 13.7 shows the use of *this*.

```
begin

  class Linker;
  begin
    ref(Linker) Next, Sex, Employment;
    text ID;

    procedure Add_to_List(LHead); name LHead; ref(Linker) LHead;
    begin
      Next :- LHead;
      LHead :- this Linker
    end..of..Add..to..List;

    procedure Onto_Lists(Gender,Occupation);
        name Gender,Occupation;
        ref(Linker) Gender,Occupation;
    begin
      Sex :- Gender;
      Employment :- Occupation;
      Gender :- Occupation :- this Linker
    end..of..Onto..Lists;

    InImage;
    ID :- Copy(SysIn.Image);
    InImage;
  end--of--Linker;
```

```
Linker class Male_Dancer;
begin

   ! Should contain full details;

end--of--Male--Dancer;

Linker class Female_Dancer;
begin

   ! Should contain full details;

end--of--Female--Dancer;

Linker class Male_Accountant;
begin

   ! Should contain full details;

end--of--Male--Accountant;

Linker class Female_Accountant;
begin

   ! Should contain full details;

end--of--Female--Accountant;

procedure Write_List(Heading, ListHead); text Heading;
                                ref(Linker) ListHead;

begin
   Boolean SexList;
   SexList := (ListHead==Males or ListHead==Females);
   OutImage;
   OutText(Heading);
   OutImage;
   OutImage;
   while ListHead=/=None do
   begin
      OutText(ListHead.ID);
      OutImage;
      if SexList then ListHead :- ListHead.Sex
             else ListHead :- ListHead.Employment
   end
end--of--Write--List;
```

```
ref(Linker) NextEntry,List,Males,Females,Dancers,Accountants;
text Line;

comment First read the input onto a single list;

InImage;
Line :- Blanks(80);
while SysIn.Image.Strip ne ".end" do
begin
  Line.SetPos(1);
  Line := SysIn.Image;
  if Line.GetChar='F' then
  begin
    if Line.GetChar='D' then NextEntry :- new Female_Dancer
                  else NextEntry :- new Female_Accountant
  end else begin
    if Line.GetChar='A' then NextEntry :- new Male_Accountant
                  else NextEntry :- new Male_Dancer;
  end;
  NextEntry.Add_to_List(List)
end;

comment Now process the main list, forming threaded lists;

NextEntry :- List;
while NextEntry=/=None do
begin
  inspect NextEntry

    when Male_Dancer do Onto_Lists(Males,Dancers)

    when Female_Dancer do Onto_Lists(Females,Dancers)

    when Male_Accountant do Onto_Lists(Males,Accountants)

    when Female_Accountant do Onto_Lists(Females,Accountants);

  NextEntry :- NextEntry.Next
end;

comment Now write out by lists;

if Females=/=None then Write_List("Females",Females);

if Males=/=None then Write_List("Males",Males);
```

```
if Dancers=/=None then Write_List("Dancers",Dancers);

if Accountants=/=None then Write_List("Accountants",Accountants)
```

end++of++program

Example 13.7 Using *this* in 13.5

Formally the keyword *this*, followed by a name of a class, is a reference to the class object containing it. The class name must be the one qualifying that object or on its prefix chain.

To make this clearer, consider example 13.7. Here the generation of a new object of class Linker, or prefixed by it, automatically inserts that object in the list whose head is passed as a parameter to it. Without the use of *this*, it would be impossible to perform such an action.

Using *this* many more actions can be included as local procedure attributes or local statements in the definition of a class. This is very important to the idea of object-oriented programming.

this in *inspect* statements

It is important to remember that the statement following the keyword *do* in a simple *inspect* and the statements in the *when* clauses of the extended *inspect* are treated as if they were inside the body of the object inspected. It is therefore possible to use *this* in these statements to refer to the inspected object.

Reference parameters

We have used references to objects as parameters without really considering the implications. We shall do so briefly here.

References to class objects may be declared and passed as parameters to both procedures and classes. They are passed to both by reference as a default. They may be passed by name to procedures but not to classes. They may never be passed by value. (See Tables 6.1 and 9.1.)

The actual reference passed when the procedure is called or the class object is generated, must be compatible with the class specified in the declaration. This means that its qualification must be equal or inner to the declared class, just as in a reference assignment.

Exercises

13.2 Rewrite example 13.7. Add a procedure Into to class linker. This takes one parameter which is a *ref*(Header). When Into is called it should insert the Linker object into the list of the Header passed. What mode should be used for the parameter?

13.3 Extend Into in 13.2, giving it a second parameter which is a ref to Linker. When called it should now insert the object through which it is accessed into the list after the object referenced by its second parameter. Beware of None. What modes should be used here?

Summary

- We have examined the uses, advantages and limitations of the dot notation for remote accessing.
- We have seen the full use of the *inspect* statement in both its simple and extended forms.
- We have used the *otherwise* clause to cope with cases of references to None.
- We have used the *when* clause to differentiate sub-classes referenced through a common prefix. This has allowed us to access attributes which were not available through this prefixing class. *Otherwise* allowed us to cater for unwanted sub-classes along with None.
- The use of *qua* has been shown to allow us both to extend to inner prefix levels and restrict to outer prefix levels the qualification of class-object references.
- We have examined ways in which *this* can be exploited, allowing objects to reference themselves and statements inspecting objects to reference those objects.
- A summary of the use of references to class objects as parameters has been presented.

Chapter 14

Classes as coroutines

Masters and slaves or equal partners?

Even if you had never programmed before starting this book, the use of procedures should be becoming second nature to you by now. The ability to call on a handy sequence of instructions whenever it is needed is one of the most useful aids to programming offered by high-level languages like SIMULA. Most people have a set of useful procedures which they like to use in just about all the programs they write. In fact most of us extend the SIMULA language with new features, many of which are procedures.

Although procedures are very useful, they are only one way of using independent pieces of code. The distinctive feature of procedures is that they are activated by being called from some point in the program and that when they have completed their instructions they return to that calling point. They are the slaves and the calling code is their master.

In the real world similar relationships exist. If we consider an office, the manager may need to write a report. To do this he will perhaps dictate it into a dictaphone and send the recording to the typing pool. For him the typing pool acts like a procedure. He passes it a recording of his report, like a parameter, and receives a typed version of it, like the result of that procedure.

If we broaden the scope of our view of the office, the manager may be one of several within his firm. He might be preparing his report as part of a monthly review process. This might involve all the managers preparing their own reports.

If we think of the managers as objects of class Manager, this preparing of reports would be the sequence of instructions within the class body of Manager. The facts on which the report is based would be given as parameters when the Manager is generated and the final report would be an externally visible attribute of Manager. Obviously specific managers might have extended definitions as sub-classes of Manager.

```
begin

    ref(Document) procedure Typing_Pool(Draft);
            ref(Dictaphone_Recording) Draft;
    begin
      Typing_Pool :- new Document;
    end--of--Typing--Pool;

    class Document;
    begin
      comment Holds standard document for this company;
    end--of--Document;

    class Dictaphone_Recording;
    begin
      comment Holds dictaphone version of document;
    end--of--Dictaphone--Recording;

    class Manager;
    begin
      ref(Document) Report;
      Report :- Typing_Pool(new Dictaphone_Recording)
    end--of--Manager;

    new Manager;

end++of++program
```

Example 14.1 Single manager writing report

Example 14.1 shows a pseudo-SIMULA program for this situation. Clearly this is not a program which could replace the managers in a real firm, but it does describe the operation of the firm. This is the use of SIMULA as a system description language. If you find this concept interesting, you should consult *SIMULA Begin* (Birtwistle *et al*, 1973). Here I am using it to show the limits of the concepts for producing independently acting components in our programs.

Previously, we have seen that our programs can describe service components, like the typing pool, as procedures. Now we can see that classes can be used to describe parallel components. These remain in existence once they have completed their actions, for as long as they are referenced. In this case we keep reference variables pointing at them. Thus the main program, which is the managing director or vice president, can read all the reports once they are complete.

If we include procedures as attributes of managers, the managing director can order his managers to do further things, but their independent actions cease once they have completed their reports. What is more they cannot interact. How, for instance, could we represent the situation where each manager wants to read all the other reports before allowing the managing director to read his? The ability to stop for a while and then start again, having allowed others to complete some task in the mean time, is vital to the way normal life is organized. It adds greatly to the power of a programming language, but very few allow it. It is one of SIMULA's great strengths that it does so; it is an even greater strength that it does so in a way that is simple to understand.

Example 14.2 shows the pseudo-SIMULA way of representing the situation where no manager makes his report available until all reports have been completed and revised in the light of reading the others. Notice that the managing director (main program) only starts the managers off, using Resume. All other interaction is between managers as equals. He can access their attributes once they have all terminated, however, as they are referenced by the elements of array Section_Head.

```
begin

    integer C;
    Boolean array Ready(1:4);
    ref(Manager) array Section_Head(1:4);

    ref(Document) procedure Typing_Pool(Draft);
          ref(Dictaphone_Recording) Draft;
    begin
      Typing_Pool :- new Document
    end--of--Typing_Pool;

    class Document;
    begin
      comment Holds standard document for this company;
      procedure Read;;
    end--of--Document;
```

```
class Dictaphone_Recording;
begin
  comment Holds dictaphone recording of document;
end--of--Dictaphone_Recording;

class Manager(Id_No); integer Id_No;
begin
  integer Count;
  Boolean Some_to_Read, Ready;
  Boolean array Report_Read(1:4);
  ref(Document) Report;

  Report_Read(Id_No) := True; ! No need to read his own;
  Report :- Typing_Pool(new Dictaphone_Recording);
  Ready := True;
  Detach;   ! Wait for others to be started;
  while Some_to_Read do
  begin
    Some_to_Read := False;
    for Count := 1 step 1 until 4 do
    begin
      if Section_Head(Count).Ready and (not Report_Read(Count)) then
      begin   !   Read this report for the first time;
        Section_Head(Count).Report.Read;
        Report_Read(Count) := True;
        comment Update own report;
        Report :- Typing_Pool(new Dictaphone_Recording);
      end..of..reading..another..report
      else Some_to_Read := True;
      Resume(Section_Head(Id_No+1)); ! Give the others a chance;
    end..of..one..pass..through..other..reports
  end..of..checking..other..reports
  All reports read so terminate
end--of--Manager;

for C := 1 step 1 until 4 do Section_Head(C) :- new Manager(C);
Resume(Section_Head(1))
```

end**of**program

Example 14.2 Interacting managers writing reports

The features used for synchronizing these more or less parallel sequences are Detach and Resume. They are system procedures. Let us consider a simple example of their use in a real program.

A simple game example

Most of the examples used in this book have been aimed at practical problems, largely to do with text processing. The others have been artificial programs, merely designed to show a feature of SIMULA. Here in example 14.3, for a change, is a program designed for fun. It involves the game of noughts and crosses.

```
begin

  character array Board(1:3,1:3);
  integer N,M;
  ref(Crosser) Cross_Player;
  ref(Noughter) Nought_Player;

  procedure Print_Board;
  begin
    integer N,M;
    for N := 1 step 1 until 3 do
    begin
      for M := 1 step 1 until 3 do OutChar(Board(N,M));
      OutImage
    end
  end++of++Print_Board;

  Boolean procedure Check_Board;
  begin
    comment Check for a winner;
    integer N;
    character Token;
    Boolean Check;
    for Token := 'O', 'X' do
    begin
      for N := 1 step 1 until 3 do
        if (Board(N,1)=Token and Board(N,2)=Token
          and Board(N,3)=Token) or
          (Board(1,N)=Token and Board(2,N)=Token
          and Board(3,N)=Token) then
          begin
            Check := True;
            go to Found
          end;
      if (Board(1,1)=Token and Board(2,2)=Token
        and Board(3,3)=Token) or
        (Board(1,3)=Token and Board(2,2)=Token
        and Board(3,1)=Token) then
```

```
         begin
            Check := True;
            go to Found
         end

   end--of--Token--loop; Found:
   if Check then
   begin
      OutText("Winner is ");
      OutChar(Token);
      OutImage;
      Check_Board := True
   end
end++of++Check_Board;

class Noughter;
begin
   comment Reads in player's move and updates board;
   integer N,M;
   Detach;
   while not Check_Board do

   begin
      OutText("Give position for nought as: n,m.");
      OutImage;
      N := InInt;
      InChar;
      M := InInt;
      Board(N,M) := 'O';
      Print_Board;
      Resume(Cross_Player)
   end--of--loop
end++of++Noughter;

class Crosser;
begin
   comment Plays for the machine;
   integer N,M;
   Detach;
   while not Check_Board do
   begin
      for N := 1 step 1 until 3 do
         for M := 1 step 1 until 3 do

            if Board(N,M)=' ' then go to Found; Found:
```

```
        Board(N,M) := 'X';
        Print_Board;
        Resume(Nought_Player)
    end--of--loop
end++of++Crosser;

    for N := 1 step 1 until 3 do
        for M := 1 step 1 until 3 do Board(Count1,Count2) := ' ';
    Cross_Player :- new Crosser;
    Nought_Player :- new Noughter;
    Resume(Cross_Player)

end**of**program
```

Example 14.3 Coroutines for noughts and crosses

For those who are not familiar with it, noughts and crosses is a two-player game, using a square subdivided into nine equally-sized squares. Each player in turn fills one of the boxes with his character, either a nought, 'O', or a cross 'X'. The first player to make a line of three of his characters, horizontally, vertically or diagonally but straight, wins.

The program contains two coroutines. One is used to read in the location where the person running the program wants to put his or her nought. This is typed in as two numbers separated by a comma, giving the location in a two-dimensional character array, which represents the game board.

The second coroutine represents the other 'player'. It selects its move according to a very simple set of rules, or algorithm. Basically, it scans each row from left to right, starting at the top. It places its cross in the first unoccupied location that it finds.

The procedures Print—Board and Check—Board are called by each coroutine, after it has placed its character, to.print the board and to check for a winner.

This may seem like a rather trivial program. It shows rather nicely, however, the operation of coroutines. They do not proceed genuinely in parallel. Instead, they take it in turns to become active. In this way they are exactly like many games, where each player has a turn and then waits idly until his turn comes again. Even the most complicated coroutine-based programs are like this.

Not all coroutines take turns in strict order, of course. The next one to be made active might depend on some condition which changes each time. Even this is like some games, where the value of a card or a number called can change the direction or sequence of play.

Because of these characteristics, coroutine programs are often called quasi-parallel systems.

Procedure Detach

Detach is a procedure which is an attribute of all class objects. A call of Detach within a class body renders the class object 'detached'. It is meaningless to try to detach a block or procedure. This will either result in the object to which the block or procedure is local becoming detached or, if there is no object containing it, there will be no effect.

The state detached is a waiting state. A detached object may be used as a coroutine and resumed from outside.

When an object detaches itself, the program goes back to the point where that object was activated, i.e. immediately after the Detach, *new* or Resume statement in the object or block which initiated the current phase of activity in this object.

Procedure Resume

Resume is a procedure which has one parameter, which may be a reference to any class object. This breaks the normal rules for the type of a reference parameter. Resume is allowed to do this, but no user-defined procedure may.

Resume restarts a detached object. The program moves to the statement following the last call of Detach or Resume which has been made by the object being resumed. If the Resume call is made from within an object, this object becomes detached. If the Resume comes in a block such as the program block, a subsequent call of Detach by the Resumed object will return activity to the next statement in that block.

If the object is not detached, trying to resume it is a runtime error.

Possible states

When an object is executing the body of code declared in its class declaration, including that of any prefixing classes, and has not executed a Detach, it is said to be 'attached' to the point at which it was generated. If it is executing, an object which is not a coroutine can only be attached. If an object executes a Detach, it forms a coroutine. It enters the 'detached' state.

An object which has been resumed is in the 'resumed' state.
An object which has just resumed another object is in the 'detached' state, i.e. it can become active either by the object which it resumed detaching or by an explicit resume.

An object, whether a coroutine or an ordinary class object, which passes through its final *end*, becomes 'terminated'. Terminated objects continue to exist as long as they are referenced from somewhere else in the program. A terminated object with no references to it is regarded as having ceased to exist.

Exercise

14.1 Write a program which uses three coroutines — Read, Sort and Check — to read in names, add them to a linked list in correct alphabetical order and check that this has been done correctly.

Text processing with coroutines

An important reason for using coroutines is to keep information, which has been accumulated by one class object, alive when that object has completed one part of its sequence of actions and then resuming it when its next sequence is required, with its data intact. This can be made even more powerful by making the whole or part of the sequence of actions loop. In this way more and more information can be accumulated as the sequence is repeated.

An example of the use of this is in the automatic generation of an index. Each time a page is complete, the indexing process can be reactivated to scan it and note any words for indexing. If a procedure were to be used, all its local data would be lost after each call. This would mean that it would have to store its information in variables outside itself. This would make it impossible to write a really self-contained indexing process. By using a coroutine, this is avoided. Instead of calling a procedure, the index coroutine is simply resumed. Once it is finished it detaches itself and waits to be resumed again.

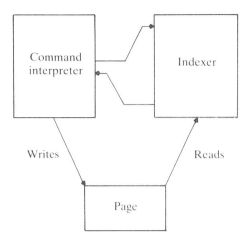

Fig. 14.1 Coroutines for text processing.

A text-processing system might have several parallel components. Example 14.4 shows the skeleton of such a system, using the sort of informal, half-SIMULA we have seen before. Figure 14.1 shows the design of the system in general terms. There are two coroutines, Indexer and Command—Interpreter.

The number of parallel components and the exact work performed by each is to some extent a question of choice. What seems an obvious design to some people, could seem odd to others. One useful rule is to build the system in a way that seems natural to you. If you think of certain sequences of actions as happening in parallel, reflect that in your programs.

Example 14.4 could have been written without coroutines. Our earlier chapter processing system did not use them, although it could have been written very simply as a set of parallel processes.

The key fact about this type of program is that none of the processes is the boss. Each has overall control whilst it is executing, but must wait to be resumed once it has detached. With procedures control passes down a chain of calls and back again to the original caller. With coroutines control can pass backwards and forwards as the situation dictates. All the coroutines can remain ready to be resumed, but none need be made active unless required. Even a terminated coroutine may still have its data accessed, as long as it is referenceable.

```
begin
  comment Outline text processer using detach/resume;

  comment General support procedures;

  text procedure InLine;
  begin
    InImage;
    InLine :- SysIn.Image.Strip
  end++of++InLine;

  procedure OutLine(T); text T;
  begin
    OutText(T);
    OutImage
  end++of++OutLine;

  comment Some list handling definitions;

  class Linker;
  begin
    comment Prefix for linked list handling;
    ref(Linker) Link;
    procedure Add_To(List); name List; ref(Linker) List;
    begin
      this Linker.Link :- List;
      List :- this Linker;   ! Requires List to be in name mode;
    end--of--Add_To;
  end++of++Linker;

  Linker class Word_List_Entry(Word); text Word;
  begin
    Add_To(Word_List)
  end++of++Word_List_Entry;

  Linker class Index_List_Entry(Word,Page_No);
         text Word; integer Page_No;
  begin
    comment Holds occurrences of words to be indexed;
  end++of++Index_List_Entry;

  Linker class Chapter(Title); text Title;
  begin
    integer Chapter_No;
    ref(Page) Page_List Current_Page;
    procedure Print
```

```
   begin
      ref(Page) Next;
      Next :- Page_List;
      while Next=/=None do
      begin
         Next.Print;
         Next :- Next.Link
      end..of..while
   end--of--Print;
   Current_Chapter_No := Current_Chapter_No + 1;
   Chapter_No := Current_Chapter_No;
   Current_Chapter :- this Chapter;
   Add_To(Chapter_List)
end++of++Chapter;

Linker class Page;
begin
   integer Page_No, Current_Line;
   text array Line(1:60);
   procedure Print;
   begin
      integer Count;
      for Count := 1 step 1 until Current_Line do OutLine(Line(Count))
   end..of..Print;
   Current_Page_No := Current_Page_No + 1;
   Page_No := Current_Page_No;
   Current_Chapter.Currrent_Page :- this Page;
   if Page_No=1 then
   begin
      Line(2) :- Current_Chapter.Title;
      Current_Line := 4
   end else Current_Line := 1;
   Add_To(Current_Chapter.Page_List)
end++of++Page;

ref(Chapter) Chapter_List;

comment Principal coroutines and records;

class Command_Interpreter;
begin
   comment Read in commands and resume appropriate coroutine.
        Implemented as a coroutine;

   text Command, Current_Line;
```

```
    while True do
    begin
      Current_Line :- InLine;
      Command :- Current_Line.Sub(1,2);
      Current_Line :- Current_Line(2,Current_Line.Length-2);

      if Command="$I" then
      begin
        new Word_List_Entry(Current_Line).Add_To(Index.Word_List)
      end else
      if Command="$I" then
      begin
        if Current_Chapter=/=None then Resume(Current_Chapter);
        new Chapter(Current_Line)
      end else
    ! if Command= etc. then
    ! begin
    ! Perform appropriate action
    ! end else;
      if Command="$E" then
      begin
        new Printer
      end==checking==command
    end..while
end++of++Command_Interpreter;

class Indexer;
begin
  ref(Index_List_Entry) Index_List, Next;
  ref(Word_List_Entry) Word_List;
  procedure Print;
  begin
  ! Sort the index list;
  ! Print the index list;
  end--of--Print;
  while True do
  begin
    Detach;
    comment Resumed at the end of each page;
  ! For each line of Current_Page, search for each word on Word_List;
    if found then new Index_List_Entry(current word).
    Add_To(Index_List)
  end--of--loop
end++of++Indexer;

class Printer;
begin
```

```
   ref(Chapter) Next;
   comment Print contents page;
   OutImage;
   OutText("Contents");
   OutImage;
   Eject(6);
   Next :- Chapter_List;
   while Next=/= None do
   begin
      OutInt(Next.Chapter_No,8);
      OutText("      ");
      OutText(Next.Title);
   end..printing..contents..page;
   comment Print chapters;
   Next :- Chapter_List;
   while Next=/=None do
   begin
      Next.Print;
      Next :- Next.Link
   end--of--printing--chapters
   comment Print index;
   Index.Print
end++of++Printer;

comment Main program;

ref(Chapter) Current_Chapter;
ref(Indexer) Index;
integer Current_Chapter_No, Current_Page_No;

Index :- new Indexer;
new Command_Interpreter

end**of**program
```

Example 14.4 Outline of a text processer using coroutines

The indexer in detail

Like all the coroutines, the first thing that the Indexer object does is to perform any initial actions and then detach itself. This is a useful start, setting all the coroutines in place and ready to be used. The main program then schedules the first to be needed, in this case the Command＿Interpreter, by calling Resume.

If we examine the Indexer coroutine in more detail we can see how it fits with Command＿Interpreter. Essentially it is activated by calls of Resume from Command＿Interpreter, each time a page of the book has been completed. It then scans the page just finished, looking for words on its wanted list. If it finds one, it creates a new entry on Index＿List for that word. This list is a linked list of index/page reference objects whose header is a ref variable inside the body of class Indexer.

Once the whole page has been scanned, Indexer detaches. A detach takes the program back to the point where the coroutine was activated. The initial detach in Indexer took it back to the place in the main program where the Indexer object was generated. This detach takes it back to the resume in Command＿Interpreter.

Indexer makes its second detach just before the end of its *while* loop. This means that every time it is resumed it goes straight to the top of this loop and repeats the sequence.

The loop is a *while* loop, but instead of a normal condition it contains the Boolean literal True. This means that the loop will continue for as long as the coroutine is resumed. This sort of indefinite loop allows 'immortal' coroutines to be created. They will always be either active or waiting.

Indexer is a fairly simple coroutine. Since Detach and Resume are procedures they can be used wherever any statement can be used, although the effect will depend on whether or not they are called from within a class object, as explained above. During its complete sequence of actions, a coroutine can detach several times or resume any coroutines with which it is operating in parallel. It is important to understand the simple logic of Indexer before moving on to more complex problems.

Making a coroutine into a slave

This chapter only deals with coroutines in a very simple manner. There remains one basic feature of SIMULA which relates to them and which is not even superficially treated by the preceding sections.

It is possible to activate a detached object by using Resume, as we have seen. This makes an independent but passive object into an independent and active one. It does not attach the resumed object to the point from which it was resumed, except that it may choose to return there by calling Detach.

When an object is generated, we have seen that it is attached to the point where it was created. It is an extension of the block where it was generated, not an independent object, until it detaches or terminates.

A detached object may lose its independence and be reattached. This can be done by any block, not just the one where it was created. It is done by the procedure Call.

Once a detached object has been called it acts as if it had been generated at the point where it was called. It restarts from its last Detach and remains attached to the calling block.

Call takes one general class-object reference parameter, just like Resume.

Restrictions on Call and Resume

The use of Call allows an object which was generated at one point in a program and which then detached itself, to be restarted later from another point, as does Resume. However, while Call is allowed for objects anywhere in the program, Resume is illegal for objects local to other class objects or to procedure bodies. Only objects which are defined by classes whose bodies are declared in sub-blocks or prefixed blocks can be resumed. We have seen the use of sub-blocks and we shall look in more detail at prefixed blocks in Chapter 16. If an object Resumes itself this has no effect.

A Call can be made on objects whose class declarations are local to classes and procedures, as well as on those allowed for Resume. An object may not Call itself without a runtime error being reported.

The use of both Call and Resume is illegal on objects which are not detached, including those which have terminated. It is also illegal on None.

The restriction on Resume is to prevent seriously ambiguous situations developing. The SIMULA Standard gives more technical detail.

Using Call

Example 14.5 shows an example using Call. Since the objects used are local to class Master, it would be illegal to Resume them. This means

```
begin

  class Master;
  begin

    class Slave;
    begin
      OutText("Action before detach");
      OutImage;
      Detach;   ! Leaves Slave detached;
      OutText("Action when reattached by Call");
      OutImage
    end--of--Slave;

    ref(Slave) Servant;

    Servant :- new Slave;
    OutText("Action of Master when Slave detaches");
    OutImage;
    Call(Servant);
    OutText("Final action by Master when Slave has terminated");
    OutImage
  end++of++Master;

end**of**program
```

Example 14.5 Use of Call

that they cannot interact as equals, but must be controlled by Master while active.

  This simple example should help to make clear how we use Call, even if the technical reasons for needing it as well as Resume go beyond the scope of this book.

Exercise

14.2 Improve the noughts and crosses program by adding a better set of rules for judging where the noughts should be placed. There is no definitive solution to this.

Some more on games

Noughts and crosses is a very simple game, but the basic principles used here can be applied to many other game-playing programs. Even a chess-playing program could be written on the same basis. The board would be more elaborate and the rules for deciding moves more involved, but that is all.

It is also possible to write programs to play multi-player games. A game of bridge, for instance, would involve four coroutines, with two phases — bidding and playing. If you enjoy bridge, this would be an interesting project to attempt. Chapter 20 will show you how to generate 'random' numbers, to represent the dealing of the cards. One last possibility is to make all the coroutines internal and to let the program play itself. This is a way of testing alternative strategies.

Summary

- We have covered coroutines and quasi-parallel systems rather informally.
- We have seen the sequencing control procedures Detach and Resume and their use.
- We have seen the possible states that a class object can be in.
- We have seen the use of Call and something of the difference between Call and Resume.

Chapter 15

Direct and byte files

Variations on the File concept

This chapter introduces a new type of Image File. It allows a file to be treated like an array of records and is called a Direct File.

We also meet a type of File which is not an ImageFile and so does not hold its contents as a series of records. It is called a Byte File and has three sub-classes, InByteFile, OutByteFile and DirectByteFile.

Direct or random access to a file

ImageFile class DirectFile implements a concept known as direct or random access to the contents of a file. It only works for files which are genuinely areas of the computer's memory and which are permanent during the running of the program. In particular, random access cannot be used on terminals, printers or other input and output devices. In this way DirectFiles are very different from InFiles and OutFiles.

The ImageFile generally views files as ordered lists of records. The DirectFile views them as numbered lists of records. The difference is rather like the difference between linked lists and arrays. To reach item 100 on a linked list you must count past the first 99, while to reach item 100 in an array you can go straight to it using a subscripted variable. With an InFile or OutFile, in order to read or write record 100, you must first read or write the previous 99, while with DirectFile you can go straight to record 100, using a procedure called Locate, which is an attribute of DirectFile.

The other difference with a DirectFile is that a program can both read from and write to the same file, without closing and reopening as a different type of file. This makes DirectFile a very useful concept for what is generally known as database work. This involves retrieving, storing and updating information.

What does a DirectFile look like?

Every SIMULA system is free to store the information in the physical locations referred to through DirectFile objects in any way that it finds suitable. What is important is how it presents this to the SIMULA program. This presentation must conform to the rules of SIMULA. The real, physical storage of data should be given in the user's guide or programmer's reference manual for the SIMULA system you are using.

When a DirectFile is first created it is empty, but it has certain properties. One of these is the record length, which must be the same for all its records. Another may be the maximum number of records that the file can hold, but not all systems will fix this in advance.

Once some output has been transferred to a DirectFile, through OutImage, it will contain one or more non-empty records. Each of these will have a sequence number, called its Location. As it is not necessary to write to records in the order of their sequence numbers, these non-empty records may be mixed up with empty or unwritten records.

It is central to the understanding of DirectFile to realize that there can be 'holes' in the sequence of Locations of written records and that these represent unwritten records. This is particularly crucial when an attempt is made to read from a particular location. The effect will depend upon whether or not a record has been written there.

Consider example 15.1. The only unfamiliar concept is that of Locate. This simply moves the current position of the program within the sequence of records in a DirectFile to the record whose location is given as a parameter to Locate. Figure 15.1 shows the contents of the file at the end of the program. Note the holes in the record sequence.

Having described informally what a DirectFile represents, we can now move on to consider the attributes of ImageFile class DirectFile. These are as specified in the 1986 SIMULA Standard and may not all be implemented on some older systems. As usual, you should check the documentation for the system you are using.

The attributes of DirectFile

Since DirectFile is a sub-class of ImageFile, it contains all the attributes of ImageFile. This means the Image, Pos, SetPos, Length and More

```
begin

    ref(DirectFile) Direct;
    Direct :- new DirectFile("Data");
    inspect Direct do
    begin
        Open(Blanks(80));
        OutText("First");
        OutImage;
        Locate(4);
        OutText("Fourth");
        OutImage;
        Locate(10);
        OutText("Tenth");
        OutImage;
        OutText("Eleventh");
        OutImage;
        OutText("Sixth");
        Locate(6);
        OutImage;
        Close
    end--of--inspect

end**of**program
```

Example 15.1 Writing to a DirectFile

Location	Content
1	'First'
2	unwritten
3	unwritten
4	'Fourth'
5	unwritten
6	'Sixth'
7	unwritten
8	unwritten
9	unwritten
10	'Tenth'
11	'Eleventh'

Fig. 15.1 Contents of file after example 15.1

are defined in the same way as for the other sub-classes of ImageFile. These are all attributes concerned with the current Image text.

Other attributes of ImageFile are redefined slightly for DirectFile. The differences depend on the current value of Location and what is found there. We shall consider the attributes dealing with the image locations first, to make it easier to understand these redefinitions.

Locate, Location, MaxLoc and LastLoc

The highest permitted image number in the file is fixed on some systems and can be any number on others. The integer procedure MaxLoc returns the limit for any given file. Where no limit is imposed, the procedure will return the largest value allowed to an integer minus one.

Since not all the images in a DirectFile object's permitted range may be filled, the integer procedure LastLoc is provided. This gives the index number of the highest numbered image location currently in use.

Location is an integer procedure which gives the index number of the image location which is currently being accessed. It is legal for the current location to be unused.

Procedure Locate takes one integer parameter. It resets the currently accessed image location to the one whose index matches the parameter. An attempt to exceed the value of MaxLoc causes a run-time error.

These procedures allow programs to access image locations in any order and to check that the locations being accessed match the current contents of the file.

Now let us look at attributes with, mostly, familiar names. First let us consider image-handling procedures.

InImage, OutImage and DeleteImage

These three procedures all deal with the contents of the currently accessed image location.

InImage reads the contents of the current location into text attribute Image, in a similar way to the InImage of InFile. It is different since the contents of the current location can produce more possibilities. Essentially there are three cases.

1   The current location has an image which has been written to. This image is transferred to Image and the current location is updated to point to the next location.

2   The current location has had no image written to it, but is not beyond the highest currently used location, as given by LastLoc. Image is filled with null characters, Pos is set to Length + 1, making More give False. The current location is again increased by one.

3   The current location is beyond LastLoc, but less than or equal to MaxLoc. This causes EndFile to return True and Image is given the single character representing end of file, ISOChar(25), as its contents.

OutImage transfers the contents of text attribute Image to the current location. It makes a previously unwritten location into a written one. If the current location is initially greater than LastLoc, LastLoc will be updated to the current location. The current location is then increased by one.

DeleteImage removes the current location's image. This leaves the current location unwritten, i.e. as if it had never been filled. If the location deleted is the same as LastLoc, LastLoc will be reduced to the index of the next highest position written to.

Note on sequential access to DirectFile

If Locate is never used to read images out of order, DirectFiles can be read or written to in the same way as InFiles and OutFiles. The incrementing of the current location by one after InImage or OutImage is identical to what happens in these types of file.

EndFile

EndFile is a Boolean procedure, like that of InFile, with the same purpose. It checks whether the current location is greater than LastLoc, i.e. the highest location currently holding a written image. If it is beyond LastLoc it returns True, otherwise False. It also returns True if the file is currently closed.

CheckPoint

As with OutFile and PrintFile, the system may not actually update the memory of the computer each time an OutImage is performed. Instead it may hold several outstanding requests until a suitable limit for the system and then write them together. In order to be secure, it is sometimes desirable to force the updating of the physical file before proceeding. CheckPoint is particularly important for DirectFile objects, where access is both for reading and writing and files are often shared. It works in the same way as in OutFile.

SetAccess

For database applications, shared and readwrite modes are especially important. The use of SetAccess is described in Chapter 7. If readwrite mode is set to readonly or writeonly, the DirectFile in question may only be accessed in that way from the program. This can prevent corruption of data.

Locking a DirectFile

As a major use of DirectFiles is in database applications, where a file may well be shared amongst several users, it is often important to allow one user to gain exclusive access to the file for a limited period, to prevent it being written to while someone is trying to read from it. This is known as locking the file.

In fact it may be better to lock only that part of the file which the particular program wants to access, leaving the rest free for others to access. This may or may not be possible, depending on the system.

Three procedures are provided for this.

1 Lock is an integer procedure with three parameters. The first is a real, which specifies how long the program is prepared to wait for the file to be locked. If this time is exceeded, the system returns a result of −1. If the lock fails for any other reason, a value less than minus one is returned, with a system-defined meaning. If the time passed is zero or negative, Lock returns without doing anything.

The other two parameters are both integers. They indicate the range of locations within the file which this program wishes to lock. Some systems will lock the whole file regardlessly. If both integers are zero, the whole file is to be locked. If the system does not support locking of files, it returns a negative result to indicate this. If Lock succeeds within its time limit, zero is returned.

A second call of Lock, with the file already locked, will cause it to be first unlocked and then locked again. This may mean that it becomes locked first by another program.

2   Unlock is a Boolean procedure with no parameters. It cancels any current locking of the file by this program, having first called CheckPoint to preserve any unwritten changes made by it. The result of the CheckPoint call is returned as the result of Unlock.

3   Locked is a Boolean procedure, returning True if the file is currently locked by this program.

Open and Close

Procedures Open and Close work in the same way as for InFile and OutFile, except that the length of the text passed to Open will be taken as the fixed length of all records in the file. This length may not be changed.

Item-oriented procedures

All item-oriented input and output procedures from InFile and OutFile are also found in DirectFile. There is one difference: any unwritten locations are skipped by the input procedures and the first location containing a non-empty image becomes the current location.

An example of the use of DirectFile

An obvious use of DirectFile is to hold information with some kind of numerical key. Example 15.2 shows a simple program which adds a new employee record to a personnel database. The records are listed according to the works number of the employees.

Not all records contain a convenient number of this sort. It may be necessary to scan a file checking for the required record. Even so, there is often an advantage in being able to search and write to a file without copying it into a new file. Think back to our earlier label programs and see how much simpler they would be with a DirectFile.

A particular example of efficient searching on a non-numerical key is known as hashing. DirectFiles are very useful for simple hashing. Most textbooks on searching and sorting will explain this in full.

```
begin
  ref(DirectFile) Records;
  ref(InFile) InPut;
  InPut :- new InFile("Additions");
  InPut.Open(Blanks(86));    ! First 6 hold employee number;
  Records :- new DirectFile("StaffRecs");
  Records.Open(Blanks(80));
  while not InPut.EndFile do
  begin
    Records.Locate(InPut.InInt);
    Records.OutText(InPut.InText(80));
    Records.OutImage
  end--of--reading--in--records;
  while not Records.EndFile do OutText(Records.InText(80))
end**of**program
```

Example 15.2 Use of DirectFile for numbered records

Exercise

15.1   Rewrite exercise 9.5 using a DirectFile.

Files without records

So far we have only considered files as lists of records or images. All the reading and writing has been in terms of the current record and what happens when we reach its end. Even the item-oriented input and output procedures have worked on items within records.

This approach is often quite natural. It has its origins in the use of punched cards, usually holding up to 80 characters, for input and line printers, printing up to 132 characters per line, for output. The name Image is a contraction of the old term 'card image', referring to how the contents of a punched card is stored in a particular computer's memory.

This view of the world has never covered all the possible devices for input and output for computers. It certainly does not represent the memory in which most information is stored on modern computers. Neither does it represent 'screen oriented' input and output, nor graph-plotter output.

In fact, most computers use a large number of different structures for representing data. Some are held in memory, others are connections to external sources and destinations. Only some of them can be adequately thought of in terms of records.

Even when it is possible to pretend that an unstructured file is made up of records, this may slow down access as make-believe records are constructed or disassembled. In recognition of the need to provide a solution, SIMULA has a type of file called a ByteFile. This attempts to provide the most general way of reading or writing information, with no assumptions about what that information looks like. This approach is sometimes called 'stream oriented' input and output.

Bytes and files

It is beyond the scope of this book to explain the details of how a computer works. The following explanation is as complete as it needs to be, but does not cover everything.

As far as most programmers are concerned, the way in which a computer stores information is irrelevant. They are normally interested in manipulating characters and numbers. Numbers are held in most computers as sequences of binary digits (bits) with a fixed maximum length. In real numbers some of these digits represent the position of the decimal point, the others the decimal digits. In integers they all represent the digits. In general the number of bits in an integer and the number of bits in a real is the same and this number of bits is called a 'word'.

Long reals and short integers may be stored in longer or shorter locations as appropriate.

A computer's memory is an enormous number of bits, divided into fixed-size locations which are words. The number of bits in a word is usually several times larger than that needed to represent one ISO character, which requires a minimum of eight bits for the full set. Most computers divide the words in their memory into smaller locations called bytes. Each byte can hold one character and so is, normally, at least eight, but possibly more, bits long.

Figure 15.2 shows some typical memory locations on what is called '32 bit' computer architecture. Computers are often categorized by the number of bits in one word of their memory.

integer	Ibyte1Ibyte2Ibyte3Ibyte4I $\rightarrow$ 1 word $\rightarrow$ 32 bits
real	Ibyte1Ibyte2Ibyte3Ibyte4I $\rightarrow$ 1 word $\rightarrow$ 32 bits
character	Ibyte1I $\rightarrow$ 1 byte $\rightarrow$ 8 bits
long real	Ibyte1Ibyte2Ibyte3Ibyte4Ibyte5Ibyte6Ibyte7Ibyte8I $\rightarrow$ 2 words $\rightarrow$ 64 bits
short integer	Ibyte1Ibyte2I $\rightarrow$ 2 bytes $\rightarrow$ 16 bits

NB These vary from system to system, even among 32-bit machines. Consult your documentation carefully if you use ByteFiles.

Fig. 15.2 32-bit memory locations.

Clearly most programs handle information by the word (integers and reals) or by the byte (characters and texts). Furthermore, it is usually possible to treat a word as a sequence of bytes. Thus a file type which allows byte by byte access to memory can be used to read words.

Records are also sequences of bytes. They contain a fixed number of bytes (fixed-length images), are prefixed by a byte or word indicating their length (variable-length images), end with a special character (also variable-length images) or are marked in any of a large number of possible ways. Thus reading a byte at a time allows records to be accessed as well. In fact many new ways of structuring files can be built on top of the ByteFile.

A simple example

Most practical uses of ByteFile are likely to be extremely technical. It is a concept which is likely to be useful to all of us, but in very different situations. Example 15.3 shows an important use in a realistic situation, and demonstrates the main attributes of InByteFile and OutByteFile.

The program will convert a file from ISO into local characters, by reading it as a stream of bytes. Each of these will occupy the standard eight bits for an ISO character and the value read will be the ISORank for it. By passing this to ISOChar a local character corresponding to this ISO internal code is generated. By passing this to Rank, the local internal code is generated. This is written out to a file as a local byte, with the appropriate number of bits.

```
begin

   ref(InByteFile) LocalChars;
   ref(OutByteFile) ISOChars;

   LocalChars :- new InByteFile("SOURCE");
   ISOChars :- new OutByteFile("OUTPUT");
   inspect LocalChars do
   begin
     Open;
     inspect ISOChars do
     begin
       Open;
       SetAccess("bytesize:8");   ! Standard for ISO/ASCII files;
       while not EndFile do OutByte(Rank(ISOChar(InByte)));
       Close
     end--of--inspecting--ISOChars;
     Close
   end..of..inspecting..LocalChars
end**of**program
```

Example 15.3 Use of ByteFiles

File class ByteFile

ByteFile is a sub-class of File, but not of ImageFile. As it deals in
bytes, not records, it does not need an Image or any of the associated
attributes.

It has a short integer procedure ByteSize, which will return the
number of bits in a byte on that SIMULA system. The value of
ByteSize is fixed.

ByteFile also has an Open procedure. Note that this requires no
parameters, since there is no Image.

SetAccess also works for ByteFile. The mode bytesize is especially
provided for use when files with non-standard byte sizes for a particular system, such as those brought from another computer, are to be
processed.

ByteFile class InByteFile

InByteFile is used to represent input to the program as a sequence of
bytes. It is used in a similar way to InFile. Its only attributes are:

- EndFile — defined as usual as a Boolean procedure to say when the input is exhausted. Initially set to True.
- Open — a Boolean procedure. Sets EndFile to False. Has no parameters. Acts in a similar way to Open for other File sub-classes.
- Close — a Boolean procedure. Sets EndFile to True. Acts in a similar way to Close in other File sub-classes.
- InByte — a short integer procedure. Reads in the next byte and returns its value as a short integer. If there are no more bytes to read, sets EndFile to True.
- InText — a text procedure with a text-reference parameter. It fills the text parameter with the next N bytes, where N is the length of this text. It returns a reference to this, with its Pos reset to one.

ByteFile class OutByteFile

OutByteFile is the equivalent of OutFile. It is used to output to a file representing a sequence of bytes. It has the following attributes:
- Open — a Boolean procedure, like that for InByteFile.
- Close — a Boolean procedure, like that for InByteFile.
- OutByte — a procedure with one short integer parameter. If this is greater than the largest value which can be represented as a binary number by one byte on this system, it is a runtime error. If it is a legal value it is written as the next byte to the output defined by this file.
- OutText — a procedure with one text-reference parameter. The characters of this text are written as the next N bytes to the file, where N is the length of the text.

ByteFile class DirectByteFile

In a DirectByteFile, the file represents a numbered sequence of bytes. The highest permitted number is fixed or set to the highest possible integer value on that SIMULA system minus one.

In effect the DirectByteFile is the byte equivalent of a DirectFile. Unwritten bytes have a value of zero. It is possible to both read and write. The attributes are:
- Open — a Boolean procedure with no parameters.

- Close   — a Boolean procedure with no parameters.
- EndFile   — a Boolean procedure returning True when the file is unopened or closed or the location being read from is greater than the highest currently written to.
- MaxLoc — an integer procedure returning the highest byte number allowed for this file.
- LastLoc — an integer procedure returning the highest byte number so far written to.
- Location — an integer procedure returning the number of the current byte.
- Locate   — a procedure with one integer parameter, which moves the current location to the byte whose number is passed as a parameter. This value must be less than or equal to MaxLoc.
- InByte   — a short integer procedure which reads the current byte if its location is less than or equal to LastLoc and returns its value. It then moves the current location to the next byte. If the current byte is unwritten, a zero is returned. If the current location is beyond LastLoc or is a previously unwritten location, zero is returned. If it is beyond MaxLoc, a runtime error is reported.

OutByte, InText and OutText are all like their equivalents in InByteFile and OutByteFile.

Summary

- This rather brief chapter has outlined a new type of ImageFile and three types of File which do not use an Image.
- The concepts of direct access and byte-oriented access have been outlined.
- We have seen the attributes and uses of ImageFile class DirectFile.
- We have seen briefly the attributes of ByteFile and its sub-classes InByteFile, OutByteFile and DirectByteFile.

Chapter 16

Prefixed blocks as packages

Avoiding re-inventing the wheel

One of the most labour saving aspects of high-level languages, like SIMULA, is the provision of features which allow a piece of the program with a well-defined function to be used wherever needed without rewriting it each time. Loops, procedures, recursive calls, classes and coroutines all help with this. Even these features must be written again in each program where they are used and not simply named.

Certain commonly used features are available in all programs, without any declarations being necessary. These are the system features. This is very useful, but not all the procedures or classes required for a particular programmer to produce his programs will be found in the list of SIMULA system features.

Some versions of SIMULA have extra system features, but programs written for such systems will not run on standard systems. Even the best of these extended systems cannot have all the features which may be required.

In practice each type of program will probably want to use a set of features suited to the problems being solved. We have seen that word-processing programs can make use of many features which might appear in several different parts of a system or in completely different programs. The word-processing programmer would like to have these available as system features. On the other hand, a mathematical programmer would probably find little to interest him in line breakers, chapter classes or whatever. He would prefer to have complex number procedures, matrix classes or things of that sort.

There are two possible solutions to the problem. One is to keep extending the language to try to provide all the possible features which will be required. This leads to impossibly complicated languages and cumbersome compilers and runtime systems. I will not name any of the languages which have fallen into this trap. If you ever meet any, you will recognize the description.

253

SIMULA is already a fairly substantial language. Its origins in Algol 60 have made it larger than it needs to be; to add further complication is not a good idea. In general, the system features in SIMULA only provide facilities which would be impossible or very inefficient if they were written in SIMULA itself. This leaves the second solution.

If a programmer could produce a library of procedures and classes suited to his particular needs and make it available wherever he needed it, in a simple way, the problem would be solved. This concept is sometimes called a library and sometimes a package.

It is also useful sometimes to be able to use just one or two features, independently of a package. If these can be included in a concise way, it can save effort. This can be done as well, using 'separate compilation'.

Finally, it is useful to be able to compile a package separately, as well as odd procedures or whatever. The advantage is that this part of your program is already compiled. It does not need to be completely reprocessed by the compiler. This can make compilation of the program using the separately compiled feature much faster. Since it is often necessary to recompile a program several times before it is correct and working, the saving can be considerable.

Making packages with prefixed blocks

When we want to make the features of a class available in another class, we prefix the new class with the old one. In a similar way, we can prefix a block with a class. This makes all the features of the class available inside that block. Example 16.1 shows a prefixed block, using the features available in class MyFeatures.

Clearly this example gains no advantage from using a prefixed block. We could simply have declared the two procedures outside of MyFeatures and called them anywhere in the program. It merely serves to illustrate the nature of a prefixed block.

In its simplest form, a prefixed block is a prefixing class identifier, followed by the keyword *begin*, followed by a sequence of declarations and statements, followed by the keyword *end*.

All the visible attributes of the prefixing class are available inside the block that it prefixes without further declaration.

The declaration of the prefixing class must be made in the block which immediately encloses the block that it prefixes. In the example,

```
begin

    class MyFeatures:
    begin

        procedure OutLine(T); text T;
        begin
          OutText(T);
          OutImage
        end..of..OutLine;

        procedure DoubleSpace(T); text T;
        begin
          OutLine(T);
          OutImage
        end..of..DoubleSpace;

    end--of--MyFeatures;

    MyFeatures
    begin
      OutLine("First");
      DoubleSpace("Second");
      OutLine"Fourth")
    end--of--prefixed--block

end**of**program
```

Example 16.1 A simple prefixed block

the class MyAttributes is declared in the program block. This is also the block immediately surrounding the prefixed block and so the program is legal SIMULA.

Note that the use of the keyword *this* inside the prefixing class is both meaningless and forbidden.

In general, this simple kind of prefixed block is only of academic interest. One simple extension is to prefix more than one block with the class. This is possible only where the blocks meet the condition in the last paragraph but one, i.e. they are both sub-blocks of the block where the prefixing class is declared. Different blocks can also be prefixed with different classes, but again the usefulness is limited if the full class declaration has to be made in the immediately enclosing block.

A rather more interesting possibility is to use parameters to the prefixing class. This allows different blocks with the same prefix to be set up differently. A somewhat contrived example is shown in example 16.2. Note that the parameter values must follow the class identifier which prefixes each block.

```
begin

    class Printing(Spaces); integer Spaces;
    begin

        procedure OutLine(T); text T;
        begin
            integer Count;
            OutText(T);
            for Count := 1 step 1 until Spaces do OutImage
        end..of..OutLine;

    end--of--Printing;

    Printing(1)
    begin
        OutLine("First");
        OutLine("Second")
    end--of--first--prefixed--block;

    Printing(2)
    begin
        OutLine("First");
        OutLine("Third")
    end--of--second--prefixed--block

end**of**program
```

Example 16.2 Prefixed blocks with parameters

Still, there is no great benefit to be seen from such a device. In itself the prefixed block provides no great power. It is, however, immensely powerful in practice, when combined with other features.

The first benefit is that two system classes are provided for use as prefixes. Each covers a particular area which is not of sufficiently general interest to be included in the basic language. These are SIMSET, which provides powerful list handling, and SIMULATION, which provides discrete-event simulation features. They are described in Chapters 17 and 19 respectively.

The second benefit is that a class can be compiled on its own then brought into the programs you write by a single line 'external' declaration. It is this second point that we shall consider next.

Using separately compiled prefixes

A class like MyFeatures is suitable for separate compilation. It contains no uses of non-system identifiers, other than those declared inside itself. It is self-contained.

The precise way of specifying that a class is to be compiled on its own rather than as part of a program, varies amongst SIMULA systems. You should check the documentation for the one you wish to use. Some older systems may not even allow it, in which case you are advised to move to one that does, if at all possible.

When a class is separately compiled one or more extra files are generated, compared with a normal compilation. These are called attribute files and contain details of the visible attributes of the class. They will be needed by the compiler whenever you compile a program which contains an external declaration of the class. Again, you should consult carefully the documentation for the system you are using.

To use a separately compiled class, you must include an external declaration in the place of the full class declaration. Example 16.3a shows example 16.1 with MyFeatures assumed to have been compiled separately.

The syntax of this external declaration is quite simple. The keyword external is followed by the keyword class, followed by the class identifier. The identifier will enable the compiler to locate the attribute file or files for MyFeatures. These contain all the information it needs about the class. The parameters, if any, should not be specified. They will be described in the attribute file or files.

Note that the external declaration is given at exactly the place where the full class declaration was given, so as not to violate the rule concerning declaration inside the block enclosing the prefixed block.

Example 16.3b shows the same program with a slight twist. It may be that the particular SIMULA system has file names which do not conform to the syntax of SIMULA identifiers. It may be that you need to show that the attribute files for the class are in another directory or belong to a different user. It may even be that you wish to give the class a different name in your program to the one it had when it was

(a)   begin

      external class MyFeatures;

      MyFeatures
      begin
        OutLine("First");
        DoubleSpace("Second");
        OutLine(Fourth")
      end- -of-- prefixed-- block

    end**of**program

(b)   begin

      external class MyFeatures = "ERCS12.MYFEATURESATR";

      MyFeatures
      begin
        OutLine("First");
        DoubleSpace("Second");
        OutLine("Fourth")
      end--of--prefixed--block

    end**of**program

Example 16.3 Using a separately compiled class as a block prefix

separately compiled. The use of an 'external identifier' as well as an 'internal identifier' can allow for all of these.

The external identifier is an optional addition in an external declaration. It follows the internal identifier, separated by an equal sign and enclosed in double quotes. The use made of this string is system dependent, although I have tried to give examples of typical uses.

The example in 16.3b shows how it would be possible to specify on the 2900 EMAS SIMULA system that the attribute files for the class known with the program as MyFeatures actually belong to user ERCS12.

Yet again, read the documentation carefully to see how your system interprets the external identifier.

Note how much more compact even such a trivial program can become.

Exercises

16.1 Try out the separate compilation features of your SIMULA system, using example 16.3.

16.2 Rewrite example 16.2 using separate compilation.

16.3 Start building your own libraries. Remember to include only items needed for a particular type of programming in each one.

Other possibilities with prefixed blocks

It is possible to have classes as well as procedures inside the prefixing class. This would allow us to have the list-processing facilities which we developed in Chapter 10 available in a package.

It is also possible to use one separately compiled class to prefix another. This would allow one package to be an extension of another. This is important, because a block can only be prefixed by one class. To make the attributes of two separately compiled classes available, it is necessary to make one a sub-class of the other and use the sub-class as a prefix.

A common way of organizing this is to have your most widely used features declared in a basic class. This is then used to prefix a wide range of more specialized classes. These can, in turn, be used to prefix even more specialized ones and so on. Examples 16.4a, b and c show how this works.

(a) The parent class, compiled separately

```
class MyFeatures;
begin
    procedure OutLine(T); text T;.......;
    procedure DoubleSpace(T); text T;.......;
    etc.
end--of--MyFeatures;
```

(b) A more specialized sub-class, also compiled separately

```
external class MyFeatures;
MyFeatures class LinkList;
begin
    class Linker;.......;
    class ListHead;.......;
    etc.
end--of--LinkList;
```

(c) A program using LinkList

```
begin

    external class LinkList;

    LinkList
    begin
      ref(Linker) L;
      Linker class LinkObj;.......;
      etc.

      OutLine("Hello");
      etc.
    end--of--prefixed--block;

end**of**program
```

Example 16.4 Sub-class prefixing of blocks

This ability to extend the language according to the special needs of a user led the original designers of SIMULA to call it the 'Common Base Language'. Their intention was that very few people would need to write in straight SIMULA. Most would use packages of ready-built components suited to their needs.

Instructions in prefixing classes

The class which prefixes a block can contain instructions and an inner statement, in the same way as any other class. These are executed in the same way as for a class which prefixes another class.

The instructions up to the inner statement, if present, or the final end, if not, are executed when the block which is prefixed is entered. If there is an inner statement, the instructions which follow it are executed when the prefixed block is left through its final end. Example 16.5 shows a trivial example of this.

The initial sequence can be used to set values in variables, print headings and any other preliminary tasks. The prefixed block is then executed. The sequence after an inner can then be used to tidy up, print summaries, close files or any concluding tasks.

(a) The separately compiled class

```
class TopandTail;
begin
   OutText("Top and Tail, version 1.1");
   OutImage;
   inner;
   OutText("Top and Tail has finished");
   OutImage
end--of--TopandTail;
```

(b) A program using TopandTail

```
begin

   external class TopandTail;

   TopandTail
   begin
      OutText("The prefix block's actions come here");
      OutImage
   end--of--prefixed--block

end**of**program
```

Example 16.5 Prefixed block with actions

Programs as prefixed blocks

In fact the program block is really inside a prefixed block, whose prefix does not have to be written. This brings into the program two libraries of system features, one of which prefixes the other.

The outermost class is called Environment. This contains the system procedures not connected with files, such as Call.

This class prefixes one called BasicIO, which contains the declarations of File and all its sub-classes. SysIn and SysOut are declared here.

These classes can be regarded as having been separately compiled to produce the runtime system. We have already seen most of the contents of BasicIO. The environment is covered more fully in Chapter 20.

When you write

```
begin
    . . .

    . . .
end + + of + + program
```

it is interpreted by the system as

```
BasicIO(InLength,OutLength)
begin
  inspect SysIn do
    inspect SysOut do
    begin

        . . .

        . . .
    end + + of + + program
end − − of − − prefixed − − block − − and − − inspections
```

Fig. 16.1 The program as a prefixed block.

A normal program can be regarded as being as shown in Fig. 16.1. Note that BasicIO is shown as having two parameters. These are the image lengths to be used for SysIn and SysOut respectively. They are set by the system to match the devices being used for default input and output.

Using externally declared items directly

It is also legitimate to compile a class or procedure separately for use as a simple class or procedure. It is not just prefixes of blocks which can be treated in this way.

Such classes and procedures are introduced by external declarations, as we have seen with prefixing classes. For a procedure, the keyword *procedure* is used where previously the keyword *class* was. Having been declared in this way, these procedures may then be used as if they had been fully declared inside the program.

The types of block in a SIMULA program

We have now covered all the types of block which can occur in a

SIMULA program, and so a brief summary is perhaps in order.

Program block is the outermost block of a full program. Everything from its *begin* to its *end* is part of the main program. It acts as if it were enclosed by an invisible block prefixed by BasicIO and as if it was within nested inspection blocks for both SysIn (the outer inspection) and SysOut (the inner). BasicIO is a sub-class of class Environment (see Chapter 20).

Sub-block is any sequence of instructions enclosed within a *begin/end* pair, containing at least one declaration and not falling into any other category of block. Note that it might contain only declarations. If it contains only statements and no declarations, it is a compound statement and not a block.

Procedure body is the statement following the header of a procedure, which specifies the actions to be performed by that procedure. It is regarded as a block even if it is a simple statement or a compound statement, containing no declarations.

Class body is the equivalent of a procedure body for a class.

Prefixed block is any sequence of instructions enclosed within a *begin/end* pair and prefixed by a class identifier. It is regarded as a block even if it contains no declarations, unlike a sub-block.

Inspection block occurs inside inspection statements. Those statements within the *when* clauses, *otherwise* clauses or, within simple inspection statements, following the *do* are all inspection blocks. They are regarded as blocks even when they are simple statements or compound statements containing no declarations.

The significance of declarations within blocks, especially on access to those items, is considered further in Chapter 18, when the concept of 'scope' is considered in some detail.

External declaration of non-SIMULA procedures

As well as useful libraries of SIMULA classes and procedures, it is often important to be able to use libraries of procedures written in other programming languages. Mathematical and graphical libraries are common examples, which are often written in FORTRAN or the assembly language of a particular computer. The syntax of SIMULA allows for such procedures being used in SIMULA programs, but, unfortunately, different SIMULA systems have interpreted the meaning of such declarations rather differently.

It is not sensible to cover all the variations here. The only reliable guide is the documentation for the system you are using.

Be especially careful that such differences do not cause problems when moving your programs from one system to another. Check also the range of parameter types allowed, which can be very different between systems where 'foreign' language procedures are used.

One useful device is to create a separately compiled class containing SIMULA procedures which call all the non-SIMULA procedures in a particular library. This class is then the only place where the non-SIMULA procedures need to be declared. Any programs using them can be prefixed with the class containing their declarations and use the SIMULA procedures which call them. This means that when you move to another system, only the interfacing class needs to be changed to match the form of non-SIMULA external declaration for that system.

Summary

- We have seen how to make a package of features available, using a prefixed block.
- We have seen how separately compiled SIMULA modules, especially packages contained in classes, can be used through external declarations.
- The notion of the program block as being enclosed in an invisible prefixed block and two inspections has been introduced. This explains the presence and meaning of system features in SIMULA.
- A summary of the types of block possible in SIMULA has been given.
- We have noted that it is possible to use separately compiled procedures from other programming languages by making external declarations. We have also noted that the use of such declarations varies widely amongst existing SIMULA systems and the problems that this can cause, when moving programs from one to another.

Chapter 17

More complex list handling — SIMSET

Back to real problems

We have spent several chapters learning new features of SIMULA. Let us spend rather more time on their application in the next few pages.

The importance of lists was demonstrated in Chapter 10. It is widely accepted today that list processing is a very powerful part of programming. Several languages have been developed which are based on this idea.

Like many languages, SIMULA includes facilities which make handling lists of objects possible. The key ones are reference variables, which allow pointers or links, and sub-classes, which allow objects of different types to be linked together, so long as they have a common parent. The ability to distinguish to which sub-class each item on a list belongs enhances the second of these. The use of *is*, *in* and *inspect* allows lists of objects to be processed safely.

Safe access

The concept of security in accessing objects is more important than may sometimes be realized. Some languages do not allow lists of objects of different types at all. This is safe, since a location in an object cannot be accessed in the mistaken belief that it is an attribute of an object of another type. On the other hand, some languages allow pointers to reference any object, regardless of type. This allows lists to be used more widely, but is totally unsafe.

Consider Fig. 17.1. It shows three objects, which might correspond to the class declarations under them. What would happen if the same pointer could be used to access the attributes of all three? With no way of checking which was which type, it would clearly result in chaos.

As an example, the program might wish to assign to the integer location in object A. If it does not know whether the object is an A, B or C object its task is hopeless. It either assigns to that location, whatever the object, or does nothing. If it assigns to a B object by

A	B	C
class A;	class B;	class C;
begin	begin	begin
integer Var1;	real Var1;	ref(B) Var1;
real Var2;	ref(A) Var2;	character Var2;
Boolean Var3;	text Var3;	integer Var3;
end + + of + + A;	end + + of + + B;	end + + of + + C;

Fig. 17.1 Potential access conflicts in objects.

mistake, the location is actually used to hold a real. If it assigns to a C object, the location actually holds a reference variable. Clearly the only safe thing is to do nothing and so such a language is much weaker than SIMULA. To be fair, some languages allow a limited sub-typing capability. This is usually done through 'variant records'. This means declaring all the possible sub-classes as alternatives inside the parent class declaration. This can be more secure, but is also much more restricting. It does not allow a parent class to be separately compiled and then extended at will in the main program, for instance. All possible variations are fixed in the original declaration.

This type of language usually has no equivalent of *inspect* or *is*. It may allow you to say what sub-type you wish to use rather like half an *inspect* or a limited *qua* or it may check the actual type and behave accordingly, but not as flexibly as SIMULA.

SIMULA is almost alone in allowing secure and flexible access to sub-types and in allowing the range of such sub-types to be easily extended. It is uniquely suited to certain kinds of list processing.

A first practical example

Consider a firm wishing to keep records of all its customers. From time to time it sends out brochures on various types of goods that it sells. It only wishes to send such information to customers who have bought goods of that type before. It will want to build up lists of customers on this basis. Since some customers will have bought several types, some records may be on several lists.

One way of coping with the problem is to use a class with pointers for each type of goods to be considered. Each record can be read from a DirectFile and a class object generated to correspond to it. Instead of copying the contents of the record into the object, the index number is entered. The object is then entered on the lists corresponding to its previous purchases.

A skeleton for this program is shown in example 17.1. It assumes that the Image read from the DirectFile has fixed-length fields, corresponding to the details of that customer. These include the categories of goods available, each a one-character field set to 'N' for no purchase and to 'P' for a past purchase. Where such a field is a 'P' that record's indexing object is added to the corresponding list in the program.

This simple example is intended to refresh your memory and get us back to practical problems. It demonstrates simple one-way lists and the use of multiple lists or cross referencing as it is more widely known.

```
begin

   class Customer(Index); integer Index;
   begin
      ref(Customer) Gears, Bearings, Bolts;
      text Ident;
   end--of--Customer;

   ref(Customer) Gears, Bearings, Bolts, NewRecord;
   ref(DirectFIle) PastRecords;
   text Record;

   PastRecords :- new DirectFile("Purchases");
   PastRecords.Open(Blanks(132));

   inspect PastRecords do
   while not EndFile do
   begin

      Record :- InText(132);
      NewRecord :- new Customer(Location);
      if Record.GetChar='P' then
      begin    ! Previous purchaser of Gears;
         NewRecord.Gears :- Gears;     ! Add to Gears list;
         Gears :- NewRecord
      end;
      if Record.GetChar='P' then
```

```
begin    ! Previous purchaser of bearings;
   NewRecord.Bearings :- Bearings; ! Add to Bearings list;
   Bearings :- NewRecord
end;
if Record.GetChar='P' then
begin    ! Previous purchaser of bolts;
   NewRecord.Bolts :- Bolts;        ! Add to Bolts list;
   Bolts :- NewRecord
end;

NewRecord.Ident :- Copy(Record.Sub(4,129))
end..of..while..loop..and..inspect

end**of**program
```

Example 17.1 Customer records on multiple, one-way lists

Exercise

17.1 Complete the program in example 17.1 to print out lists of customers in each category as labels for mailing. Create a file of records and test it out. Refine it to prompt for the category wanted for this mailing and to produce only that list.

Backwards and forwards

One limitation of our lists so far has been the difficulty of moving backwards along them. How, for instance, could we find the preceding record once we had printed an object on our list of Gear customers in example 17.1? We would have to go back to the start and read through until we found the object pointing to the one currently being accessed.

A practical application where this might be a problem is in searching lists held in alphabetical order. If the name we want begins with the letter Z, we still have to read through all the other letters to find it. A human searching in a telephone book would probably save a lot of time by starting at the last page and searching backwards.

Another application, which returns to our text-editing project, is to hold the current document as a list of line objects, with a text attribute to hold the contents. It would clearly be highly desirable to be able to move backwards as well as forwards when editing. To do this we need a two-way list.

Example 17.2 shows a simple version of such an editor. It reads in a file's contents as a linked list. Each object represents a line in the file and has two pointers to other line objects. These are called Previous and Next. Previous always points to the line before the current one, Next always points to the line after.

```
begin

   ref(InFile) Input;
   ref(OutFile) Output;

   text procedure InLine;
   begin
      InImage;
      InLine :- Copy(SysIn.Image.Strip)
   end++of++InLine;

   procedure OutLine(T); text T;
   begin
      OutText(T);
      OutImage
   end++of++OutLine;

   class LineRec(Tex); text Tex;
   begin
      procedure AddTo(List); ref(Link_List) List;
      begin
         if List.Last=/=None then List.Last.Next :- this LineRec;
         this LineRec.Prev :- List.Last;
         List.Last :- this LineRec;
         if List.First==None then List.First :- this LineRec
      end--of--AddTo;

      procedure Add_Before(Record); ref(LineRec) Record;
      begin
         if Record.Prev=/=None then
         begin
            Record.Prev.Next :- this LineRec;
            Prev :- Record.Prev
         end..of..if;
         Record.Prev :- this LineRec;
         Next :- Record
      end--of--Add_Before;

      ref(LineRec) Next, Prev;
   end++of++LineRec;
```

```
class Link_List;
begin
   ref(LineRec) First, Last;
end++of++Link_List;

ref(LineRec) Current;
ref(Link_List) Lines;
character Command;
integer Reps, Count;

Input :- new InFile("Source");
Output :- new OutFile("Output");
Lines :- new Link_List;

comment First read in the file;
inspect Input do

begin
   Open(Blanks(80));
   while not EndFile do new LineRec(InText(80)).AddTo(Lines);
   Close
end++of++inspect++Input;


comment Now process commands from SysIn;
Current :- Lines.First;
while Command ne 'E' do
begin
   if Command ne '!0!' then Reps := InInt;
   InImage;
   if Command='M' then
   begin   ! Move forward or backwards;
      if Reps>0 then
      begin
         for Count := 1 step 1 until Reps do
         begin
            if Current.Next==None then OutLine("***End of file***")
               else Current :- Current.Next
         end
      end else
      if Reps<0 then
      begin
         for Count := 1 step 1 until -Reps do
         begin
            if Current.Prev==None then OutLine("***Start of file***")
            else Current :- Current.Prev
         end
```

```
       end
     end else
     if Command='I' then
     begin   ! Insert new lines;
       for Count := 1 step 1 until Reps do
          new LineRec(InLine).Add_Before(Current)
     end else
     if Command='D' then
     begin   ! Delete lines forwards or backwards;
       if Reps>0 then
       begin
          Current :- Current.Prev;
          for Count := 1 step 1 until Reps do
          if Current.Next==None then OutLine("***End of file***") else
          begin
             Current.Next :- Current.Next.Next;
             Current.Next.Prev :- Current
          end
       end else
       if Reps<0 then
       begin
          Current :- Current.Next;
          for Count := 1 step 1 until -Reps do
          if Current.Prev==None then OutLine("***Start of file***") else
          begin
             Current.Prev :- Current.Prev.Prev;
             Current.Prev.Next :- Current
          end
       end
     end==of==D;

   OutLine(Current.Tex);
   Command := InChar
end++of++command++loop;

Comment Now write out file;
Current :- Lines.First;
inspect Output do
begin
   Open(Blanks(80));
   while Current=/=None do
   begin
      OutText(Current.Tex);
      OutImage;
      Current :- Current.Next
   end;
```

```
    Close
  end++of++inspect++Output;

  OutLine("Edit finished")
end**of**program
```

Example 17.2 A line editor using a two-way list

The program will accept four commands, given as single characters followed by an integer. Several commands may be given on a single line.

The letter 'M' means move forwards or backwards; the integer specifies how many lines to move. Positive integers mean forwards, negative integers mean backwards.

The letter 'D' means delete the number of lines specified, starting with the current line. A positive number means delete forwards, a negative number means delete backwards.

The letter 'I' means insert the number of lines specified in front of the current line. Only positive numbers are accepted. The lines are read from SysIn until the required number have been given. The next line is again assumed to contain commands.

The letter 'E' means end the editing session, write the lines out to a file and stop the program.

Note the use of pointers. Check that you follow the way the program works.

Exercise

17.2 Add a command to move a line to a new location forwards or backwards. The integer should specify how far.

Lists held as 'trees'

There is one more type of list that is very useful and deserves to be covered in some detail before we look at SIMULA's built-in, list-handling package. This last type is very different from the one- and two-way lists that we have used so far. It is usually known as a 'tree structured' list.

The idea of a tree structure is to allow very rapid storage and retrieval of data which is held in some order — usually numerical or

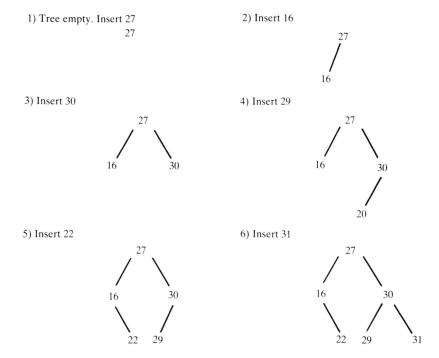

1) Tree empty. Insert 27

2) Insert 16

3) Insert 30

4) Insert 29

5) Insert 22

6) Insert 31

Fig. 17.2 Building a tree sorted list.

alphabetical. It may also be used for other special purposes, but we are not concerned with those here. The use of trees is, incidentally, a nice example of recursion.

Figure 17.2 shows the building up of a tree-structured list, used to hold items in numerical order. Study it closely before reading on, as a diagram is probably the easiest way to understand such a structure.

The most obviously striking feature of such a tree is that it is shown growing downwards. This is only a convention, but I have shown it that way to avoid confusion if you see it elsewhere. More importantly, the tree always branches into two, or one, new twigs. This type of tree is called a 'binary' tree, because it always subdivides into two new paths.

The building of the tree follows a simple pattern. Each new value is attached to an existing value, so that it forms the left branch from that value if it is smaller than it or the right branch if it is greater. Only values with an unfilled left or right branch may be used to attach a new value. These are either at the ends of branches, and have both left and right free, or next to the end, and have only one of left or right free.

The important rules governing this process of construction are the ones which govern which existing value in the tree is chosen to have the new branch for the new value attached to it. These rules ensure that the final tree is indeed held in order and, consequently, allows other related rules for searching the tree for a value.

The rules for adding a value are as follows.

(a) Start at the head of the list, i.e. with the first value put into the tree.

(b) If the head is empty, use that to hold the new value. This is now the first value to be put into the tree.

(c) If the head contains a value, compare it to the new value. If the new value is less than the head's, follow the left branch; if it is greater, follow the right. (The question of how to behave if the two values are equal can only be answered in the light of the use to which the list is to be put.)

(d) If the branch followed is empty, use it to hold the value.

(e) If the branch is not empty, compare its value to the new value. If the new value is less, follow the left branch; if it is greater, follow the right.

(f) Repeat (d) and (e) until a home is found for the value.

Follow these rules through using Fig. 17.2. Check that they really do describe how the tree was built.

You will have noticed that rule (f) simply tells us to repeat (d) and (e) until we succeed. It might be sensible to use a mechanism which embodies this idea. The *while* loop is one such mechanism, but recursion provides the most compact solution. The set of rules (or algorithm) given above is a recursive one. The same actions are performed for a succession of sets of data (objects) until some condition is satisfied. A *while* loop is more suited to repeating the same actions on the same object.

Example 17.3 builds the tree shown in Fig. 17.2, using a *for* loop to supply the values. The building rules are encapsulated in the procedure AddOn. This is given two ref(Val) parameters. The first is the branch to be followed, the second the new Val object which is to be found a home. Check this through once more comparing the rules, the procedure and the diagram.

The second part of the example searches for three of the values in the tree and one which is not present. It too uses a recursive procedure

```
begin

   class Number(Val); integer Val;
   begin

      procedure AddOn(Link); name Link; ref(Number) Link;
         if Link==None then Link :- this Number else
         if Val>Link.Val then AddOn(Link.Right) else AddOn(Link.Left);

      ref(Number) Left, Right;

   end..of..Number;

   procedure LookFor(Val,Link); integer Val; ref(Number) Link;
      if Link==None then
      begin
            OutText("Value not in tree ");
            OutInt(Val,4);
            OutImage
      end else
      if Val=Link.Val then
      begin
         OutText("Number found");
         OutInt(Val,4);
         OutImage
      end else
      if Val>Link.Val then
      begin
         OutText("Following right link");
         OutImage;
         LookFor(Val,Link.Right)
      end else
      begin
         OutText("Following left link");
         OutImage;
         LookFor(Val,Link.Left)
      end..of..Look..For;

   ref(Number) Head;
   integer Count;

   for Count := 27, 16, 30, 29, 22, 31 do new Number(Count).
               AddOn(Head);
   for Count := 27, 22, 33, 31 do LookFor(Count,Head)

end**of**program
```

Example 17.3 Building the tree in Fig. 17.2

and prints out the route taken at each branch, so that we can follow its working. Run it and see if it behaves as you expect.

Exercises

17.3 Write down the algorithm used by the search procedure in example 17.3, as a set of rules.

17.4 It is also useful to be able to find a value which follows one already known. Add a recursive procedure to example 17.3, called Next, which returns an integer value when passed an integer parameter. The value returned should be the one in the list which is the nearest one following that given. Note that the value passed need not be in the tree for a result to be found.

The advantages of trees

In most cases the use of tree structured lists for the purposes shown is quicker than the use of simple linked lists. The number of values checked in a search is fewer, since whole branches are eliminated at once. You may wish to try reworking Fig. 17.2 and example 17.3 with a simple list structure and see, by hand or by using the measure of time taken for the program to run, whether this holds true. The bigger the list, the greater the benefit.

A tree is not better when you merely wish to follow a list. Insertion, deletion and location of specified entries are what it is good at.

System class SIMSET

The remainder of this chapter is concerned with one of SIMULA's two ready-made packages. It is held in a class called SIMSET and contains building blocks for two-way linked list handling. It is different from our earlier two-way lists in that it holds its lists as circles of objects rather than straight lines. In SIMULA, such a list is known as a Set.

Example 17.4 shows most of the attributes. We shall look at it first and then consider a full list of the features of SIMSET.

The example is a program for reading and printing examination marks. It reads a name, followed by an integer mark. It then prints a list of names and corresponding marks. Finally it prints a sort of inverted histogram, with ten columns. Each student whose results fall

within the appropriate range is printed in that column. A maximum
name length is printed, to keep the columns straight.

```
SIMSET
begin
   ref(Head) array HistoChart(0:9);
   ref(Head) MixedList;
   integer Count;
   Boolean MoreLeft;
   text Student;
   ref(Link) NextRec, ThisRec;
   ref(Link) array CurrentRec(0:9);

   Link class MarkHolder(Student,Mark); integer Mark;text Student;;

   MixedList :- new Head;
   Student :- InText(32);
   while Student.Sub(1,1) ne "*" do
   begin
      new MarkHolder(Student,InInt).Into(MixedList);
      InImage;
      Student :- InText(32)
   end--of--reading;

   for Count := 0 step 1 until 9 do HistoChart(Count) :- new Head;
   NextRec :- MixedList.First;
   while NextRec=/=None do
   begin
      ThisRec :- NextRec;
      NextRec :- ThisRec.Suc;
      inspect ThisRec when MarkHolder do
      begin  ! Must inspect to allow access to Mark and Student;
         OutText(Student);
         OutInt(Mark,8);
         OutImage;
         if Mark=100 then Into(HistoChart(9))
         else Into(HistoChart(Mark//10))
      end..of..inspect
   end--of--sorting;

   for Count := 0 step 1 until 9 do
   begin
      CurrentRec(Count) :- HistoChart(Count).First;
      if CurrentRec(Count)=/=None then MoreLeft := True
   end;
```

```
    if MoreLeft then OutText( "  0-9    10-19   20-29   30-39
40-49  50-59" "  60-69   70-79   80-89   90-100")
            else OutText("Lists empty");
  OutImage;
  while MoreLeft do
  begin
    MoreLeft := False;
    for Count := 0 step 1 until 9 do
    begin
      inspect CurrentRec(Count) when MarkHolder do
      begin
        if Mark=100 then

        begin
          OutText("*");
          OutText(Student.Sub(1,7))
        end else OutText(Student.Sub(1,8));
        if Suc=/=None then MoreLeft := True
      end..of..clause
      otherwise OutText("        ");
      if CurrentRec(Count)=/=None
          then CurrentRec(Count) :- CurrentRec(Count).Suc
    end--of--for;
    OutImage
  end++of++while

end**of**program
```

Example 17.4 The use of SIMSET

The record for each student is kept in an object which is a sub-class of Link. Link is defined in SIMSET with a forward pointer, Suc, and a backward pointer, Pred, both of which are returned by procedure calls rather than being directly accessible.

The complete list is held in the Set defined by the Head object, MixedList. Head has a pointer to the start of the list, First, and a pointer to the end, Last. Again, these are only accessible as results from ref (Link) procedures.

Once the list is complete, which is indicated by an asterisk for the next name, the list headed by MixedList is read through and each record is printed out, before being moved to the list headed by the appropriate entry in the ref(Head) array HistoChart. This has ten elements, which correspond to results in the range $0-9$, $10-19$, etc. up to $90-100$.

The 'histogram' is then printed. Students with a perfect mark of 100 have an asterisk printed by their names.

The program could, of course, have been more concise. It is intended as a demonstration of SIMSET, not of how to perform a particular task. On the other hand, this program is capable of extension to perform more complex functions, where a no-nonsense program might not be.

A formal description of SIMSET

SIMSET is a special, separately compiled class available as part of every SIMULA system. It does not need to be declared before use. It can be used to prefix a block anywhere in a program, including, as example 17.4 showed, the program block itself.

As with all prefixed blocks, sub-classes of the classes declared within SIMSET may only be declared within the actual block which is prefixed, not within blocks local to this. References may be made to all such classes and sub-classes within local blocks, however.

There are three classes declared within SIMSET, one of which is a prefix to the other two. Let us look at them in turn.

Class Linkage

Linkage is the prefix of the other two classes in SIMSET. There are Link, representing Set members, and Head, representing the start and end of the Set. Prefixing by Linkage allows a reference to be made to either, where appropriate.

Linkage contains the basic linking attributes for forming lists. Here is a brief description.

ref(Link) procedure Prev returns a pointer to the item before this one in the list, if it is a Link object. If the previous item is the Head object it returns None.

ref(Link) procedure Suc returns a pointer to the item behind this one, if it is an object of class Link or a sub-class of Link. If the next item is the Head it returns None.

ref(Linkage) procedure Pred returns a pointer to the item before this one, whether it is a Link or Link sub-class object or a Head or Head sub-class object.

Notice how all the attributes of Linkage available to us are procedures, not simply ref(Linkage) variables. This prevents us assigning

H1 :- new Head

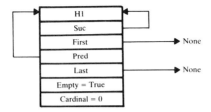

L1 :- new Link; L1.Into(H1)

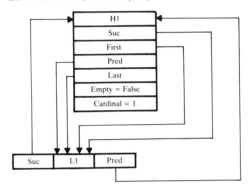

L2 :- new Link; L2.Into(H1)

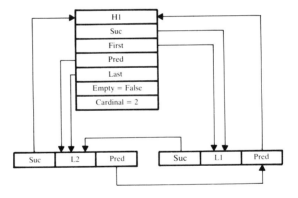

new values to them, except by the use of procedures local to Link and Head. This restriction stops us 'tinkering' with the objects and makes us think in object-oriented terms. This is a way of producing safe packages for use by inexperienced programmers. We shall look at how to write such packages in Chapter 18.

L3 :- new Link; L3.Precede(L2)

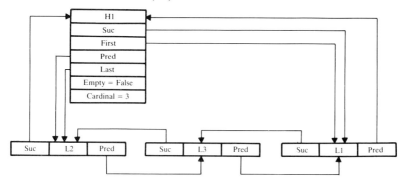

L1.Out

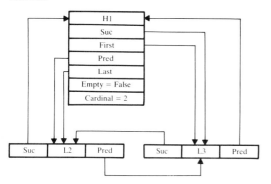

L1.Follow(L3)

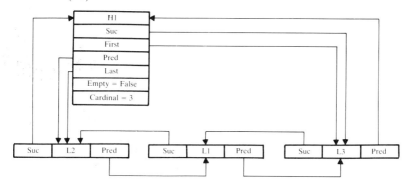

Fig. 17.3 SIMSET lists.

Linkage class Link

The items in the list of a Set are represented by objects of class Link or, more usefully, of sub-classes of Link. It adds four procedures to those inherited from Linkage.

procedure Out removes this item from the list. Its predecessor and successor will be linked, to heal the breach. If it is not currently in a Set, this procedure has no effect.

procedure Into has one ref(Head) parameter. It removes this object from any Set it is in at present and makes it the last item in the Set whose head is given as parameter.

procedure Follow has one ref(Linkage) parameter. It places this object after the one referred to by the parameter in the appropriate Set, after removing this object from any Set that it is currently in. If the parameter refers to a Head object the effect is to put this object into first place in the set. The effect is the same as Out if the parameter is None or does not belong to a Set and is not a reference to a Head object.

procedure Precede is exactly like Follow, except that it will attempt to place this object before the one referred to by the parameter. If the parameter refers to a Head object, the effect is the same as Into. (Think about the last statement, bearing in mind that this is a circular list structure.)

These include the only procedures that can be used to add items to a Set. Removal can only be achieved using these or one of the attributes of Head.

Linkage class Head

Head represents the whole Set. It will give pointers to both ends of the list and other information concerning it.

ref(Link) procedure First returns a pointer to the first item in this list. If the list is empty it returns None. It will always give the same result as a call of Suc for this Head object.

ref(Link) procedure Last returns a pointer to the last item in this list. If the list is empty it returns None. It will always give the same result as a call of Pred for this Head object.

procedure Clear removes all the Link items from this list, by calling Out for them.

Boolean procedure Empty returns True if this list is empty, otherwise it returns False.

integer procedure Cardinal returns the number of Link items currently in this list.

What a SIMSET list looks like

Figure 17.3 shows two SIMSET lists, starting with them empty and applying the various procedures mentioned in turn.

All of the features provided in SIMSET could be written in SIMULA. The reasons for providing them as a predefined package are first to encourage safe list-handling packages and second to allow them to be provided in an efficient form for even inexperienced programmers to use. The SIMULA Standard gives the SIMULA code for all of SIMSET, if you are interested.

Summary

- We have seen further uses of list structures, including new forms of list.
- We have used multiple lists, tree structures and two-way lists in various examples.
- We have seen the ready-defined list-handling facilities available in the system class SIMSET and learned of the features which it contains.

Chapter 18

Scope rules, virtuals and attribute protection

The scope of identifiers

It is a fundamental rule of SIMULA that an identifier cannot be used unless it has a matching declaration. The declaration defines the meaning of that identifier.

We have seen that a declaration made in an outer block is valid inside blocks which are enclosed by that block or which are prefixed by it, but not vice versa. This rule covers the use of identifiers declared in prefixing classes within sub-classes.

Further, we have seen that a declaration in an inner block will supercede that in an outer block where the names of the identifiers are the same. This is true even when the type of the declaration is the same in both outer and inner blocks. A different location is indicated for a variable, a different body for a procedure or a class.

This is a brief summary of the scope rules that we have used so far. They are very important and it is essential to grasp them fully.

In addition to these basic rules, we have seen that *when* and *qua* are provided and allow the scope rules for classes and sub-classes to be bent. They allow a reference to a parent to be extended to access an object of a sub-class or access to attributes of a class from a reference to a sub-class in which their identifiers have been redeclared. There are three more features of SIMULA which concern themselves with relaxing the scope rules for classes. This chapter will examine these in some detail.

The concept of virtual quantities

One feature of SIMULA which is found in almost no other programming language is the virtual declaration. This allows a declaration to be made in a parent class for a label, switch or procedure without a matching definition or with a definition which will only be used if no redefinition is made in a sub-class.

This reverses the normal rule about identifiers in inner blocks being inaccessible to outer blocks. As long as a virtual declaration is made in the prefixing class, any uses of that identifier in the body of the prefixing class will be assumed to refer to the declaration of that identifier within the body of the innermost class containing such a declaration.

This is rather simpler in practice than it sounds in theory. Let us use an example to show how it works in the simplest cases.

Example 18.1 shows a class Prefix containing two virtual declarations, a procedure Banner and a label Dest. Of these, only Dest is matched by an actual label in the body of Prefix. Banner is unmatched.

```
begin

    class Prefix;
        virtual: procedure Banner; label Dest;
    begin
        Banner;    ! Call a virtual procedure with no match here;
        goto Dest;
Dest:      ! Default match for goto, skips nothing;
        OutText("Dest in Prefix used");
        OutImage
    end++of++Prefix;

    Prefix class Stars;
    begin
        procedure Banner;
        begin
        OutText("**********************************");
        OutImage
        end--of--Banner;
        OutText("This should not be printed");
Dest:   ! This will replace the Dest in Prefix;
        OutText("Dest in Stars used");
        OutImage
    end++of++Stars;

    Prefix class Dashes;
    begin
        procedure Banner;
        begin
        OutText("---------------------------------");
        OutImage
        end--of--Banner;
        OutText("This should be printed"); ! No local match for Dest;
```

```
    OutImage;
    OutText("Dest in Prefix used");
    OutImage
  end++of++Dashes;

  new Stars;
  new Dashes;

end**of**program
```

Example 18.1 Virtual quantities

Prefix is used as a parent class to both Stars and Dashes. Each of these contains a procedure called Banner, providing a match for the virtual procedure in their parent. Only Stars contains a label called Dest to match the virtual declaration in Prefix.

Prefix contains a call on Banner. Since it has no match for this itself, the statement

    new Prefix

would be reported as a runtime error.

The statements

    new Stars   or
    new Dashes

are prefectly legal, however. The procedure declared in the sub-class is called from the parent's body, via the parent's virtual declaration, which is matched in the sub-class.

Prefix also contains a *go to* statement, which uses label Dest as its designational expression or destination. Since there is a matching label in the body of Prefix, this would cause no problems if *new* Prefix were used. For *new* Dashes, the only match would be the label in Prefix itself and so the goto would lead to this, with no effect from the virtual declaration. For *new* Stars the existence of a declaration of label Dest inside the body of the sub-class would cause the goto to jump to this rather than to the label in the parent. The scope rules are reversed.

Consider the example carefully and try to work out what its output would be like. Then, of course, you should run it to check.

What use is the virtual concept?

The virtual concept allows the writing of much more powerful classes, with the intention of using them as prefixes to specialized sub-classes. This is particularly useful when we want to create packages of such parent classes.

The parent class can be written as a template. Its actions can be calls on virtual procedures and jumps to virtual labels. These can be left as blanks, to be filled in by the sub-class, or given default matches in the parent class, which can be overidden by a sub-class.

Take a practical example. We want to provide a class for use as a prefix and we want this class to write messages at the start of its actions and at the end. It also contains some procedures for writing headings, and starting paragraphs. It is a simple component in a package.

These are all candidates for virtual procedures. They provide clearly defined facilities, for which meaningful defaults can be given. They are all likely to need to be tailored to fit some purposes.

Formal description of the virtual concept

The list of virtual specifications for a class comes after any parameter type specifiers and immediately before the statement which makes up the class body.

The syntax is the keyword *virtual*, followed by a colon, followed by a list of type specifiers separated by semi-colons. These are of the same form as the type specifiers for parameters, but only the types *label*, *switch*, *procedure* and type *procedure* are allowed.

Each identifier specified as virtual is either matched by a normal declaration inside the class body which follows or unmatched. It is not an error to use an unmatched virtual identifier inside this class body, so long as this class is only used to prefix sub-classes which contain a match.

When an object is created which has virtual quantities specified in one or more classes on its prefix chain, all these must be matched by declarations in those classes or in classes inner to them. Where matches exist at more than one equal or inner level, the innermost is used.

A final example of the virtual concept: The use of a virtual label

The virtual procedure has some obviously beneficial uses, but what about the virtual label? Example 18.2 shows one very important case, which could not be dealt with adequately in almost any other way.

The class SafeMaths is a package of specially safeguarded arithmetic features. Most are shown only in outline, but SafeDivide will demonstrate the general idea and is given in full.

Class SafeDivide has two virtual labels, ZeroAction and Perform, defined. Before performing its division the divisor is checked. If it is zero, the division will result in a runtime error. (I am sorry to get mathematical again. I am sure we all remember that an attempt to divide by zero is illegal in normal arithmetic.) To allow the program to continue, a goto is performed to ZeroAction when a zero divisor is

```
class SafeMths;
begin

   class SafeDivide(Dividend,Divisor); real Dividend, Divisor;
      virtual: label ZeroAction,Perform;
   begin
      real Result;
      if Divisor=0 then go to ZeroAction;
      go to Perform;
ZeroAction:
      Divisor := 0.0001;
      Inner;
Perform:
      Result := Dividend/Divisor;
Complete:
   end++of++SafeDivide;

   class SafeAdd(Val1,Val2); real Val1,Val2;
      virtual: label SafeLab;
   begin
      ! Various actions;
   end++of++SafeAdd;

   ! Various other maths classes;

end--of--SafeMaths;
```

Example 18.2 Use of virtual label in a package

found. If a non-zero divisor is found, a goto is carried out to the other virtual label, Perform, to avoid the zero actions. Here a normal real division is performed. This is followed by a non-virtual label at the end of the class, called Complete. Note that ZeroAction is placed before the Inner statement, while Complete and Perform are placed after it.

The instructions following ZeroAction provide a default sequence in the event of an attempt to divide by zero. The decision has been taken to replace zero with a suitably small decimal fraction and then divide. This removes the possibility of a runtime error, but may not give a suitable result. Example 18.3 shows a program using SafeMaths, where division is handled by a sub-class of SafeDivide. The sub-class has provided its own default action when a zero divisor is found.

```
begin
   external class SafeMths;
   SafeMths
   begin

   SafeDivide class MyDivide;
   begin
ZeroActions:   ! Override the default ZeroActions;
       Result := 9999999999999.9999999;
       go to Complete;
   end++of++MyDivide;
                 .
   OutFix(new MyDivide(6,0).Result,4,20);
   OutImage
   end..of..prefixed..block
end**of**program
```

Example 18.3 Use of package with virtual label, SafeMaths

By providing its own match for ZeroAction, the sub-class can choose to substitute a very large value for the result of the division. This would probably represent the largest legal value for a real on the particular system. The value in the example is chosen at random.

A tighter specification

Up-to-date SIMULA systems will allow you to specify the type of any result and of any parameters to a virtual procedure in its virtual specification (see example 18.6). Older systems will not support this.

Once such a virtual procedure is specified, all matches must have exactly the same form.

Exercises

18.1 Rewrite example 18.2 to redefine the normal actions for a divide to be those of subtraction. (NB Perform.)

18.2 What would be the effect of removing the inner statement in example 18.2?

18.3 Rewrite example 18.2 using a virtual procedure to replace the virtual label.

Keeping it in the family

One property of the classes that we have written so far is that all declarations made in them have been accessible remotely, by inspection if not always by dot notation. Yet when considering SIMSET I indicated that some attributes of class Linkage were not accessible in user programs. This feature is known as attribute protection and can be used to stop any attempts to meddle with attributes which are designed for internal use only. The file references returned by calls on SysIn and SysOut are also protected from direct use by programs. Although the files they represent are attributes of Environment class BasicIO which prefixes the main program block, these can only be reached by calling type procedures.

SIMULA allows two levels of protection of attributes. The first protects the attribute from use outside the body of the class, any subclasses or blocks prefixed by the class or its sub-classes. This is achieved by specifying that attribute as protected. Example 18.4 shows the use of a protected specifier.

Notice that the form of a protected specifier is the same as a type specifier or a mode specifier, although it is only allowed for classes.

The example shows the integer Tally specified as protected. This means that it can be accessed directly inside class Counter and Counter class DoubleCounter, but only through calls on Increment, Decrement and Total from the main program. The central attribute is kept safe from outside manipulation.

This feature allows object-oriented programming to become a much more powerful concept. A data structure can be defined which

```
begin

    class Counter;
        protected Tally;
    begin
        integer Tally;
        procedure Increment; Tally := Tally + 1;
        procedure Decrement; Tally := Tally - 1;
        integer procedure Total; Total := Tally;
    end++of++Counter;

    Counter class DoubleCounter;
    begin
        procedure Increment; Tally := Tally + 2;
        procedure Decrement; Tally := Tally - 2;
    end++of++DoubleCounter;

    ref(Counter) Count1;
    ref(DoubleCounter) Count2;
    integer I;
    Count1 :- new Counter;
    Count2 :- new DoubleCounter;
    for I := 1 step 1 until 10 do
    begin
        Count1.Increment;
        Count2.Decrement
    end..of..for;
    OutInt(Count1.Total,8);
    OutInt(Count2.Total,8);
    OutImage

end**of**program
```

Example 18.4 Use of *protected* specifier

can only be manipulated in ways which are also defined in the same
class declaration, as procedure attributes. Attempts at cheating by
manipulating them directly will be prevented.

At the same time, the range of defined operations on the data can
be extended, as can the data structure. This can be done by creating a
sub-class of the original definition.

The protected specification allows extensible but externally secure
objects for use in programming. The second level of protection allows
complete internal security as well.

An attribute must be specified as protected in the class where it is declared, not in an inner one.

Keeping it from the children

Once a class has been fully defined for a particular purpose it may be prudent to hide some of its attributes even from its own sub-classes. This is the case with the references returned by Suc and Pred in Linkage class Link of SIMSET. Even in sub-classes of Link they can only be accessed by procedure calls.

To achieve this an attribute must be specified as hidden as well as protected. It is not necessary to make an attribute hidden until some sub-class of that in which it is declared and specified protected.

The hidden specifier has exactly the same form as the protected specifier, except that the keyword *hidden* replaces *protected*.

If an attribute has been specified as virtual at an outer level, specifying it as hidden at the current level means that no matches will be made at levels inner to the current one.

Example 18.5 shows the use of hidden. Example 18.5a is a package used to prefix 18.5b. The integer Tally is not directly accessible outside the package, since it is specified hidden in classes Count and Double Count. The integer CheckValue is only accessible inside the class BasicCount, which prefixes both Count and DoubleCount.

You will notice that it is possible to specify an attribute both hidden and protected at once. This is done by using both keywords, *hidden* and *protected*, separated by at least one space, in the specifier. They may be used in either order.

The order of specifiers

We have now encountered all the specifiers in SIMULA. The complete list is mode, type, protection and virtual specifiers.

Procedures only use mode and type specifiers as appropriate. These were described in Chapter 6. The mode specifiers always come before the type specifiers, when both are present.

Classes use type, protection and virtual specifiers. Type specifiers are the same as those for procedures. The others have been described in this chapter. The order, when present, is type followed by protection followed by virtual specifiers.

(a) Package using both

```
class TallyPack;
begin

    class BasicCounter;
    hidden protected CheckValue;
    begin
        integer CheckValue;
        integer procedure CVal; CVal := CheckValue;
        CheckValue := 1;
    end++of++BasicCounter;

    BasicCounter class Counter;
        protected Tally;
    begin
        integer Tally;
        procedure Increment; Tally := Tally + 1;
        procedure Decrement; Tally := Tally - 1;
        integer procedure Total; if Total<CVal then Total := CVal
                                          else Total := Tally;
    end++of++Counter;

    Counter class DoubleCounter;
    begin
        procedure Increment; Tally := Tally + 2;
        procedure Decrement; Tally := Tally - 2;
    end++of++DoubleCounter;

    end--of--TallyPack;
```

(b) Program using 18.5a

```
begin
    external class TallyPack;
    TallyPack
    begin
        ref(Counter) Count1;
        ref(DoubleCounter) Count2;
        integer I;
        Count1 :- new Counter;
        Count2 :- new DoubleCounter;
        for I := 1 step 1 until 10 do
        begin
            Count1.Increment;
            Count2.Decrement
```

```
      end..of..for;
      OutInt(Count1.Total,8);
      OutInt(Count2.Total,8);
      OutImage
   end
```

end**of**program

Example 18.5 Use of *hidden* and *protected*

```
class Virtuous;
   virtual:procedure CharVal is character procedure CharVal(IntVal);
                                       integer IntVal;;
begin
   ! Declarations and actions;
end--of--Virtuous;
```

Example 18.6 Fully specified virtual procedure

Summary

- We have revised the basic scope rules which define where an identifier may be used once it has been declared. We have also covered the effects of redeclaring an identifier in an inner block.
- The concept of virtual specification has been introduced, allowing procedures, switches and labels to be used at prefix levels outer to their declarations or to be redefined at levels inner to their use.
- The concept of attribute protection has been dealt with. The two levels of protection specifications have been explained.
- We have now covered all the features of the SIMULA language. Only certain system features remain.

Chapter 19

Class SIMULATION

SIMULA and simulation

There is a widespread belief that SIMULA is a simulation language. This is the result of a misunderstanding which confuses the reason for the development of the language with its range of application. SIMULA was developed as a language with features which allowed certain kinds of simulation to be performed more easily on computers. These features were not then available in other languages. Some, like hierarchical types and virtual specification, are still almost unique to SIMULA.

Because it was developed with one application in mind, this does not mean that it was not intended as a general purpose language. Its authors always aimed at a design with the widest range of use. The idea of a common base language, referred to earlier, was central to their purpose. The language called SIMULA is extremely powerful and has proved suited to many areas of programming. Its recent evolution has taken it further in this direction.

The area where SIMULA reveals the background of its designers is not in the language itself, but in the standard packages which it provides. We have seen SIMSET, which is useful in all sorts of programs. The other package builds on SIMSET to provide tools for discrete-event simulation. This package is called SIMSET class SIMULATION.

It is not the purpose of this book to describe how discrete-event simulation works. If you are unfamiliar with it, consult the bibliography for references. You should still be able to follow the examples in this chapter, since they are intended as demonstrative of the features of class SIMULATION, not of the underlying theory.

A simple example

Example 19.1 introduces the two most important features of class SIMULATION, the real procedure Time and Link class Process. These are combined to produce a very simple model of a man operating a machine.

```
SIMULATION
begin
  integer Count;

  Process class Man(Mill); ref(Machine) Mill;
  begin
    while Time<400 do
    begin
      OutText("Loading starts");
      OutFix(Time,2,10);
      OutImage;    ! Report made;
      Count := Count + 1;    ! Keep a tally;
      Hold(5.0);
      Mill.Components := Mill.Components + 50;    ! Load up;
      Activate Mill;    ! Restart machine;
      while Mill.Components>0 do Hold(0.5);    ! Check regularly;
      Cancel(Mill);    ! Switch off;
      Hold(10.0);    ! Unloading takes longer;
      OutText("Unloading finishes");
      OutFix(Time,2,10);
      OutImage;    ! Report made;
    end--of--loop;
    Passivate
  end++of++Man;

  Process class Machine;
  begin
    integer Components;
    while True do
    begin
      OutText("Machine starts");
      OutFix(Time,2,10);
      OutImage;
      while Components>0 do
      begin
        Hold(2.0);    ! Machining time for one component;
        Components := Components - 1
      end..of..inner..loop;
      Passivate
    end--of--loop
  end++of++Machine;

  ref(Man) Worker;
  Worker :- new Man(new Machine);
  Activate Worker;
```

```
    OutText("Count = "); OutInt(Count,4); OutImage;
    Hold(800);
    OutText("Simulation ends"); OutImage
end**of**simulation
```

Example 19.1 Simple simulation using Time and Process

Process class Man shows the actions of the man. He performs four basic actions. He loads the machine with a new supply of components. He starts the machine. He checks at regular intervals to see if the machine has finished. He unloads the machine when it is finished.

Each action involves two things. The first is some representation of what the action achieves, such as adding 50 to the attribute Components of the machine that he is operating, to represent loading it. The second is some representation of the time taken for this. In the case of loading, this is a call of procedure Hold (5.0), where 5.0 is the time taken to complete the loading.

The starting of the machine involves specifying that the machine is to become active. Since we are dealing with coroutines this implies that the man will cease to be active at the same moment. The time element specifies that the activation is instantaneous. There are other scheduling possibilities when reactivating another Process, as we shall see.

The unloading involves a Hold to represent time taken.

A third, optional element of the representation of an action is a report from the program. This can be made before or after an action, or both. Clearly the program would have no point if it did not report on what was happening.

An alternative to printing every time an action is performed is to keep a count of the number of times it is carried out. Other statistics can also be accumulated. In the program, the number of times the machine is loaded is counted and printed at the end.

What is happening?

The coroutines in the program are both sub-classes of Process. This prefixing class contains a ref attribute which can link each Process object to an object of a class called EventNotice. When a Process object is scheduled it is linked to an EventNotice object and the EventNotice is placed in a list called the sequencing set.

Each EventNotice has a real attribute called EvTime. This is the time at which the associated Process coroutine is to be restarted. The list of EventNotices is in order of increasing time. The Process whose EventNotice has the lowest EvTime is the currently active Process and its EvTime is the current time, which is returned by real procedure Time.

Figure 19.1 shows the sequence of events in our simple program as changes in the sequencing set. This list is shown as a simple SIMSET Set, but is not necessarily held in that form. A tree list is often used.

Note the effects of Hold, Cancel, Passivate and Activate. Hold adds the specified amount to the EvTime of the EventNotice for that Process. Since the list is EvTime ordered, the EventNotice is shifted to its new place in the list. This will result in the next EventNotice's Process becoming active if the new place is not still first in the list.

Activate has the effect of moving the EventNotice of the specified Process to the head of the list. There are other forms of this statement which will move it to other places in the list.

Cancel removes the EventNotice for the specified Process from the sequencing set. When Man uses Cancel he stops the machine referred to by Mill.

Passivate cancels the current Process.

Link class Process

After an informal example, here is a more rigorous definition of class Process. Many of its internal attributes are inaccessible to programs, including the reference to its EventNotice. It may only be manipulated by the features described from here on.

All the visible attributes of Process are type procedures, giving information about the current state of the Process object. The possible states are as follows.

1 Active — the Process is the first in the sequencing set.

2 Suspended — the Process is in the sequencing set, but is not the first in the list.

3 Passive — the Process is not in the sequencing set, but its actions have not reached the final *end* in its class body. It may be rescheduled.

4 Terminated — the Process has passed through the final *end* of its class body. This automatically removes it from the sequencing set. It cannot be rescheduled.

a) Time 0.0. SIMULATION activates MAIN.

b) Time 0.0. MAIN activates Worker.

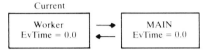

c) Time 0.0. Worker holds for 5.0.

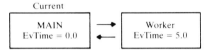

d) Time 0.0. MAIN holds for 800.0

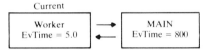

e) Time 5.0. Mill holds for 2.0

f) Time 5.0. Worker holds for 0.5.

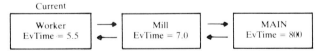

g) After numerous events: Time >= 400.0. Worker passivates.

h) Time 800. MAIN terminates.

Fig. 19.1 Starting and ending events in example 19.1.

5 Idle — the Process is either Passive or Terminated, i.e. it is not in the sequencing set. This state does not define whether the Process may be rescheduled.

State attributes

Boolean procedure Idle returns True if the Process is not in the sequencing set. Otherwise it returns False. This corresponds to the state described in 5 above.

Boolean procedure Terminated returns the value True if the Process has reached its final *end*. This corresponds to the state described in 4 above.

There is no simple way of discovering whether or not a Process is passive. The procedures Idle and Terminated must be used in combination, as follows:

passive = Idle and not Terminated.

Other attributes

Long real procedure EvTime will return the simulated time at which this Process is currently scheduled to become active. If this Process is currently Active, EvTime has the same value as the current simulated time. If this process is Idle, calling EvTime will cause a runtime error.

ref(Process) procedure NextEv returns a pointer to the next Process in the sequencing set. If there is no such Process or if that process is Idle, it returns none.

Scheduling Processes

When a Process is created, using *new*, it enters the passive state, calling Detach. It will not begin the actions defined by the programmer in the sub-class or -classes of Process, until it is scheduled and becomes active, i.e. is placed in the sequencing set and reaches the head of it.

The activate statement

It is not possible to write class SIMULATION in SIMULA because, as a prefixing class, it cheats. It contains an extra form of statement which is not allowed in SIMULA programs not prefixed by SIMULATION. When we, as ordinary users of SIMULA, write classes for use as prefixes in this way, we are not able to invent new language features. We can only build on what is already there.

This special statement is called an activation statement. It can only be used in SIMULA blocks or classes prefixed by class SIMULATION. Its task is to set the event time of a Process and insert it into the sequencing set, known as scheduling the Process.

Simple activate

The *activate* statement has a number of forms. We have already used the simplest in example 19.1.

activate Mill

This form makes the specified Process object the currently active one. This means giving it an event time equal to the currently simulated time and placing it in the sequencing set in front of the currently active Process.

Note that the previously current Process remains in the sequencing set, with its event time unchanged and one behind the newly activated Process.

Activate before and after

A second form specifies a position in the sequencing set relative to an object in the set. Two specifiers are provided, *before* and *after*. Their use is shown below.

activate Mill6 before Lathe2

will place Process object Mill6 in front of Lathe2 in the sequencing set. Lathe2 may be anywhere in the sequencing set. Mill6 will be given the same event time as Lathe2.

activate Mill6 after Lathe2

will place Process object Mill6 behind Lathe2 in the sequencing set, giving it the same event time.

In either case, if Lathe2 happened not to be in the sequencing set, nothing would be done to Mill6.

Activate with a delay

A third form allows a Process object to be activated a specified time after the current simulated time. Its simple form is shown by

activate Mill6 delay 6.5

which will give Mill6 an event time equal to the current simulated time plus 6.5. It is then added to the sequencing set at the appropriate place. If one or more Process objects are already present in the sequencing set with the same event time, the newly scheduled one will be placed after them.

If it is wished to place a newly scheduled Process object in front of any which are already in the sequencing set with the same event time, an additional keyword specifier is used, as in

activate Mill6 delay 6.5 prior

Activate at

Finally, it is possible to specify an event time absolutely rather than relative to the current simulated time. This has the same variants as when *delay* is used.

activate Mill6 at 10.2

The statement above gives Mill6 an event time of 10.2 and adds it to the sequencing set. If other Process objects are already present with the same event time, it is added behind them. To force it to be inserted in front of any such objects, the final version of the *activate* statement must be used, as in the example below.

activate Mill6 at 10.2 prior

Reactivate

activate statements have no effect if the Process is not already a passive member of the sequencing set. If you wish to schedule an object regardless of whether it is active, passive or suspended, you must use a *reactivate* statement. (Attempts to schedule terminated objects will cause runtime errors to be reported.)

The *reactivate* statement has exactly the same forms as the *activate* statement, with the keyword *activate* replaced by the keyword *reactivate*. Equivalent statements to those used above are:

> reactivate Mill6;
> reactivate Mill6 before Lathe 2;
> reactivate Mill6 after Lathe 2;
> reactivate Mill6 delay 6.5;
> reactivate Mill6 delay 6.5 prior;
> reactivate Mill6 at 10.2;
> reactivate Mill6 at 10.2 prior;

New keywords in activation and reactivation

The words *activate*, *reactivate*, *delay*, *prior*, *at*, *before* and *after* are all keywords in blocks and classes prefixed by class SIMULATION. Using them elsewhere in a SIMULA program will result in a compiler reported error.

Other scheduling mechanisms

Activation explicitly places Process objects in the sequencing set, in accordance with the implicit or explicit scheduling criteria given. Identical effects can often be produced by different forms.

There are other scheduling mechanisms and scheduling support mechanisms, all in the form of procedures. These are not language extensions and do not introduce new keywords. Thus they could, in theory, be written in SIMULA.

None of the following procedures are attributes of Process and so they are all used without remote accessing.

ref (Process) procedure Current returns a reference to the currently active Process. Since this contains the sequence of statements currently being executed, its EvTime attribute defines the current simulated time. In fact, all actions inside a class SIMULATION block can only occur when the object in which they are contained is Current or when they are in the main block.

long real procedure Time returns the current simulated time, which equals Current.EvTime.

procedure Hold has a single, long real parameter. It increases the event time at which the Process in which it is called by the amount of this parameter and moves it to the appropriate place in the sequencing set. If the new event time is greater than the event time of the second Process in the set, this second Process now becomes Current. Hold is used to specify the passage of time in a process which is being modelled as a Process object. This can correspond to a period of activity or a period of waiting.

procedure Passivate removes the Process object in which it is called from the sequencing set. This makes the object passive. It represents the start of an inactive, waiting period. Unlike Hold, it does not specify a duration for this period. The object may only be restarted by an Activate or Reactivate statement outside its own body, i.e. by the actions of another Process. This includes the main program block, as we shall see later.

procedure Wait has a single ref(Head) parameter. The Process in which it is called is removed from the sequencing set, in the same way as by Passivate. The Process object is then added to the list represented by the Set whose Head is passed as the parameter to Wait. It is inserted at the end of this Set. This represents the Process joining a queue, where it waits, passively. When it reaches the front of this queue or is selected from it by some other criterion it may be rescheduled, but again, only from outside itself.

procedure Cancel has a single ref(Process) parameter. It will remove the specified Process object from the sequencing set and make it passive. It differs from Passivate and Wait, in that any Process object may be passivated by another, not just by itself. It represents a Process making a decision to halt another.

A further example of SIMULATION — a receptionist

Example 19.2 shows a more complex model, using some of the features described above. In particular it shows the use of Wait to represent queuing.

The model shows an employment office, with two interviewers and a shared receptionist. New arrivals looking for work must register with the receptionist and then wait in one of the queues (lines), according to their desired type of employment. When the job hunter has been interviewed, he leaves.

Job hunters, the receptionist and the two interviewers are all active participants and so are represented as Process sub-class objects. Each

```
SIMULATION
begin

   ref(Head) ReceptionistQ, InterviewQ1, InterviewQ2;
   integer I, Manual;

   Process class Interviewer(Title, MyQueue); text Title;
                                   ref(Head) MyQueue;
   begin
      ref(Link) Next;
      inspect MyQueue do
         while True do ! Indefinite loop;
         begin
            if not Empty then
            begin
               Hold(3.5); ! Interview time taken as 3.5 minutes;
               Next :- First;
               Next.Out;
               activate Next after Current;
               Hold(3.0);    ! 3 minutes to clear desk;
            end else
            begin
               Hold(5.0);    ! Wait 5 minutes before checking queue again;
            end--of--one--sequence
         end++of++loop

   end==of==Interviewer;

   Process class JobHunter(SkillCategory); integer SkillCategory;
   begin
      OutText("Job hunter "); OutInt(SkillCategory,4);
      OutText(" joins receptionist queue at time "); OutFix(Time,4,8);
      OutImage;
      Wait(ReceptionistQ);
      OutText("Job hunter "); OutInt(SkillCategory,4);
      OutText(" joins interview queue"); OutImage;
      Hold(1.0);    ! 1 minute to join new queue;
      if SkillCategory=Manual then Wait(InterviewQ1)
                         else Wait(InterviewQ2);
      OutText("Job hunter "); OutInt(SkillCategory,4);
      OutText(" leaves employment office"); OutImage
   end==of==JobHunter;

   Process class Receptionist;
   begin
      ref(Link) Customer;
```

```
      while True do
      begin
        if not ReceptionistQ.Empty then
        begin
           Hold(2.0);
           Customer :- ReceptionistQ.First;
           Customer.Out;
           activate Customer;
        end else Hold(1.0)
      end
    end==of==Receptionist;
    Manual := 1;
    ReceptionistQ :- new Head;
    InterviewQ1 :- new Head;
    InterviewQ2 :- new Head;
    activate new Receptionist;
    activate new Interviewer("Manual",InterviewQ1);
    activate new Interviewer("Skilled",InterviewQ2);
    for I := 1,2,2,1 do
    begin
      Activate new JobHunter(I);
      Hold(2.0)
    end;
    Hold(100)
  end**of**program
```

Example 19.2 An employment office queuing model

has appropriate attributes and actions, including reporting on their actions, defined in the body of their sub-class.

Arrivals are parameterized, allowing job hunters with different skills to be generated from the same basic class. These attributes will determine which interviewer they see.

The queues are represented by sets and arrivals join them by calling Wait with the Set appropriate to their skill or the initial queue for the receptionist as parameter. The receptionist and the two interviewers check the queue of arrivals waiting to see them and take the first member of the Set, if any, each time they have completed an interview. They then reschedule this Process, allowing it to move to the next stage in its job search.

The delays are all given as real constants in this example. To produce a more realistically random effect, random drawing procedures could be used to provide delay values, according to appropriately chosen distributions. Those provided in SIMULA are outlined briefly in Chapter 20. Others are usually available from standard libraries on particular systems, such as the NAG library.

The Main Process

We have already implied that the block prefixed by class SIMULATION may be regarded as a Process, in that it can Hold, be the Current object, etc. Indeed for symmetry it is often useful to be able to schedule the prefixed block in the same way as user-defined Process objects. Within a block prefixed by SIMULATION, usually called the main block for the simulation model, all the actions of a Process object are legal.

To achieve this, class SIMULATION includes a hidden declaration of a sub-class of Process called Main_Program. This is used to create the main block's representative in the sequencing set. The body of this sub-class consists of a single statement, as shown below.

```
Process class Main_Program;
begin
   while True do Detach;
end--of--Main_Program;
```

As the last of its initialization actions, class SIMULATION creates a Main_Program object and schedules it for simulated time 0.0. This means that when the actions of the prefixed block commence, they follow a call of Detach inside this Main_Program object. This object is still at the front of the sequencing set and remains the currently active Process, but its Detach causes the statements in the prefixed block to be performed. Thus the currently active Process object uses the actions in the prefixed block as its own.

If Hold is called inside this block, it will act on the currently active Process object, i.e. the Main_Program object, rescheduling it for a later event time. This will cause the currently executing actions to leave the prefixed block's statements and enter those of the body of the new first in the sequencing set.

When the Main_Program object again reaches the front of the sequencing set and becomes active, it immediately calls Detach again. This takes it back to the prefixed block, at the instruction immediately following the one which caused the Main_Program object to be rescheduled, in this case Hold. Thus the Main—Program object again uses the actions of the prefixed block as its own and the effect of rescheduling it is seen to be equivalent to rescheduling the prefixed block.

This explains the method used to set the period of time covered by all or part of a simulation program. Both our examples so far contain a call on Hold in the main program block. This follows the setting up and starting of the other Process objects and puts the Main—Program object at the end of the sequencing set, with an event time equal to the desired length of time to be simulated. When this object reaches the front of the sequencing set it detaches back to the program block, allowing final reporting and termination of the program.

Where a simulation consists of several phases, it is possible to use several Holds in the program block. Each represents a particular part of the period being simulated.

If Passivate were to be called instead of Hold in the program block, the Main—Program block would never be re-entered and the simulation would continue for as long as any Process object remained in the sequencing set. Such a simulation's duration would be hard to predict, possibly running indefinitely. Normally Hold is used to fix a limit to the duration.

Warning over the use of Detach and Resume

The Process objects in a SIMULATION program should only be scheduled by using the mechanisms described in this chapter. All of these procedures depend on the use of Detach and Resume internally to achieve the correct effects, as we have seen with Main—Program. The Process objects exist as coroutines.

If you attempt to Detach or Resume a Process object explicitly, the effects could be disastrous for the scheduling mechanisms of SIMULATION. Detach and Resume should never be used in SIMULATION programs.

Utility procedure Accum

SIMULATION provides one further procedure, which is designed to be used for collecting certain information over a period of time during a simulation program. If you are not a mathematician you may skip

this section. If you are, the following formal description may be of
interest.

The procedure Accum is used to accumulate the 'system time
integral' of a real variable, C. This is regarded as a step function of
simulated time. Its integral is collected in long real variable A. B is the
time of the last update and D the current increment. Accum is given in
full.

```
procedure Accum (A,B,C,D); name A,B,C; long real A,B,C,D;
begin
    A:= A + C * (time — B);
    B:= Time;
    C:= C + D;
end ** of ** Accum;
```

A final example

Example 19.3 is another simulation using the features outlined in this
chapter. It shows a model of an office. Documents are written by
writers who pass them to the typing pool. The documents are typed by
typists who pass them to the photocopier. Copies are made and passed
to the mail room.

```
SIMULATION
  begin

    procedure Report;
    begin
      OutText("   *** Report ***"); OutImage;
      OutInt(Count,6); OutText(" documents printed, at time");
      OutFix(Time,2,8); OutImage
    end--of--Report;

    Process class Writer;
    begin
      ref(Typer) Typist;
      ref(Document) Doc;
      while True do
      begin
        Hold(8.0);
        Doc :- new Document;
        Typist :- TypingPool.First;
        Typist.Out;
```

```
        activate Typist
      end
   end--of--Writer;

   Process class Typer;
   begin
      Wait(TypingPool);
      while True do
      begin
         Hold(4.0);
         activate PhotoCopier;
         Wait(TypingPool);
      end
   end--of--Typer;

   Process class Copier;
   begin
      while True do
      begin
         Hold(1.0);
         Count := Count + 1;
         OutText("Document printed at ");
         OutFix(Time,2,10);
         OutImage;
         Passivate
      end
   end--of--Copier;

   class Document;;

   ref(Head) TypingPool;
   ref(Copier) PhotoCopier;
   integer I, Count;

   TypingPool :- new Head;

   for I := 1 step 1 until 10 do activate new Typer;
   PhotoCopier :- new Copier;
   activate new Writer delay 2.0;
   activate new Writer delay 4.5;
   Hold(100);
   Report;
   Hold(100);
   Report
end++of++program
```

Example 19.3 Simulation with two time periods

The model runs for 100 time units and then reports. It then restarts for a further 100 time units, reports and stops.

Note that the main program makes two holds in this time. It is often useful to create models which report at regular intervals, not just at the end. It may also be useful to change some factors at certain points. This may represent day and night, changes in weather, the seasons, rest breaks or many other alterations in the conditions under which the model is operating.

Summary

- This chapter has outlined very briefly the working of the standard prefixing class, SIMSET class SIMULATION. It has not dealt with the theory of simulation.
- The class Process has been explained.
- The procedures for scheduling and enquiring about the state of the simulation have been explained.
- The mechanism for scheduling the main program block has been outlined.

Chapter 20

The environment

The system facilities of SIMULA

The system facilities of SIMULA which are always present are attributes of class Environment and Environment class BasicIO. In addition, the attributes of class SIMSET and SIMSET class SIMULATION, which are declared in Environment, can be made available by using one of these as a prefix. We have considered all the attributes of SIMSET (Chapter 17) and SIMULATION (Chapter 19) and most of the attributes of BasicIO (Chapters 7 and 15). The first part of this chapter completes BasicIO and gives a complete list of the contents of Environment, only some of which have been covered so far.

The contents of both BasicIO and Environment have been enlarged considerably in recent years. It is likely that further extensions, such as new sub-classes of File, will be made in the next year or two. The lists given here cover the attributes defined in the 1986 SIMULA Standard.

It is important to check the documentation for the SIMULA system that you are using against the lists given here. Some features may be missing and extra ones may be present. The preceding chapters have tried, with the exceptions of ByteFile and some parts of DirectFile which are new in this standard, to use only the most generally available features in examples.

Terminate_Program — the missing part of BasicIO

As well as the File features described in Chapters 7 and 15, BasicIO contains a system procedure called Terminate_Program. This has no parameters.

When Terminate_Program is called the program ends as if a goto had been made to the final end of the program. Where the program is prefixed, the final end refers to the end of the prefixing class body.

Where the program is prefixed by a class containing an *inner* statement, this is the only way to guarantee that it stops immediately, except by forcing a deliberate runtime error.

312

The complete environment

Parts of the environment have been described earlier, some in mathematical appendices. The following is a complete list of the attributes of class Environment, to allow easy reference. Where a description has already been given, only a reference to this is given. Where it is mentioned for the first time, a brief definition is supplied.

Basic arithmetic operations

integer procedure Mod(I, J); integer I, J;   Returns the arithmetic modulo of I with respect to J, i.e.

> zero if I=J
> I−(I//J)*J if I and J have the same sign
> J+I−(I//J)*J if I and J have different signs.

integer procedure Rem (I, J) integer I, J;   Returns the remainder of I integer divided by J, i.e.

> I−(I//J)*J.

type procedure Abs (I); type I;   Returns the absolute value of I, where I may be of any type and the result will be of the same type, i.e.

> if I>=0 then result =I
> if I<0 then result =−I.

integer procedure Sign (I); type I;   Returns zero if the parameter, which may be of any type, is zero, plus one if it is positive and minus one if it is negative.

integer procedure Entier (R); real R;   Returns the integer value nearest to and less than or equal to R, i.e. 1.8 gives 1, −1.8 gives −2.

(long) real procedure AddEpsilon (R); (long) real R;   Returns the nearest real or long real value greater than the real or long real R, that the particular system is capable of distinguishing. See appendices A and B.

(long) real procedure SubEpsilon (R); (long) real R;   Returns the nearest real or long real value less than the real or long real R, that the particular system is capable of distinguishing. See appendices A and B.

Basic text and character handling

The following are described in Chapter 5:

text procedure Copy (T); text T;
text procedure Blanks (L); integer L;

The following are described in Chapter 12:

integer procedure Rank (C); character C;
integer procedure ISORank (C); character C;
character procedure Char (I); integer I;
character procedure ISOChar (I); integer I;
Boolean procedure Digit (C); character C;
Boolean procedure Letter (C); character C;

The following are described in appendix B:
character procedure LowTen (C); character C; Returns the current floating-point exponent marker and resets it to C.
character procedure DecimalMark (C); character C; Returns the current decimal-point character in real texts and resets it to C.

There are two further text-handling procedures:
text procedure UpCase(T); text T; Converts all characters which are letters in T to upper case, leaving T with its Pos at the end of the text frame. Returns a new reference to the text frame of T, with its Pos at the start of the frame.
text procedure LowCase(T); text T; Converts all characters in T which are letters to lower case, leaving the Pos of T at the end of the text frame. Returns a new reference to the text frame of T, with its Pos at the start of the frame.

Mathematical functions

SIMULA possesses a fairly extensive library of mathematical functions. Most are assumed here to be self-explanatory. All may be passed as either real or long real parameters. The values returned match the type of the parameters.
[long] real procedure SqRt(R); [long] real R; ! Square root;
[long] real procedure Sin(R); [long] real R; ! Sine;
[long] real procedure Cos(R); [long] real R; ! Cosine;
[long] real procedure Tan(R); [long] real R; ! Tangent;
[long] real procedure CoTan(R); [long] real R; ! Cotangent;

[long] real procedure ArcSin(R); [long] real R; ! Arcsine;
[long] real procedure ArcCos(R); [long] real R; ! Arccosine;
[long] real procedure ArcTan(R); [long] real R; ! Arctangent;
[long] real procedure ArcTan2(Y,X); [long] real Y,X; ArcTan2 returns a value in the range −Pi to +Pi. If Y is positive, the value returned is positive. If Y is negative, the value returned is negative. If Y is zero, the value returned is also zero if X is positive, or Pi if X is negative. If both X and Y are zero a runtime error occurs. The value is generally the same as ArcTan(Y/X).
[long] real procedure SinH(R); [long] real R; ! Hyberbolic Sine;
[long] real procedure CosH(R); [long] real R; ! Hyperbolic Cosine;
[long] real procedure TanH(R); [long] real R; ! Hyperbolic Tangent;
[long] real procedure LN(R); [long] real R; ! Natural logarithm;
[long] real procedure Log10(R); [long] real R; ! Base 10 logarithm;
[long] real procedure Exp(R); [long] real R; ! e to the power R;

Extremum functions

type procedure Max(V1, V2); type V1, V2;
type procedure Min(V1, V2); type V1, V2;

These return respectively the larger or smaller of the values of their two parameters. Legal types are character, text, long real, real, short integer and integer. The type returned matches the evaluated parameters, following the rules given for types of evaluated expressions in Chapter 3.

Environmental constants

Environmental constants allow programs to find out information about the particular SIMULA system on which they are running. This can be of great help in writing portable programs.

The first set reveal the range of arithmetic values and internal character values.

integer MaxRank is the highest internal representation of a character using the normal collating sequence of the system.

integer MaxInt is the longest value that can be held in an integer on the system.

integer MinInt is the smallest negative value that can be held in an integer on the system.

long real MaxLongReal is the largest value that can be held in a long real on the system.

long real MinLongReal is the smallest negative value that can be held in a long real on the system.

real MaxReal is the largest value that can be held in a real on the system.

real MinReal is the smallest negative value that can be held in a real on the system.

The others give information recorded by the compiler.

text procedure SIMULAId returns a text which identifies the current SIMULA system, the installation on which it is running and so on. For the details of what can be learned about a particular system, consult its documentation.

integer procedure SourceLine returns the line number in the SIMULA source where it is called.

User-defined errors can be signalled by calling the following:

procedure Error (T); text T; This causes the program to stop as if an error had occurred. The text T is printed as the runtime error message.

Array characteristics can be found from the following:

integer procedure UpperBound (A,I); type array A; integer I; Returns the upper bound of dimension I in array A. A can be of any type.

integer procedure LowerBound (A,I); type array A; integer I; Returns the lower bound of dimension I in array A. A can be of any type.

Date and time information are given by the following:

text procedure Date__Time; Returns a text containing the current date and time in the form

> YYYY-MM-DD HH.MM.SS.sss...

An example is   1985-11-26   08.39.23.00

long real procedure CPUTime; Returns the number of processor seconds used so far by the program.

long real procedure ClockTime; Returns the number of seconds since midnight.

Random numbers and drawing

There is an extensive library of random-number generating functions. All use a basic drawing from a uniform distribution from 0 to 1. This drawing uses an integer seed, which is passed by name to the appropriate function. The variable U is always used to represent this seed in the following descriptions. The matching actual parameter must always be an integer variable, which is set to the desired seed value before the first call and is never, normally, assigned to again in the program.

The use of the negative value of a seed as the seed to a second series of drawings will produce an antithetic series of random numbers. For suitable sizes of seeds, consult the documentation for your system.

Boolean procedure Draw (A,U); name U; long real A; integer U; Returns True and False. A is the probability that True will be returned.

integer procedure RandInt (A,B,U); name U; integer A,B,U; Returns an integer in the range A to B with uniform probability.

long real procedure Uniform (A,B,U); name U; long real A,B; integer U; Returns a long real in the range A to B, not including B, with uniform probability. A must be less than B.

long real procedure Normal (A,B,U); name U; long real A,B; integer U; Returns a long real value normally distributed about mean A, with standard deviation B.

long real procedure NegExp (A,U); name U; long real A; integer U; Returns a long real value from the negative exponential distribution with mean 1/A, defined by −LN(d/A), where d is a basic drawing.

integer procedure Poisson (A,U); name U; long real A; integer U; Returns an integer value from the Poisson distribution with parameter A. If A is negative, the result is 0.

long real procedure Erlang (A,B,U); name U; long real A,B; integer U; Returns a long real value from the Erlang distribution with mean 1/A and standard deviation 1/A*SqRt(B).

integer procedure Discrete (A,U); name U; long real array A; integer U; A is a one-dimensional long real array holding values corresponding to a step function. It is augmented by an extra value, corresponding to an imaginary element A(UpperBound(A,1)+1). This extra value is assumed to be 1. The step function is a cumulative distribution, rising from 0 to 1.

An integer in the range LowerBound(A,1) to UpperBound(A,1)+1 is returned. It is the lowest value of I such that A(I) is greater than some basic drawing.

long real procedure Linear (A,B,U); name U; long real array A,B; integer U; Returns a long real value from a cumulative distribution function, F. This is found by a linear interpolation in a non-equidistant table defined by A and B, such that A(I) = F(B(I)).

A and B must be one-dimensional long real arrays and have equal numbers of elements. The first element of each must be 0 and the last 1.

integer procedure HistD (A,U); name U; long real array A; integer U; A is a one-dimensional long real array assumed to represent a histogram. A value in the range LowerBound(A, 1) to UpperBound(A,1) is returned, according to the relative frequencies of the values in the histogram.

Finally there is one statistical reporting procedure:

procedure Histo (A,B,C,D); real array A,B; real C,D;   Updates a histogram defined by one-dimensional real arrays A and B, according to observation C with weight D.

Formally, A(LowerBound(A,1)+I) is increased by D, where I is the smallest integer such that C<= B(Lowerbound(B,1)+I). A should normally be one element longer than B. If it is not, the system reacts in any appropriate way.

The highest element of A corresponds to observations larger than all elements of B.

Appendix A

Arithmetic expressions

This appendix gives a rather fuller and more formal description of arithmetic expressions for readers who are interested in using SIMULA's very powerful facilities for mathematical programming.

The order of evaluation of expressions was said in Chapter 2 to be from left to right. This is obviously not the whole story and SIMULA actually follows normal rules of operator precedence and bracketing.

Parentheses

Any sub-expression within an expression may be enclosed in parentheses. This may be done recursively to any desired depth, allowing sub-expressions to be nested.

When an expression is evaluated, any parenthesized sub-expressions within it are evaluated fully first. This rule is applied recursively, so that nested sub-expressions are always evaluated before their enclosing expression. Where an expression contains more than one parenthesized sub-expression, these are evaluated left to right.

Thus the following Boolean expressions are true.

$$2 * 2 + 3 + 4 * 5 = 27$$
$$2 *(2 + 3) + 4 * 5 = 30$$
$$(2 *(2 + 3) + 4)* 5 = 70$$

Precedence

Terms separated by operators form triples and arithmetic expressions are made up of such triples. Each triple yields a value. Parentheses and operator precedence determine the order of evaluation of triples and, by implication, the combinations which yield triples. The order of operator precedence is as follows:

First exponentiation	**
Second multiplication and division	*, /, //
Third addition and subtraction	+, −

Within these categories, triples are evaluated from left to right.

Thus the following are true.

$$4 + 2 \,/\!/\, 2 = (2 \,/\!/\, 2) + 4$$
$$7 * 8 + 3 * 11 ** 4 = ((11 ** 4) * 3) + 7 * 8)$$

Note how parentheses can make expressions easier to read, even if they do not change the meaning.

Implicit conversion

Implicit coversion is performed, where necessary, each time a term-operator-term triple is evaluated. This may mean several conversions of the intermediate values in an expression, with possible rounding errors each time, during the evaluation of a complete expression.

The following rules govern where conversion is performed.

1   If the operator is integer divide, $/\!/$, both terms must be integer or short integer. Use of reals or long reals constitutes a runtime error.

2   All short integer values are converted to integer. This can never cause a conversion error.

3   If the operator is real divide, $/$, both terms are converted to real or long real, in accordance with (4) below.

4   Where the terms are of different types and at least one is real or long real conversion is performed. If one term is long real the other is converted to long real otherwise the non-real term is converted to real.

The type of the final value will depend on the type of the terms after application of these rules. Type conversion is always performed before the operation is performed.

Implicit conversion and conditional expressions

Where the alternatives of a conditional arithmetic expression yield values of different types, rules (2) and (4) above are applied to determine the type of the overall expression.

Appendix B

Arithmetic types

This appendix deals with conversion, reading and writing of arithmetic values. It is intended to be read in conjunction with appendix A.

Implicit conversion

The circumstances in which implicit conversion occurs were outlined in Chapter 3. The rules for expression evaluation were described formally in appendix A. This section explains the rules for rounding.

Short integer to integer conversion is always exact.

Integer to short integer conversion resulting from assignment of an integer value to a short integer location or passing an integer value as a short integer parameter is exact where it is possible. Where the integer's value lies outside the range of short integer values for that system, the attempted conversion will cause a runtime error. All value ranges are system dependent.

Real to long real conversion should involve no loss of precision, since long reals are required to allow greater or equal precision. Some systems restrict the range of long real values to obtain greater precision, compared to reals. In these systems it is possible to cause a runtime error by attempting to convert a real to a long real.

Long real to real conversion may result in loss of precision. If the value range of long real exceeds that of real for the system, a runtime error will result if the long real is outside the real range.

Integer to real or long real conversion is exact within some system defined range, which must include zero. Outside that range it may be non-exact. In general no range errors should be possible.

Real or long real to integer or short integer conversion is defined as equivalent to adding 0.5 to the value and taking the integer part of the result. Thus 3.5 becomes 4, while −3.5 becomes −3. It will cause an error if the value is outside the range for integers.

Precision

All non-integer arithmetic values are stored with a finite precision. The

321

effect of certain mathematical operations is dependent on the sensitivity of the expression to rounding errors.

The system procedures AddEpsilon and SubEpsilon (see Chapter 20) are provided to help with advanced numerical programming. They determine the sensitivity of real or long real values to addition and subtraction respectively.

Floating-point representation

SIMULA recognizes the following real number forms, both within source programs and in input from ImageFiles.

> <sign?> <spaces?> <integer—part> <exponent?>
> or
> <sign?> <spaces?> <integer—part?> <decimal—mark>
>   <fractional—part> <exponent?>
> or
> <sign?> <exponent>

A plus or minus sign is optional. A plus has no effect; a minus denotes a negative number.

The integer part is optional when a decimal mark and fractional part are given. It consists of a sequence of digits. When no fractional part is given an integer part followed by an exponent is regarded as a real or long real constant.

There must be a decimal mark if there is a fractional part. The system will normally expect a full stop (period), but this can be reset using the system procedure DecimalMark (see Chapter 20). This also allows the current mark to be checked.

The fractional part is another, non-empty, string of digits.

The exponent is optional where at least a fractional part is given, but may be used on its own. It consists of the low-ten symbol followed by an integer value. It specifies a power of ten by which the value of the rest of the number is to be multiplied or is itself, combined with a sign part if present, the value of the number.

The low-ten character is normally ampersand (&) for real numbers and double ampersand (&&) for long reals. Note that this allows the precision of the number to be specified for constants. The ampersand is replaced by any character passed to the system procedure LowTen (see Chapter 20). This procedure also returns the current character.

Valid real constants include:

2.67
0.54
 .54
−12.68&−6
&&12

Floating-point output

OutReal and PutReal generate texts in floating-point form, using the fullest variant of the above.

PutReal has two parameters. The first is the real or long real value to be represented, the other controls the precise format. Real values are printed with a single low-ten character, long reals with a double.

The second, integer parameter of PutReal has the following effects:

- where zero, only the exponent, with a preceding sign is output;
- where one, only an integer with one digit followed by an exponent is output;
- where greater than one, an integer with one digit, followed by N−1 fractional digits and then an exponent is output.

Thus the following calls produce the output given:

PutReal(34.56,0) → &+01
PutReal(34.56,1) → 3&+01
PutReal(34.56,2) → 3.5&+01

Systems may vary in the number of digits output for the exponent. You should consult the documentation for the system you are using.

OutReal takes a third parameter, which is an integer used to specify the total width allocated for the number to be output, as explained in Chapter 8.

Appendix C

Alternative number bases

SIMULA allows integers to be specified to number bases other than 10. This applies to integer parts, fractional parts and exponent values, as well as all uses of integers (see appendix B).

The format of such an integer, which may be preceded where appropriate by a sign (not in fractional parts), is:

<radix>R<appropriate_digits>

Radix is the number specifying the base to be used and must be one of 2, 4, 8 or 16.

The digits which may be used will depend on the choice of base, as follows:

$2 \rightarrow 0,1$
$4 \rightarrow 0,1,2,3$
$8 \rightarrow 0,1,2,3,4,5,6,7$
$16 \rightarrow 0,1,2,3,4,5,6,7,8,9,A,B,C,D,E,F$

Examples of this form for simple integers are:

2R1010
16RFFFE
8R76501

Appendix D

Conditional expressions

SIMULA allows any expression to contain a number of alternatives, one of which is chosen for evaluation according to one or more conditions. These are all extensions of the simplest form, which may be nested to produce arbitrarily complicated variants. In practice it is wise to use these with caution.

Some simple examples are:

(a) Integer expression.

   IntVal:= if A=B then IntVal + 1 else InVal = 2

Here IntVal is increased by 1 if A=B, otherwise it is increased by 2.

(b) Object expression.

   (if A=B then Obj1 else Obj2).Val:= 6

Here the value 6 is assigned to attribute Val of Obj1 if A=B, otherwise it is assigned to attribute Val of Obj2. Note that the reference expression must be enclosed in brackets to avoid ambiguity and that Obj1 and Obj2 must be qualified by the same class.

These examples should give a sufficient idea of the use of this feature.

References

1986 SIMULA Standard. SIMULA a.s., Oslo, 1986.

Birtwistle G.M., Dahl O-J., Myrhaug B. & Nygaard K. (1973) *SIMULA Begin.* Student-litteratur, Lund, Sweden.

Birtwistle G.M. (1979) *A System for Discrete Event Modelling on SIMULA (Demos).* Macmillan Press.

Franta W.R. (1977) *The Process View of Simulation.* North-Holland Publishing Co.

Implementors List

The list below gives the addresses of the organizations distributing the various SIMULA Systems.

DEC 10/DEC 20/
VAX/VMS & VAX/UNIX
Stockholms Datorcentral (QZ)
Box 27322
S-102 54 Stockholm, Sweden

VAX/UNIX/SUN/MASSCOMP
DS90/ABC9000/Ohio Scientific 700
SIMPROG AB
Østermalmsgatan 21
S-114 26 Stockholm, Sweden

VAX BERKELEY/UNIX 4.2
Unger Huntsinger and Associates Ltd.
5001 13th Ave. N. W.
Calgary, Alberta
Canada T3B 1J1

CDC 3000
Computer & Automation Institute
Hungarian Academy of Sciences
P. O. Box 63
H-1502 Budapest 112, Hungary

CDC 6000/CYBER
Control Data Norway A/S
P. O. Box 112, Refstad
0513 Oslo 5, Norway

HB DPS8
CII HONEYWELL BULL
94 Avenue Gambetta
75960 Paris Cedex 20
France

IBM SIMULA
Simula a. s.
Postbox 335, Blindern
0314 Oslo 3, Norway

S-2000
Simulation Technology a. s.
P. O. Box 15, Refstad
0513 Oslo 5, Norway

DG Eclipse/DG Desktop/MV-Series
Department of Computer Science
Lund Institute of Technology
Box 725
S-220 07 Lund, Sweden

BESM 6
ADW der DDR
ZI für Mathematik und Mechanik
Mohrenstrasse 39
108 Berlin, DDR

NORD 100/500
Norsk Data A/S
P. O. Box 25, Bogerud
0621 Oslo 6, Norway

CROMEMCO
A/S OMNIBUS
Wdm. Thranes gate 75
0171 Oslo 1, Norway

PR1ME
PR1ME Computer Scandinavia AB
Box 18
S-163 93 Spånga, Sweden

ICL 2900/PERQ
ERCC
University of Edinburgh
59 George Square
Edinburgh EH8 9JU, Scotland

SPERRY
Sperry Corporation
P. O. Box 500
Pennsylvania 19424-0001
USA

Index